D1069222

# MUSLIM ZION

FAISAL DEVJI

# Muslim Zion

## *Pakistan as a Political Idea*

Harvard University Press
Cambridge, Massachusetts
2013

First published in the United Kingdom in 2013 by
C. Hurst & Co. (Publishers) Ltd.,
41 Great Russell Street, London, WC1B 3PL

First Harvard University Press edition, 2013


*Library of Congress Cataloging-in-Publication Data*

Devji, Faisal.
Muslim Zion: Pakistan as a Political Idea / Faisal Devji.
p.  cm.
Includes bibliographical references and index.
ISBN 978-0-674-07267-1 (cloth : alk. paper)
1. Islam and politics—Pakistan.   2. Islam and state—Pakistan.
3. Pakistan—Politics and government—20th century.
4. Pakistan—History—20th century.   5. India—History—Partition, 1947.
I. Title.
DS384.D43 2013
320.54095491—dc23      2013014319

# CONTENTS

FEB     2014

# ACKNOWLEDGEMENTS

The idea for this book was prompted by an invitation to deliver the Kingsley Martin Memorial Lecture at the University of Cambridge in 2009. The project I sketched out in my lecture was subsequently elaborated over many conversations with Shruti Kapila, as well as receiving much productive commentary in workshops and talks organized by Chris Bayly, Sunil Khilnani, Uday Mehta, Henning Trüper, Ravinder Kaur and Thomas Blom Hansen. Some of the book's themes possessed an earlier incarnation at Yale, as a paper on Jinnah inspired by the late Carol Breckenridge, which received the careful consideration of Arjun Appadurai, Achille Mbembe and Vyjayanthi Rao, to all of whom I'm very grateful. My thanks also go to those who have generously read and commented on draft chapters. In addition to the two anonymous press reviewers, these include Derek Penslar, Neguin Yavari, C. M. Naim, Ahmed Zildzic and Kelly Grotke. As always, Rachel and Michael Dwyer as well as Christophe Carvalho have made my task as a writer easier and more pleasurable.

Faisal Devji                                          Oxford, March 2013

# INTRODUCTION

In an early essay called "Is Judaea, then, the Teutons' Father-land?" a great philosopher of the modern state wondered if his homeland would ever give rise to a nation. Reflecting upon the patchwork quilt of principalities that was Germany in his day, G. W. F. Hegel noted that its history seemed to provide only fragments for the building of a collective imagination:

Thus we are without any religious imagery which is homegrown or linked with our history, and we are without any political imagery whatever; all that we have is the remains of an imagery of our own, lurking amid the common people under the name of superstition. As a belief in ghosts it retains the memory of a hill where knights once did their mischief or a house where monks and nuns walked or where a supposedly faithless trustee or neighbor has still failed to find rest in the grave. As a product of fancy, drawing nothing from history, it befools weak or evil men with the possibility of witchcraft.[1]

Instead of turning to their own country and its past, suggested Hegel, Germans were only able to imagine a homeland in the landscape of biblical Judaea, whose image they had inherited from the centuries of Christianity that preceded the politics of nationalism:

Christianity has emptied Valhalla, felled the sacred groves, extirpated the national imagery as a shameful superstition, as a devilish poison, and given us instead the imagery of a nation whose climate, laws, culture, and interests are strange to us and whose history has no connec-

1

tion whatever with our own. A David or a Solomon lives in our popular imagination, but our country's own heroes slumber in learned history books, and, for the scholars who write them, Alexander or Caesar is as interesting as the story of Charlemagne or Frederick Barbarossa. Except perhaps for Luther in the eyes of Protestants, what heroes could we have had, we who were never a nation?[2]

Hegel's despair about Germany's future as a nation state was shared by so many of his compatriots as to become a historical cliché. And this sentiment may well have played a part in the extraordinarily violent way by which some Germans sought to create a nation where there seemed to be none, including the attempt to make of it a world-historical power in two world wars. After many vicissitudes, Germany has finally achieved the status of a unified nation state, one founded upon the powerful myth of common blood and a rootedness in the soil of a historical fatherland. But what interests me here is Hegel's suggestion that his compatriots in the early nineteenth century could only recognize their homeland in the landscape of Palestine. I want to argue that this ambiguously religious way of imagining nationality in an alien geography, without a necessary reference to shared blood and a rootedness in the soil, represents a tradition of collective belonging that differs from the conventional narratives of European nationalism.

In Hegel's day such a vicarious cartography of national belonging characterized utopian communities and settler societies in the New World, some of whose political vocabularies also alluded to the Holy Land, and in particular the Children of Israel's millennial return to it, whether in the journey of Moses out of Egypt or in that of the Jews' final ingathering before the coming of the Messiah. The biblical elements of this political vocabulary, however, did not descend in a single file from ancient times, but were characteristic of Protestant thinking in particular.[3] For the Reformation's dissent from Roman Catholicism was expressed in the name of a return to origins, whether this return was to scripture, the primitive church or indeed Judaea. And in this sense Zionism, too, can in one of its dimensions be seen as a Protestant enterprise, dedicated as it was to the literal accomplishment of a biblical prophecy, even and especially when those who sought this fulfilment were themselves not believers of any traditional kind. But it is also clear that such a return needn't be religious at all, to say nothing of Protestant, nor need it be directed towards Palestine, for its desired homeland could just as well be thought of as another Athens, a new Rome or a Workers' and Peasants' Republic.

In the way I am using it in this book, then, Zion serves to name a political form in which nationality is defined by the rejection of an old land for a new, thus attenuating the historical role that blood and soil play in the language of Old World nationalism. Moreover I wish to claim that the Zionist movement leading to the creation of Israel in 1948 was simply one example of this political form, with Muslim nationalism, resulting in the founding of Pakistan a year earlier, constituting both its precedent, and perhaps its closest political relation as well. I shall return to the relationship of Pakistan and Israel in the chapter that follows, but for the time being I wish to stress that they both emerged from situations in which minority populations dispersed across vast subcontinents sought to escape the majorities whose persecution they rightly or wrongly feared. For it was only the emergence of national majorities in nineteenth-century Europe and India that turned Jews and Muslims there into minorities, whose apparently irreducible particularity posed a "problem" or "question" for states newly founded on notions of shared blood and the ancestral ownership of a homeland.[4]

As a result of representing a problem or question for the national movements within which they were formed, both Zionism and Muslim nationalism held such forms of collective belonging to be deeply suspect, even as they sometimes attempted to fashion similar nationalities for themselves elsewhere. Or as the literary critic Jacqueline Rose puts it in *The Question of Zion*, "Israel inscribes at its heart the very version of nationhood from which the Jewish people had to flee."[5] Yet the effort to make oneself at home in a new land, in the same way that one's oppressor had in the old, remained an incomplete and ambiguous one, giving the lie both to attempts at defining Zionism merely as a form of colonialism, as well as to the movement's obsessive insistence on belonging to the land.[6] So the Zionist attempt to create a nationality by living and dying for a land remade by Jewish labour, for instance, could only occur after the fact and as a way of compensating for the absence of a naturalised relationship with it, in this way making Israeli nationalism into a remarkably dynamic enterprise. Its ironic if not contradictory nature is signalled by the novel that stands as one of the earliest works of Zionism's founder, Theodor Herzl, graced as it was with the title *Altneuland* (Old-New Land), and a content that brought together the utopian ideology of settler societies in the New World with the ancestral pieties of nationalism in the Old.[7]

Marked as they are by the paradox of rejecting nationalism while desiring it at the same time, neither Zionism in Europe nor Muslim nationalism in India has ever managed to escape the naked abstraction of a homeland lacking historical roots, with Israel, for example, often seen as "returning" to a history made by nation-states only at the cost of denying a Jewish past in the diaspora.[8] But this abstraction also links Pakistan and Israel to the twentieth century's ideological states, generally communist but sometimes fascist as well, whose rejection of the past and radical orientation to the future they both share. So as President of Pakistan, Zia ul-Haq was only stating the obvious when in a 1981 interview with *The Economist* he pointed out that "Pakistan is, like Israel, an ideological state. Take out the Judaism from Israel and it will fall like a house of cards. Take Islam out of Pakistan and make it a secular state; it would collapse."[9] Not only did Zia take religion to be the ideology of a state, he also made it clear in this interview that by excluding other forms of collective belonging, such as blood and soil, it came to be the solitary basis for nationality, yet one whose power was for this very reason remarkably vulnerable. For we shall see that religion was itself little more than an idea for Muslim nationalism in India, one that no longer referred to any life-world of belief and practice. So however peremptory the claims of Islam might be upon its followers, no other country has made of religion the sole basis of Muslim nationality. When on the rare occasion Pakistan's ideologists attempted to give it a basis in blood and soil, they could only do so by turning to their future homeland's religious minorities, as in the following passages from a text published by the Muslim League in 1943, which describes that part of India watered by the Indus River and its tributaries as Pakistan's "natural" homeland:

The people of Pakistan differ from the rest of India in religion, race, and language, and possess all the necessary essentials which go to form a nation. Among themselves, the Muslims, Hindus and Sikhs have more in common than they have with the people living in the rest of India. In religion, the Sikhs and Arya Samajists have more identical views on the unity of God and belief in a revealed religion than with the Hindus elsewhere. By race, the people belong to the same Aryan stock while Urdu with its Persian script is treated as the court language throughout this area. Untouchability, the caste system, music before the mosque and cow protection do not present such difficult problems as in the rest of India.[10]

The creation of a bigger Punjab with natural expansion in the north-west and south, so as to include Kashmir, the Frontier Province, Sind and Baluchistan, is in reality the regeneration of the old historical kingdom which the Sikhs tried to keep united in their time of glory and which now will be supported by the combined might of Muslims and Sikhs.[11]

These arguments represented, of course, fairly transparent attempts to woo Hindu and Sikh minorities into supporting the idea of Pakistan, or at least to give the impression that the country would be an inclusive and pluralistic one, but what is striking about them is the fact that they can only conceive of old fashioned territorial nationality in the name of non-Muslim groups. Only religious minorities in Pakistan and Israel, after all, can claim nationality on the basis of blood and soil alone, something that both denationalizes their majority populations further, and stands as a permanent challenge to them. This is surely why the autochthony of such minorities, at least in Israel, is so hotly contested by some elements of the national majority.

Whether or not Zion is identified with some holy land, it works as a distinctive political form to create a new kind of geography, so that countries like Pakistan and Israel can be said to share more with each other than they do with their immediate neighbours, despite the common histories and geographies that otherwise link them with the latter. Yet while Israel is routinely seen by friends and foes to be a stranger in her own neighbourhood, the same might also be said of Pakistan, which unlike India didn't even inherit a name from the past, and which was literally unimaginable before the 1930s. Indeed Pakistan was created in less than a decade after it had first been proposed as a political goal, representing in this way a success so astonishing as to be unique in the history of the nation state. And yet the very rapidity of her founding suggests that Pakistan possessed no nation in any conventional sense, and in fact Muslim nationalism was pressed from the very beginning to define itself by partisans and enemies alike. Even during its brief career, the Pakistan Movement was imagined so variously, with such wildly fluctuating borders and an equally variable constitutional status, that like Zionism it must be seen as a psychic projection as much as anything else. For as Jacqueline Rose puts it, "Precisely because Zionism had to make itself out of nothing—create a unity, a language, a homeland where there was none before—it knows itself as a child of the psyche, a dream, a figment of the brain."[12]

Pakistan's ambiguous heritage and sheer abstraction as a political idea have become the stuff of popular legend, so that

Salman Rushdie was immediately understood when he described it in one of his novels as a country "insufficiently imagined," while the historian Farzana Shaikh has recently demonstrated its lack of political foundations.[13] Most scholars have dealt with Pakistan's vacillating and unanchored reality in two important ways. Some speculate that Muslim nationalism was intended by its leaders, and in particular the country's founding father, Mohammad Ali Jinnah, as a movement whose goals were open-ended enough to allow for the possibility of a new political relationship between India's Hindu majority and Muslim minority.[14] Such a relationship, they claim, might even have precluded the creation of Pakistan, had the Indian National Congress been willing to compromise with the Muslim League. A reprise of arguments familiar from colonial times, this theory was known in a somewhat cruder form in Jinnah's own day, with Pakistan seen by some of its supporters as well as detractors to be a "bargaining counter" that the Congress finally made into a reality—whether by design or accident it is difficult to tell. Indeed the focus of this group of historians on hidden motives and intentions resolves Pakistan's history into nothing more than a failed conspiracy—which is only appropriate given the conspiratorial nature of political thought in that country.

Others see this narrative of elite manipulation as insufficient, and emphasize instead the many different ways in which Pakistan became a popular idea that was reworked by ordinary Muslims in local political arenas.[15] But this kind of explanation "from below," which Bernard Cohn, who taught me at the University of Chicago, used to call the proctological view of history, deprives the Pakistan Movement of all integrity. Indeed the partisans of local history subscribe to some version of Zeno's Paradox, where an arrow's movement through space is denied because it is stationary at every point of its trajectory. They can only account for Jinnah's success by arguing that the League had to capture the bases of local politics, embodied in clan and caste loyalties, from its opponents and by extension the colonial state, thus suggesting that everything and yet nothing actually changed with Pakistan's achievement. In any case Muslim nationalism cannot simply be seen as the sum of its provincial parts, with the ideas that characterized it as an India-wide project possessing their own autonomy as part of a distinct political logic. Such minor histories, after all, could not exist without a countrywide one in the increasingly centralized political arena of the colonial state, while the reverse is manifestly not true, however important the political support of these provinces was for Pakistan's achievement. Moreover the effort to regionalize history can become ever more localized, with each successive step downwards implying the irrelevance of the one above, until we arrive at the psychological and even physiological conditions that motivated individuals. This joined-up view of history, as if its subjects were neatly stacked one inside the other like a Russian doll, has little to recommend it in comparison with one for which economies of scale are incommensurable.[16]

For both groups of historians, moreover, the abstract and empty idea that founds Muslim nationalism is not worthy of consideration in its own right, with Pakistan requiring only the cutting and pasting by scholars of historical content to fill it out, this being furnished by elite or popular politics according to the historian's taste. For ideas here are subordinated to interests in such a way that a causal relationship is posited between the latter's significance and the former's influence. Yet this way of writing history ignores the fact that however "material" they might be, interests are the most transient of things. Ideas invariably exceed them and are the great survivors of history, living beyond the political conjunctures within which they were produced to shape new futures. My task in this book, then, is not to trace causal relationships between interests, ideas and events in some mechanistic way, nor to show which ideas were the most common or "influential" in Indian politics, but to describe the lines of argument or debate that have emerged as the most important and productive ones in the history of Muslim nationalism. This is a task that can only be fulfilled retrospectively, in a strong sense of that word, and not by providing a blow-by-blow account of what "actually" happened in a merely belated fashion. Precisely this latter kind of history, written as a police report or judicial decision to make someone "responsible" for it, and thus connected by links of desire to the procedures of the state, especially in its colonial incarnation, is what I want to reject here. Instead of focussing in good legal style on the "motives" or "intentions" of groups and individuals, which can only be known, if at all, in the most superficial or "criminological" way, I am interested in the forms of argumentation and lines of reasoning that both transcend and survive such intentionality to shape the prose of history.

What concerns me especially is the abstract idea at the heart of Muslim nationalism, one created by the forcible exclusion of blood and soil in the making of a new homeland for India's diverse and scattered Muslims. Such conventional forms of belonging only worked to divide Muslims from one another while tying them to Hindu, Sikh and other neighbours in particular parts of the country. Even the ethnic and cultural identities of those Muslims who constituted a majority in the areas that were to become Pakistan, were unable to provide it with the foundations of a nationality, since this was at least theoretically meant to include all the subcontinent's Muslims. It was, after all, those Muslims living in Hindu-majority areas who proved to be the League's strongest supporters. And so it was that Urdu, which was not the mother tongue of any group in the regions that became Pakistan, should have been chosen as its national language. In some respects like the adoption of Hebrew as Israel's national language, this was an attempt to create a nationality by reaching for a unity that necessarily broke with the past of those who had to be made into the citizens of either state.

9

Indeed the Pakistani state has from the very beginning been deeply suspicious of "provincialism," the culture and characteristics of those who actually constituted the majority of its citizens, preferring instead to unite them under Islam as a universal idea having little to do with anything given to a people either by history or geography.

As early as 1948, in a speech made at a mammoth meeting in Dacca, the Governor-General of a recently created Pakistan made it clear that his new nation would have to repudiate not simply its colonial and more generally Indian past, but even the regional identities of its own Muslim majority, which he fearfully compared to nations in waiting. It was as if Jinnah's own "two-nation theory" had returned to haunt Pakistan with the spectre of more partitions to come, leading him to recommend a politics of unity that was, in appearance, at least, difficult to differentiate from that which characterized his rivals in the Indian National Congress. What distinguished Pakistan's unity from that of its giant neighbour's, however, was the elimination of everything that its people had inherited from their past. This was why the Qaid could invoke his country's unity by referring to the United States of America as a paradigmatic New World model:

Take America. When it threw off British rule and declared itself independent, how many nations were there? It had many races: Spaniards, French, Germans, Italians, English, Dutch and many more. Well, there they were. They had many difficulties. But mind you, their nations were actually in existence and they were great nations; whereas you had nothing. You have got Pakistan only now. But there a Frenchman could say 'I am a Frenchman and belong to a great nation', and so on. But what happened? They understood and they realized their difficulties because they had sense, and within a very short time they solved their problems and destroyed all this sectionalism, and they were able to speak not as a German or a Frenchman or an Englishman or a Spaniard, but as Americans.[17]

"Zionism," writes Jacqueline Rose, "always involved a form of 'insubordination' against reality and the demands of reason."[18] It is the insubordinate character of the demand for Pakistan, too, that interests me in this book, one whose unreality was so widely recognized at the time that historians even today must struggle to explain it by various forms of rationalization. What are the implications of founding a country on nothing but an idea, one that represented a desire both to join and reject the world of nation states? The rhetoric of exceptionality that marks the politics of Israel and Pakistan not only serves as an illustration of this contradiction, but it also links both countries to settler societies in the New World and the ideological states which in some ways were their heirs. And without taking these factors into consideration, I will argue, it is impossible to have any broad understanding of either country's creation as part of a larger, international project, within which religion takes on a new meaning and of which I am concerned here only with its Pakistani exemplar. For interesting as the structural similarities between Zionism and Muslim nationalism undoubtedly are, more important might be the role that world Jewry played in the latter's imagination. It was not only the story of the Jews as a scattered minority who chose to become a national majority, in other words, that occupied Muslim nationalists, but also, and conversely, their international or rather non-national character. However minor its role in Muslim nationalism appears to be, then, Zionism's imaginative as much as historical link with Pakistan allows us to rethink the latter's politics in what I believe are productive new ways. For nationalism and anti-nationalism join these otherwise very different projects into a single if thoroughly ambiguous political narrative in which the nation never coincides with a state.

# 1

## ANOTHER COUNTRY

In March 1946, little over a year before the end of Britain's Raj and the emergence of India and Pakistan as its successors, Gandhi met with the Member of Parliament and president of the World Jewish Congress's British section in Poona. Sydney Silverman was seeking the Mahatma's support for a Jewish "national home" in mandated Palestine, claiming that his people were "the only nation on earth without a country." Having been dealing for some half a dozen years with similar claims by another people without a territory for its own "national home" in India, Gandhi was no doubt familiar with this position, though he was too polite to mention the comparison to his interlocutor at once. What followed was a kind of Socratic dialogue in which Silverman and his associate, Camille Honig, were brought to recognize their kinship with Mohammad Ali Jinnah, President of the All-India Muslim League and soon to be founder of Pakistan. This dialogue, as transcribed by the Mahatma's secretary Pyarelal, proceeded in the following way:

Gandhi: "Let me try to understand the question. Why do you want a national home in Palestine?"

Mr Silverman: "Two reasons. Firstly, because six and a half *lakhs* [650,000] of Jews are already settled there. We cannot throw them away and begin anew. Secondly because there is nowhere else we can go to."

Gandhi: "Are there not waste spaces enough in the world to receive you?"[1]

The Mahatma began not by questioning the need for a Jewish homeland but asking what connection it had with Palestine. Since invocations of biblical history would not have been an adequate response, Silverman pointed to the presence of Jews already in the territory as the strongest reason for establishing a state there, holding that no other place was available for them to settle in. Like that advanced by Jinnah for carving a Muslim state out of India, Silverman's argument was premised upon the existence of a people in a land, but without holding this connection to be natural or inevitable, to say nothing of being sacred. And indeed Pakistan and Israel were both conceived as accidental countries, settled by nations founded outside their borders not for reasons of sentiment as much as convenience. It was the administrative convenience of this peculiar form of nationalism whose consequences Gandhi proceeded to examine, when asking Sydney Silverman the same questions he had posed Jinnah so many times before:

Gandhi: "Then you want to convert the Arab majority into a minority?"

Messrs Silverman and Honick [sic] admitted that the status of the Arabs was affected to that extent and injustice done to them. But they maintained that even if they lost their status in Palestine there would still be five independent kingdoms left which they can call their own, and with the addition of Syria and Lebanon at no distant date there will be seven. "But if we lose Palestine, we have nothing left to us. That is our plea. It means 5 per cent of injustice to the Arabs to avoid a denial of all justice to the Jews."[2]

In India this familiar argument had the merit of being universally convertible, with Hindu and Muslim nationalists both being able to claim that the other party had many more territories occupied by co-religionists to which they might retreat. We

14

don't know if the Mahatma smiled when he heard it on the lips of the President of the World Jewish Congress, though he went on to ask Silverman another set of questions that he might easily have posed the President of the All-India Muslim League:

"So the Arabs do stand to lose something?"

"Something which they never had."

"Before the Jewish immigration into Palestine began in 1917?"

"Yes, but under Turkish rule."

"So you want the Arabs to sacrifice something which you want for yourself?"

"We only want them to make a little sacrifice so that justice might be done to the general situation."[3]

Seen as the unwillingness of a populous and widely dispersed majority to compromise with a disadvantaged minority looking for a piece of land to call its own, the opposition to Jewish as well as Muslim nationalism gave rise in both to fears of plots to exterminate them politically. Whatever the truth behind these fears, and however different the circumstances in Palestine and India, the similarity between these minority nationalisms that managed to create the first two religious states of the twentieth century is interesting enough to merit examination. Gandhi was certainly struck by the comparison:

"I can only hope that a just solution may be found which will give satisfaction to the Jews. But after all our talk I am unable to revise the opinion I gave you in the beginning. You should see the Congress President and Qaid-e-Azam Jinnah too and try to gain their sympathy. Unless you can get the active support of the Muslims nothing is possible in a substantial way in India."

"It is well nigh impossible," they remarked.

"I do not minimise the difficulty," replied Gandhi, "but I won't say it is impossible."

"Would Mr Jinnah listen? He won't."

"He may."

"Perhaps he may by the same token which he demands a Pakistan."

"You can tell him that also," said Gandhi, and they all had a hearty laugh.[4]

My purpose in citing this conversation is to point out that new political forms, such as the religious nationalisms that gave rise to Pakistan and Israel, took shape in an international arena and cannot be studied as part of regional histories alone. It is not simply a coincidence, therefore, that the Jewish State and Islamic Republic share so much in the way of ideology and even politics, despite the narratives of exceptionality within which they have hitherto been mired. Indeed most of these accounts, which take a nineteenth-century model of the nation state as their conceptual framework, are belied by the words and deeds of the Zionists and Muslim nationalists who created these twentieth-century states. For Israel and Pakistan were both founded in the wake of the Second World War, which destroyed the kind of nationality whose claims to autochthony were couched in the language of Romanticism. And so the task I have set myself is to describe the religious state not only as a modern political form, whose international dispersal prevents it from becoming a regional exception, but also as one that challenges nationalism itself, if only by questioning its attachment to the territory that makes a common history and culture possible. Established both in the name of minorities and as a result of vast migrations, these religious states have had to reject the principle of territorially based community that gives meaning to majority nations. Pakistan and Israel, I will argue, have opened up new ways of structuring political communities whose consequences go far beyond the highly publicized travails of either one.

## States of mind

The comparison between Jewish and Muslim nationalism was made over and over again during the career of both movements, much to the displeasure of the latter's champions. Choudhry Khaliquzzaman, for instance, a Muslim League politician from the United Provinces, found his attempts to win the support of Arab politicians for his cause rebuffed at the 1938 Palestine Conference held in Cairo, because it was seen as being too close to Zionism and other forms of minority nationalism:

> Before my onward journey to London I met Mustafa Nahas Pasha, who had for a long time been the Prime Minister of Egypt, although at the time he did not hold office. I found that Nahas Pasha was singularly ill-informed about the history of the Muslims in India or their differences with Congress and applied his experience of life in Egypt to India so literally as to make the Muslim problem of India exactly as the Jewish or Christian problem which Saad Zaghlol Pasha had to face in Egypt, thus completely ignoring the difference in the size of the two countries and the magnitude of the minority [...] five times the total Muslim population of Egypt. I implored him to leave us to our fate if he found himself unable to sympathize with us.[5]

Despite their annoyance, however, advocates of the League were saddled with the comparison to Zionism, not least because they insisted on using practically the same terminology as their Jewish peers, including the ambiguous but still, even in our own day, crucial term Muslim or Jewish "homeland," which could refer either to an independent or merely autonomous state. But there was also a move from the term "national home" to a "national state," as the possibility of a singular and sovereign country came to dominate earlier visions of autonomous regions, federated states and partnerships in empire for both movements. So B. R. Ambedkar, for example, the Dalit or "Untouchable" leader who published one of the most detailed and widely cited books on Pakistan during the heyday of its national movement in 1941, pointed to this disavowed similarity and made it clear, with lengthy citations of legal documents, that the Muslim League had willy-nilly to follow the constitutional precedent set by Zionist dealings with Britain—beginning his argument with the following preamble:

Some speak of Pakistan as a Muslim National State, others speak of it as a Muslim National Home. Neither care to know whether there is any difference between a National State and a National Home. But there can be no doubt that there is a vital difference between the two. What that difference is was discussed at great length at the time of constituting in Palestine a Jewish National Home.[6]

And indeed the League's propagandists had frequently compared themselves with Zionists, as in a book on the idea of Pakistan by the anonymous author M.R.T. that began with a foreword by none other than Mohammad Ali Jinnah:

The Indian Muslims who form one fourth of the total population and number 90 million are in their opinion comparable to minorities in European countries or even to the Jews who are scattered all over the world.[7]

Interesting about this statement is that it compares the position of India's Muslims to the worldwide dispersion of the Jews, suggesting therefore the global dimension of Muslim nationalism, for which Pakistan's role, like that of Israel's for the Jews, was a world-historical one and not confined only to the fate of India's Muslims. I shall return to this theme in later chapters, but want to note here that it was probably the conception of Jews as a global community, rather than a regional minority or even a nation, that made it such an attractive mirror for the League's spokesmen. Apart from the general category of minority they had come to represent in European thought and politics, after all, there was little that Jews held in common with the subcontinent's Muslims. And so their invocation by Muslim nationalists, which we shall see occurred in private correspondence as well as in literary genres like Persian verse, going well beyond any merely instrumental form of public argumentation, was both eccentric and excessive in the comparison it set up. It is almost as if the Jews were interesting to Muslim intellectuals because they represented not simply a minority that sought to become a nation so much as a potentially international or global polity. Curious also was the fact that the League's supporters did not hesitate to compare their Indian constituency to Christian and Jewish minorities in the Middle East which were opposed by Muslim majorities there:

Thus if small peoples like the Protestant Irish in Ireland, the Christian Arabs in Syria and the Jews in Palestine do not wish to lose their separate political identity, and are supported in this desire for separate existence by two of the foremost democratic nations, there is no reason why Indian Muslims should be forced to accept the position of a minority.[8]

When seen as a national majority in a future Pakistan, of course, Muslims were no longer to be identified with Jews and other Middle Eastern minorities, but even so they retained a kind of non-national character. Comparing the economic situation of Punjab's Muslim majority to that of the Turks, for instance, M.R.T. can only do so by referring to the malign dominance of autochthonous and national minorities, saying that though "the Turk had ruled over Asia Minor for over 800 years, and formed the majority of its population, yet economically he stood no comparison with the subject peoples like the Greeks, Armenians, and Jews."[9] But there was no clear shift between the Jew as model and as enemy, with the former comparison continuing to dog the Muslim League even after it had won Pakistan in 1947. For the League's achievement was invoked in the UN General Assembly as a precedent for the founding of Israel only a year later, much to the chagrin of Pakistan's representative there. Indeed Sir Muhammad Zafrulla Khan, who led the opposition to Palestine's partition at the UN, was put in the ironical position of championing the very arguments that had been used against India's division not long before.[10] He even compared the area of Palestine, though without any trace of irony, to the two provinces of West Pakistan which were at the time still grappling with the violence of India's partition, including millions of dead, injured and homeless, writing that the "area of Palestine is 10,000 square miles, equal to about, say, four average districts of the Punjab or, say, about two or three average districts of Sind."[11] Palestine would soon see similar scenes enacted following her own partition and the war that came in its immediate aftermath, just as it had in Pakistan.

While leading the fight against Palestine's partition at the United Nations, Zafrulla Khan was helped by Judah Magnes, rector of the Hebrew University of Jerusalem, whom Pakistan's representative thanked in his memoirs (or rather a set of interviews about his career), not seeing fit to mention any Arab for similar gratitude.[12] But if Pakistan's founders were reluctant to draw any comparison between their national movement and Zionism, it is clear that a number of them recognized it in some way. So of the five books on Palestine in Jinnah's library, not counting a 1901 edition of Tasso's Renaissance epic of the Crusades, *Jerusalem Delivered*, only one, a collection of papers by the Institute of Arab American Affairs, is anti-Zionist in its argument.[13] Indeed Jinnah seems to have possessed more books on the problems of European Jewry than on any Muslim people or country, including such classics as Leon Feuchtwanger's *Jew Suss* and Israel Zangwill's *The Next Religion*.[14] Given that the Qaid was often compared by his admirers to Benjamin Disraeli, that ancestor of the Zionists in politics, this reading list makes perfect sense.[15] Of course the similarity between Pakistan and Israel went further than this, since both countries had been ruled by Britain, and come into existence as the result of being partitioned along religious lines, as had their Catholic predecessor Ireland some three decades before. But Israel and Pakistan share much more than these general features, so that it is even possible to say that the Jewish State might never have come into being without its Muslim twin. For legal precedent apart, Pakistan's creation allowed Britain to free her Middle Eastern policy from Indian concerns, which had in the past taken priority over such Levantine matters.

The Indian Empire possessed the world's largest Muslim population, which provided Britain with a substantial portion of the army with which she controlled large parts of Asia, Africa and the Middle East. So it was no accident that viceroys from Curzon to Wavell had, from the Balfour Declaration to the White Paper on Palestine, strongly objected to any encouragement their government offered the Zionist cause, this being likely to inflame Indian sentiment and put pressure upon the loyalty of troops recruited there. Indeed the German-American philosopher Hannah Arendt, who wrote a great deal on Jewish politics during this period, was not alone in thinking that even Balfour's declaration should be linked to Indian politics, suggesting in an article of 1944 that:

It would certainly serve the cause of a politics free of illusion, if for our part we could come to see the Balfour Declaration in light of Indian Office politics. For even if the Declaration was indeed not dictated solely by selfish motives and the concerns of colonial policy, nevertheless over the longer term—that is, for as long as British policy in the Near East is essentially determined by British control over India—it can serve to implement only such interests and concerns.[16]

For like so many others, Arendt, too, was convinced that Palestine and the Near East in general were only important to Britain as long as she held India.

For their part British officials in India thought that by pushing the Zionist party, London was doing nothing but laying the ground for Pakistan's creation, with Lord Wavell writing in his diary about the Report of the Palestine Commission in 1946 that the:

Americans seem to have insisted on the Jewish point of view being accepted, which will ruin our policy and prestige all over the Middle East, but will do nothing to help us. We seem to have lost the will and courage to support our own point of view. The results here will be bad and will harden the Muslims in favour of Pakistan.[17]

Other British politicians, like Churchill, found it easy to support both the Zionists and the Muslim League, though no doubt for rather different reasons. Once Pakistan had become a reality, however, Israel, too, could be ushered into being without compromising imperial interests, though even so Britain could only do so by throwing the whole issue into the lap of the UN. So in a paper written in 1948 and dedicated to Magnes, Arendt attributed the British decision to evacuate Palestine to India's partition and independence in the form of two dominions, arguing that Israel's emergence that year "was caused neither by Jewish terrorism nor by the Arab League, but came as a consequence of the Labor government's liquidation of British rule in India."[18] In the event all that Pakistan could do was lead the fight against the Jewish State at the UN, though it soon became clear that her clout as an independent country counted for less in these affairs than it had as a colony.

In the imperial and international context where they belong, the Jewish State and Islamic Republic represent a profound distrust of nationalism, and an attempt to create new forms of political belonging. Unlike the confessional states of post-Reformation Europe, then, or its post-war Christian Democracies, religion in both these States does not merely serve to qualify the national life of their citizens. Instead it defines nationality outside the state, with all the world's Jews and all the subcontinent's Muslims capable of becoming its citizens, which is perhaps why the states meant to be their homelands can be imagined in such disparate and shifting ways. From an Eretz Israel that can include large chunks of Egypt, Jordan and Lebanon, to a Pakistan that would add to its territory not simply the whole of Kashmir, but also bits of the Indian provinces of Punjab, Gujarat and Andhra Pradesh, these countries have never possessed a stable form even in their own imaginaries.[19] Chaudhry Rahmat Ali, for instance, the Cambridge undergraduate who came up with the idea and name of Pakistan in the early 1930s, envisioned a country or set of countries distributed all over the map of India, in what can only be called a counter-nationalist vision, one entirely lacking territorial integrity.[20] In a later iteration of his theory, Rahmat Ali imagined India not as a country at all, but rather a continent of religious groups, which he thus renamed Dinia by transposing the letters making up the term India to get out of it a word derived from *din*, the Arabic for religion.[21] Dinia would be made up of a number of Muslim, Hindu, Sikh and other states, including one for Dravidians and "Untouchables," a vision that survives today largely intact in the ideology of Pakistan's preeminent militant group, the Lashkar-e Taiba, which is well-known for launching terrorist attacks in India as well as Pakistan.

But let us return to the curious links between Pakistan and Israel. Both Muslim and Jewish states survive with the rhetorical fear of being divided or altogether extinguished by their enemies. Yet when the time comes for either to abandon a portion of its territory, it does so without any apparent crisis of nationality. This is true whether we look at Israel's attempts to trade land for peace, of which the return to Egypt of the Sinai was the most spectacular example, or to Pakistan's loss of more than half its population and nearly as much of its territory with the independence of Bangladesh in 1971. All of this suggests that as the principle of Pakistani and Israeli nationality, religion stands distinct from the territory its followers covet, which had in any case always been seen as an accidental homeland for them. Even if it was a purely rhetorical exercise, the fact that the early Zionists had to run through a list of options that included Kenya and Argentina as potential Jewish homelands is highly instructive in this regard. Theodor Herzl was clear about this in his book *The Jewish State*, arguably the founding text of Zionism:

It is true that the Jewish State is conceived as a peculiarly modern structure on unspecified territory. But a state is formed, not by pieces of land, but rather by a number of men united under sovereign rule. The people is the personal, land the impersonal groundwork of a state, and the personal basis is the more important of the two.[22]

The same might be said for Mohammad Ali Jinnah's demands at various times for bits of territory that included the Andaman and Nicobar Islands as maritime links between East and West Pakistan, or for a corridor across the north of India as a territorial link between them, both justified largely for reasons of bureaucratic convenience. Indeed his main justification for the territory he sought, but was denied, was not the Muslim character of its population but that it alone would make for an administratively "viable" state, which curiously the Qaid-e-Azam, or Great Leader, of his people thought a state with two separated wings would do. But then viability was only a bureaucratic way of lending some reality to a country conceived of as an abstract idea, which accounts for Jinnah's famous statement that Pakistan would have to be conceded, whatever shape it took, even if it was to be the size of his handkerchief. Indeed the Qaid routinely imagined Pakistan as a piece of cloth rather than of land, as his equally famous statement about having inherited a "moth-eaten" country illustrates. But then it was not so much a given territory as the principle of territoriality that gave such states their meaning. And so rather than seeing these national forms, if such they can be called, as imperfect or incomplete versions of some standard set in the nineteenth century, it might make more sense to place them in their own times.

## After nationalism

Muslim and Jewish nationalisms became state-building enterprises only in the early years of the Second World War, the former announced in the Lahore Resolution of 1940 and the latter at the Biltmore Conference in 1942. They had until then toyed with ideas of multinational federations, autonomous zones and partnerships in empire that were common in the period following the First World War, with its mandates and minority protections guaranteed by the League of Nations. And it was the collapse of all these arrangements after 1939 that forced upon men like Jinnah the realization that however regrettable, such schemes were no longer tenable. So in his presidential address delivered to the special Pakistan session of the Punjab Muslim Students Federation in 1941, Jinnah had this to say:

Let me tell my friends, the Hindu leaders, that the League of Nations is dead. (Cheers). Don't you know that yet? Let me tell them, you are living at least a quarter of a century behind. Not only that, but you do not realise that the entire face of the world is being changed from week to week and from month to month in the European and other fields of battle.[23]

The death of the League of Nations was important for two reasons, the first having to do with the collapse of its system of minority protections, to which I shall return in the next chapter. The second reason for its importance to men like Jinnah had to do with the fact that the end of the League of Nations meant that of the international system as a whole, one that had been founded in the wake of the First World War at least in part on the basis of Woodrow Wilson's principle of self-determination. Disillusioned as they were by the rapid unravelling of an international order that had been intended to guarantee the independence of nation states as well as the minorities within them, Zionists and Muslim nationalists nevertheless felt compelled to lay claim to an even stronger form of nationality than the one in favour among the new states that had come into being under the aegis of the League of Nations. But these more cynical forms of national belonging, which saw an opportunity as much as a risk in the breakdown of the international order, could now jettison the naturalistic language of a people's territorial and historical unity, and even become indifferent to geography in some fundamental way.

Surely the historically variable and still unfixed boundaries of Pakistan and Israel indicate not only a disdain for the traditional model of a nation state, but also a geographical indifference of some kind? As far as the former is concerned, this indifference manifested itself in what might otherwise appear to be a set of

25

contradictory visions for Pakistan. Rajendra Prasad, the Congress leader from Bihar and future president of India who in 1946 published the most detailed analysis of Muslim nationalism of anyone from his party, makes an interesting observation about Pakistan's amorphous geography in his book:

Now, the words used to denote the extent of the territory to be included in the Muslim State or States are 'units', 'regions', 'areas' and 'zones'. None of these words is to be found in the present constitutional or administrative documents of the country. The words generally used are 'districts', 'tahsils', 'taluqas', 'provinces', etc., and nothing could have been easier than to use these well-known and well-understood expressions, if clarity, intelligibility and definiteness were intended rather than obscurity, vagueness and ambiguity.[24]

Prasad, of course, wants to suggest that the Muslim League's ambiguity was meant to function as a bargaining point if not a deliberate ploy to claim as much territory as possible for Pakistan. But what strikes me as being more important is the fact that the famous Lahore Resolution, to which he refers, should describe the area of a future Pakistan according to an alien but also international vocabulary, unlike the many peculiarly Indian terms that Prasad also cites. This attempt to render not only Pakistan, but the whole of India as well, into an abstraction, is illustrated by the words of Muslim leaders like Jinnah, who refused to describe Pakistan's creation as an act of territorial definition at all, but only a constitutional one, since he conceived of it as emerging directly from a kind of state of nature. The Qaid thus exhibited an indifference to India's own geographical integrity by focussing on its partition in strictly legalistic terms, as in the following message to the Bombay Presidency Provincial Muslim League Conference of May 1940:

It is amazing that men like Mr Gandhi and Mr Rajagopalachariar should talk about the Lahore Resolution in such terms as 'vivisection of India' and 'cutting the baby into two halves'. Surely, to-day India is divided and partitioned by Nature. Muslim India and Hindu India exist on the physical map of India. I fail to see why there is this hue and cry. Where is the country which is being divided? Where is the nation which is being denationalised? India is composed of nationalities, to say nothing about the castes and sub-castes. Where is the Central National Government whose authority is being violated?[25]

Rather than mark out Pakistan as a unique and entirely distinct territory, in other words, the League's ideologues simply adopted a geographically indifferent attitude towards it, with administrative boundaries or topographical features serving to define the new state more by the criterion of bureaucratic convenience than of religious demography, since it was intended to include very large numbers of non-Muslims. Indeed it was the Congress that insisted upon the partition of India along purely demographic lines. Whatever their compulsions or intentions in doing so, then, supporters of the Pakistan Movement routinely ignored the specificities of their national geography, as is only natural for a state meant to represent and protect even Muslims who lived outside its borders, just as Israel did for world Jewry. So F. K. Khan Durrani, author of a 1944 book called *The Meaning of Pakistan*, was quite happy to agree with his rivals in the Congress in maintaining that India was a geographical unity, contending only that such a unity had no bearing on the character of nations, writing, on the authority of the French philosopher Ernest Renan's celebrated essay on nationalism, that "Though geographically India is one unity, its people are not, and in the making of states and nations it is the people that count and not geography."[26] We have already seen Theodor Herzl express this idea in almost identical words.

Jinnah himself was forthright in emphasizing the national rather than territorial nature of the Pakistan demand in his 1944 talks with Gandhi, making it clear that his claim was not based on the actual territory that Muslims already happened to occupy but rather on a principle:

Apart from the inconsistencies and contradictions of the various positions that you have adopted in the course of our correspondence [...], can you not appreciate our point of view that we claim the right of self-determination as a nation and not as a territorial unit, and that we are entitled to exercise our inherent right as a Muslim nation, which is our birthright? Whereas you are labouring under the wrong idea that 'self-determination' means only that of 'a territorial unit' which, by the way, is neither demarcated nor defined yet, and there is no Union or Federal constitution of India in being, functioning as a sovereign Central Government.[27]

The new projects to found Jewish and Muslim states were also launched at a time when it wasn't clear who would win a war that had already destroyed the international system set in place by the Treaty of Versailles and put the fate of the old-fashioned nation state itself in doubt. This was after all a world dominated by communism and fascism, which also in their own ways separated the people as a political unit from the state it occupied. Whether it was class or race that constituted the political unit in new movements like communism and fascism, each transcended the territory it happened to inhabit, which could therefore take many forms as the object of administration. Of these the most original is undoubtedly Pakistan's division into two wings separated by a thousand miles, though at the time of its founding Israel, too, existed in three distinct parts inter-layered with Palestinian territory. Today Israel's early form can only be seen, miniaturized, in the existence of a Palestine made up of a Gaza Strip disconnected from the Authority in the West Bank. But Pakistan's was a situation unknown either in the history or theory of nationalism, and the only other example that comes to mind is the short-lived United Arab Republic that brought Egypt and Syria together into an ethnic and ideological state from 1958 to 1961. Yet such a divided polity did not look so out of place in the imperialist or even communist imagination. So when Jinnah was asked, in a 1946 BBC interview, about the difficulties of communication between the two wings of a state separated by a thousand miles of India, he could only respond by referring to the British Empire as an entity lacking geographical contiguity and therefore territorial integrity, saying "When you travel from Britain to the other parts of the British Commonwealth, you pass through foreign territory—the Suez Canal, for instance. It is all done by amicable arrangement."[28]

Or maybe it was the Soviet republics, with their dispersed and rapidly improvised nationalities, which provide the true models for our quickly founded monotheistic twins. And so it was perhaps no accident that the arch-imperialist Winston Churchill should on the floor of the House of Commons have supported the socialist MP Zilliacus and recommended the Soviet Union as a good model for an undivided India made up precisely of such religious and cultural republics, a suggestion echoed by India's last two viceroys in a remarkable departure from the nineteenth-century histories of nation and empire within which such personalities are routinely placed.[29] These efforts at thinking about India's future in federated or multinational terms, with the USA and USSR as examples, were also common among Indians of all religious and political persuasions, and demonstrate how the emergence of the Pakistan Movement, rather than making for a clash of nationalisms, allowed for the development of new ways of thinking about the political future, conceptions that no longer drew sustenance from the Old World and its romantic forms of national belonging. Even the Congress leader Rajendra Prasad, for example, felt compelled by the League's success to review the literature critical of nationalism that had appeared after the birth and death of the League of Nations, including C.A. Macartney's *National States and National Minorities*, A. Cobban's *National Self-determination* and W. Friedmann's *The Crisis of the National State*, concluding that the minority problem could only be resolved in a country like the Soviet Union.

Though it was not taken up by his party in any significant way, Prasad went on to suggest that:

Instead, therefore, of seeking a solution of the Indian problem in the creation of national states of Hindus and Musalmans, in each of which there will remain a considerable minority of the other community, is it not better to allow India to continue as an unnational state that she is and has been?[30]

And Prasad was certainly not a lonely voice in expressing the desire to rethink India's future as a political community outside the context of nationalism. Already in 1941 the historian Beni Prasad had reached the same conclusion in his book *The Hindu-Muslim Questions*, in which he suggested thinking of statehood apart from nationality, writing that:

One of the supreme needs of the modern age in the East as well as the West is the dissociation of statehood from nationhood: in a word de-politicization of the whole concept of nationality, a definite renunciation of the idea that those who feel themselves to be a nation should necessarily constitute an independent state of their own.[31]

Taking the Soviet Union, in particular, as their constitutional precedent while discarding its ideological foundation for the most part, these ways of thinking about India's political future went beyond the merely administrative option between a federal and unitary state to question the category of nation altogether, representing an alternative and today largely hidden genealogy of political thought for the Indian Union. For Nehru, too, was as much an internationalist as he was a nationalist, and in his book *The Discovery of India* he followed the same line of argument as both the Prasads, arguing that the war meant the end of national sovereignty of the Versailles kind, and signalled the emergence of multinational states in which the problem of majorities and minorities would be rendered irrelevant:

If there is a regional grouping of the countries bordering on the Indian Ocean on either side of India—Iran, Iraq, Afghanistan, India, Ceylon,

Burma, Malaya, Siam, Java, etc.—present day minority problems will disappear, or at any rate will have to be considered in an entirely different context.[32]

All these arguments, we shall see in the next chapter, had been proposed by leaders of the Muslim League much earlier in the century, but by the time they ended up in the possession of Congressmen, Jinnah had already abandoned them, at least in the form of a federated or greater India. He had in fact changed places with his political enemies, for now it was the Qaid who sang the song of a unitary nation, as in the foreword he wrote to M.R.T.'s book on Pakistan:

In sheer ignorance or with a view to misguide the foreign opinion deliberately in their own favour, it is urged in these days that India's case has a parallel in China, Soviet Russia or even in the United States of America and that its problems can be successfully tackled in the light of experience gained by the peoples of these countries. A cursory examination of such a plea by any intelligent man will convince him that it is completely misleading to compare India's problems with these countries.[33]

As we have seen in the introduction, however, Jinnah would himself return to the USA as a model after Pakistan's independence. And in any case the volume to which Jinnah had written his foreword was itself highly international in conception, though this was now of an exclusively Islamic kind, with the author suggesting that "if Islam had been the dominant religion of Europe, the world would not have seen the rise of a narrow and aggressive form of nationalism which has dragged the whole world to a state of chaos and disorder."[34] Apart from its anti-nationalist character, then, the Pakistan Movement would allow Indian Muslims "in view of their numerical strength and political importance to give a lead to the rest of the Muslim World."[35] Indeed it would "finally bring about the political emancipation of Muslims in India, China, and Russia where they are at present assigned the role of minorities, but will also restore to Islam its lost heritage of the Middle Ages."[36]

While M.R.T.'s fanciful views about an Islamic internationalism were certainly distinctive, they still belonged within the parameters of the kind of multinational polities that we have seen men like Nehru espouse, and which had as their background imperial forms of governance as well as the Soviet internationalism that came to join them. Such "unnational" ways of considering the political future were, in other words, by no means confined to India, with Hannah Arendt, for instance, writing in an essay of 1943 that one of the consequences of the emergence of the Soviet Union was that "for the first time in modern history, an identification of nation and state has not even been attempted. The government represents a federation of peoples and nationalities, all of them having their own, if very restricted, rights, none of them privileged and none of them dominated."[37] She goes on to claim that America had reached a similar conception of nationality in its own way, and then considers India as the great experiment in such a constitutional transformation, one which might provide a future Jewish homeland with its model within a larger federation:

If the British say, let Indians first settle all their problems among themselves, or if Indian leaders refuse the partition of India on the ground that there is one unique Indian people, they both are wrong. The Indian subcontinent contains a multitude of peoples and rather than an old national state in the European sense, where one people, the majority of the inhabitants, holds the reins of government and rules over other inhabitants as minorities, you might expect that sooner or later these peoples will get together and form a government that unites all the nationalities of the Indian subcontinent.[38]

Interestingly, Arendt mentioned a European federation emerging after the war as being less probable than an Indian "nonnation," though she was clear that the day of the old-fashioned European nation state was done, seeing in it a model that could only result in more conflict if adopted by new countries and lamenting that "If among the Zionist leadership many progressives know and talk about the end of small nations and the end of nationalism in the old narrow European sense, no official document or program expresses these ideas."[39] As far as the subcontinent was concerned, of course, the possibility of conceiving India's future in such anti-national ways was rendered moot, not only by the Pakistan Movement's success, but also by long-standing fears in the Congress that such a state would be prey to fragmentation from within and interference from without.

Many of Pakistan's votaries entertained equally international and ideological visions of their desired homeland, which invariably catapulted it out of a national context altogether. So Rajendra Prasad, quoting from a number of books written by Muslim nationalists, shows that none was content to stop at the achievement of an independent state. Instead they saw Pakistan's true or ultimate role as the liberation of Muslims oppressed in places like China and Soviet Central Asia, and even to "free" India herself by a process of conversion that would finally achieve the unification that supporters of the Congress had always longed for. Or as F. K. Khan Durrani put it:

Expansion in the spiritual sense is an inherent necessity of our faith and implies no hatred or enmity towards the Hindus. Rather the reverse. Our ultimate ideal should be the unification of India, spiritually as well as politically, under the banner of Islam; the final political salvation of India is not otherwise possible.[40]

So absurd as to lack even the sinister potential that Rajendra Prasad saw in them, such statements are important because they illustrate how the language of pan-Islamism among these visionaries had become almost identical with that of communism, speaking as it did of a universal liberation at the hands of a powerful global ideology.

Though he tended to speak only for India and Pakistan, Jinnah himself invariably couched his political rhetoric in these international terms, routinely speaking of Muslim nationalism in the context of communism and fascism, both of which he naturally wanted to avoid as ideologies more in keeping with his enemies in the Indian National Congress. So in a speech to the Muslim University Union in February 1938, he argued that Congress claims to be concerned with economic issues above all were not only disingenuous, but, in their falsely revolutionary impetus, bore comparison to the rise of European fascism out of socialist mobilizations:

When you are told of this heart-rending hunger and poverty, when somebody comes and tells you 'Oh! what is the use of anything? Let us remove these appalling conditions. The Congress is struggling to achieve independence and to establish a communistic and socialistic government. The economic issue is the only issue that faces us', you will be moved. I confess I myself sometimes feel moved. This has been constantly dinned into the ears of the youth. When you think you will be able to destroy the British Government, the zamindars, the capitalists with one stroke, refer to the conditions of Europe. In Germany Hitlerism came into existence because of socialistic and communistic movements. So did Fascism rise in Italy. What is the fight in Spain about? It is the same issue. When the question was put to the President of the Congress as to when he would be able to fulfil this wonderful programme, he said 'within my lifetime', and added 'when we have captured power we will destroy this constitution, not by the quill-pen'. But the question is how long he will hold the quill-pen or rather the reed pen which he is doing at present? (Laughter)[41]

He seemed to have thought that precisely because they were opposed to one another, communism and fascism belonged together, or rather that the latter became important only in those places where the former had already shaken the constitutional structures of the liberal state. And looking at Western Europe before the Second World War, as well as Eastern and Central Europe after the Cold War, who is to say if the Qaid was entirely mistaken? Of course it is easy to dismiss such effusions as mere rhetoric, though the historians who typically do so by looking for hidden intentions, which are counter-posed as the reality behind them, are guilty of anachronism. For such distinctions only make sense before mass mobilization comes to characterize nationalist politics, and in doing so lessening the importance of conspiracies and other forms of private motivation in public life. In modern times, after all, public statements possess as much, if not more, political reality as any of the motives behind them, which they often end up constraining in various ways. And it is because political reality cannot be confined to intentions that the international imaginary of Muslim, like Jewish, politics is so important, allowing Jinnah, in his presidential address to the Madras session of the All-India Muslim League in 1941, to be taken seriously when comparing what he saw as Britain's appeasement of the Congress in India to its appeasement of the Nazis internationally:

> But let me once more emphasise from this platform that the policy of the British Government in India, of inaction, of weakness, and of vacillation, is going to prove more disastrous than it is even in Europe. [Hear, hear]. Cannot these men see that events are moving so fast and that maps are being changed? Look at what is happening in Europe. Look at what the Axis Powers are doing—action and action; and what is the British Government doing, placating and placating, vacillation, weakness, inaction![42]

Naturally the Muslim League was also, and with some justice, accused of behaving in a fascist manner by its enemies in the Congress, but only tactically and not in a manner that seemed to depart entirely from the imagery of domestic politics. Indeed, what is interesting about the Qaid's referential world was not so much the understandable attention he paid to communism and fascism during the 1940s, but instead his relative neglect of comparisons and precedents taken from the Empire and Commonwealth, not least because these offered the juridical and historical context for India's own constitutional evolution, and were much cited by those who led the Congress. But Jinnah was grudging even in his references to Ireland, which surely provided the most important precedent for the kind of partition he desired. Instead he sought, in his rhetoric at least, to situate Pakistan in an entirely new international history and geography, one in which there could be no essential connection between nation and state. So in his famous presidential address to the Lahore session of the All-India Muslim League in 1940, in which India's division was first proposed, the Qaid set examples of peoples coming together to form nations against instances where they didn't, as if to dismiss any link between geography and history, state and nation:

History has presented to us many examples, such as the Union of Great Britain and Ireland, Czechoslovakia and Poland. History has also shown to us many geographical tracts, much smaller than the sub-continent of India, which otherwise might have been called one country, but which have been divided into as many states as there are nations inhabiting them. The Balkan Peninsula comprises as many as seven or eight sovereign states. Likewise, the Portuguese and the Spanish stand divided in the Iberian Peninsula.[43]

Not the least interesting thing about this passage is the fact that Jinnah referred to Ireland, or at least to its northern part, as an example of national unification rather than partition, thus disqualifying it as a precedent for Pakistan. His references to the Balkans, Czechoslovakia and Poland, then in the path of German conquest, were also not calculated to show them as models of national sovereignty. Moreover it was the Qaid who went so far as to compare a possible agreement between India's two great parties with the Hitler-Stalin Pact, and not even by way of criticizing it.[44] He was, in addition, fond of describing India's Muslims as being like the Sudeten Germans, a minority in Czechoslovakia but part of a majority when viewed from its own homeland; to which one of his opponents, the President of the Hindu Mahasabha, responded by saying that these Muslims were more like the German Jews, with whose fate he threatened them.[45] Indeed these international examples were so important for the League's political imagination that Beni Prasad could remark upon them in 1941, writing that "There is a curious resemblance between the grievances and demands of the Muslims against the Hindus in 1937–39 and those of the Christians and the Shia Muslims against the Sunni majority in Syria in 1938–39."[46] Far more important than Syria, however, was the Sudetenland:

The progress of the Sudetan [sic] demands from a larger share in administration and policy to a repudiation of minority status, the claim to separate nationhood, the denial of Czechoslovak unity, charges of atrocities and oppression unsupported by evidence, the demand for frontier revision, the advocacy of a virtual partition together with the claim of 50 per cent share in the residual central organisation—all these features in the Sudetan [sic] movement in 1936–38 found their counterpart in the resolutions of the Muslim League in 1939–41. In fact, some of the phrases employed are identical.[47]

Interesting about such references was the fact that unlike their Sudeten models, Muslim Leaguers seemed not to possess any outside majority to whom they could turn, since their co-religionists in the Middle East and Central Asia were never looked upon as potential saviours of India's Muslims. On the contrary, we have seen that Pakistan was meant to liberate and protect these fellow believers. The role played by Germany for the Sudetenland, then, appears to have been reserved for Britain in the eyes of many in the League, which was perhaps why its leaders tended to identify with Irish Protestants rather than Catholics. And in fact Pakistan has always linked its security to Western countries like Britain and then the United States. But this link between the minority seeking to overcome its weakness and an external power went well beyond self-interest, to form a distinctive way of thinking about international relations. So the party's first president, who went on to become president of the League of Nations General Assembly just before the war, explained in his memoirs many years later that he had supported the partition of Czechoslovakia because he was diverted by its resemblance to India:

Looking back on it all now, I suppose that I was subconsciously influenced in favour of the idea of separating the Germans from the Czechs in the regions in which they were in a majority, by my close personal connection with and understanding of the Muslim-Hindu issue in India, which afforded, on a much larger scale, an almost incredibly exact analogy. Here in miniature was what was to happen nearly a decade later in India. Konrad Henlein played at the time (though history was later to submerge him entirely) the decisive role which, in the Pakistan-Bharat issue, was Jinnah's.[48]

The Qaid, then, had done nothing less than abandon the more traditional politics of his enemies, however fascistic he thought it had become, to espouse a vision of it that was akin to the great new movements of his time. For by taking on board such international themes, Jinnah was not simply augmenting a domestic politics with foreign embellishments, but in fact negating its very domesticity by reading Muslim nationalism in world-historical terms alone. After all it was Jinnah who said that old-fashioned land borders no longer had defensive meaning, as the war had shown the real factor in the conquest and subjugation of a people to be air power, a comment that treated the territoriality of the state as a weakness rather than an asset and focussed on the nation as a more or less spiritual subject independent of it.[49] But such a statement only reveals that the territorial object of Muslim nationalism was by no means viewed in entirely positive terms. Like his Zionist twins, the Qaid saw the state he founded not only as a utopian possibility but also as a sign of failure, for both nationalisms are consumed by the loss of what might have been, and picture the state finally obtained as a last option forced upon them by the intransigence of their enemies—which is indeed an obsessively recurrent theme in both national histories. These lost opportunities to create more imaginative multinational or federal states are regretfully invoked by those who lend their support to very different ones, while also continuing to haunt such nationalisms as possible futures for the states that were in the end achieved. And so Pakistan and Israel are both conceived in some sense as second-best states, with Jinnah, for instance, routinely blaming not only Congress double-dealing for the partition of India, but also citing as cautionary events the failure of multinational states like Czechoslovakia and Yugoslavia to survive the new politics brought into being by the war. In this view of things Pakistan was simply an unfortunate necessity.

## Atlantic passage

The antecedents of both Muslim and Jewish states should be sought less in the European history of nationalism, with its focus on some mystical way of belonging to a land, as much as in the fantasy of creating a state by purely rational means, one that was founded upon its idea alone. This was in essence the fantasy of the social contract, whose role as a principle in political thought was suddenly eclipsed in the seventeenth century by efforts to make it an historical reality in the New World. The history of utopian settlements in the Americas, which were also often religious communities, dates from this period but continued into the eighteenth century and beyond, resulting in the creation of the United States of America. And in its Enlightenment form, this fantasy that had become history also returned to the Old World, in revolutionary movements that culminated in the establishment of the Soviet Union, itself a state based upon ideology rather than nationality. However for our purposes the most instructive example of such a homecoming is provided by the more modest if no less interesting founding, in the middle of the nineteenth century, of Liberia as a state to which not only the idea of a social contract, but also a people in the form of freed American slaves, could quite literally "return."

Founded in 1816 by a group of white men, the American Colonization Society sought to encourage the departure of freed slaves for Africa, not only because they believed that racial discrimination in the USA kept even free blacks there from becoming equal citizens, but also because "domestic tranquillity required resolution of the 'problem' of free African Americans. [...] Many thought a black republic outside the white republic would encourage gradual emancipation. Some among them hoped to rid the nation of a destabilizing and troublesome class and to protect slave property."[50] What made blacks a "problem," however, was not only their race but also that of white Americans, for it was the definition of the latter's nationality in racial terms that put the former's freedom in question. But in a country made out of immigration and settlement, it was clear that race here did not imply, as it might have done in Europe, some autochthonous relationship with the soil. On the contrary, it was important in the USA precisely because such romantic ways of belonging to the land were as yet incapable of describing nationality in a manner that could exclude native peoples or blacks. Race, then, like religion among Jewish and Muslim nationalists a century later, came to represent a form of belonging that required a territory but could not be identified with it, since any territory could strictly speaking suffice for its fulfilment.

Now the founding fathers of the USA had considered their revolution to be an exceptional one, possible only in the relatively egalitarian white society of the New World, and did not think it could be exported to the Old without drowning the principle of liberty itself in blood.[51] The creation of Liberia in 1847, then, exactly a hundred years before Pakistan's founding, represented the first attempt to export and replicate the American republic in the Old World, though assuredly not in Europe but a part of Africa seen to be as lacking in the hierarchies of ancient civilizations as North America itself. This African republic, therefore, constituted the first example of America's universality, but more than this it marked the "return" to the Old World of a distinctively New World polity, one whose founding was perhaps more radical, as it certainly was more original, than the republics created around Europe in the wake of the French

Revolution, whose form of "return" was to another history rather than geography (though the revolutionary practice of renaming places and redrawing internal boundaries no doubt indicates an effort to transform their geographies as well). For like Pakistan and Israel a century later, Liberia was founded for a nation without a territory, one that like a soul without a body required grounding in a state if it was not to wither away.

And yet it was precisely these displaced peoples that were held to constitute nations, not those who already lived in their future homelands, and who were destined to become the subjects of colonization and improvement. Like Muslim and Jewish nationalism many decades later, the Back to Africa movement displaced other visions of freedom that did not require the founding of a sovereign state. These visions included setting aside autonomous regions for blacks in the USA, as with Indian reservations, a project that was considered by figures as eminent as Thomas Jefferson, and survive today in the politics of the Nation of Islam. And it is no accident that so many of these racial and political projects should have drawn upon the millennial return of the Jews to their homeland for sustenance.[52] Indeed if the creation of Liberia provides the only real precedent for Zionism in particular, the Nation of Islam's program for America's partition, in order to establish a state for its "lost-found" people, bears a remarkable resemblance to the Pakistan Movement, with whose emergence its own more or less coincided. And this is to say nothing about the ambiguities surrounding the identity of the Nation's founder, Wallace Fard Muhammad, who was Elijah Muhammad's guide and apparently an Afghan, or even a member of the Ahmadi sect whose persecution in Pakistan I shall describe later in this book.[53] In this respect the debate between blacks who had left for Liberia and those who remained in the USA is striking in its similarity to the discussions that continue to occur between Jews and Muslims divided by the new countries that have been established in their names:

Despite the heated rhetoric and invective exchanged between Liberian emigrants and northern free blacks, their means of assessment of their condition were similar. Both tended to measure their status against America's vaunted republican liberty and an emerging, still uncertain, identity with Africa. The Virginian free blacks who constituted most of the leadership class in Liberia for two generations shared all the values and concerns of northern free blacks, except for one. They believed they could not rise to full citizenship in the United States despite their talents, but northern free blacks resisted this conclusion and grew eloquent in defining themselves in opposition. The Liberian enterprise, as colony and as republic, was the emigrants' form of resistance to slavery, but it was one that was denigrated by black and white northern abolitionists and proslavery southerners. Instead, they were described as avaricious, pretentious, and predatory toward the local indigenous population.[54]

This admixture of utopian republicanism and settler colonialism is the common characteristic that Israel and Pakistan share with their New World, Liberian and even Boer ancestors, one that is perhaps most evident in the Zionist slogan of a "land without a people for a people without a land," as well as in the new state's legitimization by the language of improvement, famously signalled in claims to have made the desert bloom, all features shared by Afrikaner nationalism as well. And this is to say nothing of another contractual idea characteristic of such a politics, that the whole or some part of a nation state might be purchased in a commercial transaction. Louisiana and Alaska provide instances of such a contract, but Liberia and Israel the exemplars, because there it was the land bought by private persons and companies rather than by a state that formed the basis of a claim to national territory, long before the sacrifices of war and work could bind a people to it in any sentimental way.

The very same transactions relied upon by minorities to purchase nation states were also used by already established ones to rid themselves of these groups, which often allowed the two to work together. From white abolitionists who thought blacks a threat to the American republic and helped fund their "return" to Africa, to the Nazis who for a time dealt with Zionist agencies on a commercial basis to transfer Jews to Palestine, to those in Israel today who would pay for the emigration of Palestinians in order to secure a truly national state, all these movements demonstrate the contradictions of political idealism. For these states founded in contract represented, in their own way, the coming to life of that famous theory associated with the names Hobbes, Locke and Rousseau, differing therefore from the leased, ceded or exchanged territories of dynastic and imperial politics, for which the term social contract would be a misnomer. Pakistan, of course, was not legitimized by purchase, though its creation did involve an enormously complex politics of restitution and property-exchange for migrants and refugees moving in both directions.[55] Moreover Jinnah was immensely proud of the fact that his new state had been achieved not by war or conquest, but in a negotiated settlement of unprecedented proportions that might well be compared to a social contract. Indeed he had been calling precisely for a social contract between Hindus and Muslims for years, irrespective of whether a single state or multiple ones would be produced thereby. And we shall see in chapter three that by using this phrase, the Qaid was doing nothing more than clearing the historical and geographical ground, rejecting all that was inherited by the people of India to try and begin anew in a remarkable act of New World hubris.

More than by way of a commercial agreement or civilizing mission, Pakistan joined its American and African predecessors in the fact that it was also built from large-scale transfers of population, indeed from the largest movement of people in human history, with Muslims entering the new country as Hindus and Sikhs departed it. The movement of Jews and Palestinians in and out of Israel, while it has remained politically more volatile than the vast migrations of South Asia, nevertheless quite pales in comparison. Such massive transfers of populations

losopher Mohammad Iqbal, whose political influence among the largely rural Muslims there was negligible. In this sense the areas that became Pakistan can legitimately be said to have played a largely negative role in the Muslim League, constituting, like Palestine for the Zionists or Liberia for the American Colonization Society, a crucial but at the same time unimportant factor in a politics that had at most to accommodate their angularities by some give and take. It took the establishment of these states to change this politics appreciably, but by that time their founding ideologies had been set in constitutional stone. And this means that today Pakistani governments look with great suspicion upon the regional cultures that make up the country, seeing in them only the seeds of secessionism in a self-fulfilling prophecy that has already resulted in the creation of Bangladesh out of East Pakistan. The country's Muslim majority, in other words, are even now unable to constitute its national culture in any formal way, something that only the abstract and universal religious idea can do.

The role played by religion in constituting the Israeli and Pakistani states is of course different from that played by race in the founding of Liberia, or of South Africa as a Boer homeland. Though all these can be seen as Enlightenment countries, created outside their borders on the explicit basis of an idea alone, the indivisibility of race and nation in the Liberian, Boer and to a lesser extent Israeli cases is not true for Muslim nationalism. The nation thought to be inherent in race is self-possessed to the degree that it needs no territory to uphold it, and cannot easily be separated from this racial foundation unless it is by miscegenation. This not only makes the task of state-building into one that might rescue a race from its rootless existence, but also an attempt to separate a people from itself by grounding it in territory. For it was precisely the self-contained and so ungrounded nature of racial minorities that provoked so much anxiety among national majorities. With Muslim nationalism, in the formation of which race played little or no role, the link between a people and the religion that constitutes it was somewhat different. While it was to be grounded in Pakistan, and therefore in Jinnah's eyes neutralized in citizenship, Islam couldn't be confined to the state simply as the religion of its citizens. For religion here is not some old-fashioned theological entity, but an abstract and modern idea, another aspect of the social contract mentioned earlier, whose sense of brotherhood provides a people with the foundation of its nationality. For Muslim nationalism, in other words, religion was conceived of not as a supplement to geography but as its alternative.

For the famously "secular" and irreligious Jinnah, as well as for his more observant associates in the Muslim League, religion was an abstract and even empty idea because they had no intention of defining Islamic practice for Pakistani citizens. On the contrary religion was deployed to name only the most general, disparate and shifting of qualities, like a theologically indeterminate belief in the God of Muhammad. But this is what made it so radical as a founding idea for the nation, the informal social contract between widely different regional, sectarian and linguistic groups whose more formal aspect was the negotiated settlement that produced Pakistan. At the moment of its founding, then, Pakistan comprised the world's largest Muslim country, and the first to be founded on the basis of Islam, even if this Islam represented only the empty idea of a national will untrammelled by anything given outside the idea itself. This is what makes it Israel's twin, for despite the profuse use of the word homeland in both countries, as well as the glorification of their territorial and even cultural integrity, no homelands can be more attenuated than these, based as they are on a national will the greater part of whose history lies outside their borders. Theodor Herzl's encomium to the political idea in *The Jewish State* is startlingly illustrative in this respect "No human being is wealthy or powerful enough to transplant a nation from one habitation to another. An idea alone can compass that; and this idea of a state may have the requisite power to do so."[57]

Pakistan and Israel constitute ideal forms of the Enlightenment state, more so than the settler states of the New World or their imitators in the Old. And they do so because whatever emphasis is put upon the land these minority nations have won, both countries debate and resolve their nationality by a question that in effect divests the nation of its state: who is a Jew and who a Muslim? This question, of as much concern to the constitutional lawyer as the passionate sectarian, takes the debate on Pakistani or Israeli nationality back to the Enlightenment's myth of political consent, when a people is converted to nationhood by the force of its idea alone. Perhaps minority peoples, with their effort to assume political universality by taking the national idea to its abstract limits, can do no more than this, making for a politics of radical non-coincidence between nation and state, past and present.

2

# THE PROBLEM WITH NUMBERS

The minority nationalisms that found their fulfilment in Pakistan and Israel emerged within empires rather than nation states, though their own achievement of such states only became possible once these imperial orders had collapsed. But this means that for much of their history, these minorities did not invoke the nation state as their final goal. What they did concern themselves with were ideas about finding a place of their own within the plural jurisdictions of empires like the Ottoman or the British.[1] Indeed both Zionism and Muslim nationalism were in the early part of their careers, preoccupied by imagining futures precisely within or alongside these two empires. After the First World War this imperial vision was gradually replaced by new internationalist ideas, according to which minorities could now be imagined as part of an international order, like the one presided over by the League of Nations with its famous minorities protections. Even when they were finally constituted into nation states after the Second World War, this imperial or international dimension did not disappear from Israeli and Pakistani nationalisms, concerned as they both have been with the fate of world Jewry on the one hand and pan-Islamism on the other, issues themselves originating as political ones in the imperial past. In this chapter I want to describe how Indian Muslims came to see themselves as a minority, and why such a category of belonging made them turn outwards to embrace an imperial or international identity, one that had to be demolished before they could turn inwards to establish nation states.

Like all empires, India under British rule was not a political unit, comprising instead a number of differing legal and administrative jurisdictions. There was British India on the one hand, which was directly ruled by the colonial state, and Princely India on the other, made up of hundreds of states, each ruled indirectly in accordance with treaties that various rajas, maharajas, nawabs and a nizam had signed with the East India Company. Added to these jurisdictions was a third, smaller one known as the Tribal Territories, whose greatest concentration was on the empire's North-East and North-West Frontiers. With more autonomy than princely states, and serving as buffer zones against the rival empires of Russia and China, these territories were also more likely to suffer punitive expeditions by the Indian army. Even British India was made up of differing legal jurisdictions, with Hindus and Muslims governed according to their own personal laws, as these were understood, expurgated and codified by the colonial state. And finally there was the fragmented geography of customary laws appertaining to caste groups in some parts of the country but not others.

Despite this multiplicity of jurisdictions, colonial rule depended upon the ability to grasp India as a unit, by understanding the fault-lines that ran across its vast expanse. Whether it was in order to govern such a society fairly, create allies among its population or decide which among them required more in the way of medical attention, education and representation in the country's political life, the state required detailed knowledge about its Indian subjects. This knowledge was collected and disseminated in a whole range of ways by learned and professional societies, as well as government institutions, with the decennial Census of

India representing perhaps its greatest and certainly most visible form.[2] Demography was of course an indispensable category for all such forms of knowledge, and it soon became clear to Indians that their numbers, as caste, religious and other groups, was important in the making of policy at every level of administration. Colonial forms of knowledge tended towards the development of standardized categories for people who might identify themselves by very particular ones. But such forms also encouraged Indians to agitate for the use of one category rather than another, if only to take advantage of such benefits as their demographic visibility could bring.

In general, Indian efforts to popularize some categories of identity rather than others were informed by the desire to augment the numbers of some communities by rejecting local categories for countrywide ones. Caste and religious groups became the chief categories for such augmentation, and by the early twentieth century it had become common for Hindu and Muslim movements of religious reform, for example, to attempt the standardization of believers' practices with an eye to building up the numbers of their respective communities. Not coincidentally, the colonial state introduced limited forms of franchise during these very years, thus making of numbers the most important factor in Indian politics. But even by the end of the previous century, before any kind of representative government had been introduced in India, those who were recognized by the colonial state to "represent" the "Muslim community" had begun to worry about the purely numerical, rather than, say, theological, sense in which both this community and its representation had come to be defined within a colonial sociology of knowledge. It was worrying, on the one hand, that religious or even political authority among Muslims should now be determined by its popularity instead of qualification; and on the other hand that Muslims should occupy the position of a "minority" compared to the Hindu "majority."[3]

For as long as they could do so, then, Muslims in public life tried to push away the problem of numbers, both as it had to do with the representation of their co-religionists inside the community, and with the latter's diminution to a minority in the world outside. And this resistance was phrased in a defence of the empire's multiple jurisdictions, which did not allow for the emergence of such purely numerical categories of identity. Thus the nineteenth-century Delhi intellectual Zaka Ullah told his English biographer that:

My own experience has shown me that there is a place for the English in India, just in the same way as there is a place for the Musalmans and a place for the Hindus. You have one destiny to fulfil in India; we Musalmans have another destiny to fulfil; and the Hindus have a different destiny of their own.[4]

Such a politics of imperial pluralism, itself rather congruent with the caste and religious practices of Indians, was broken down by the end of the nineteenth century, and the Muslim community forced into being as a minority in the early years of the twentieth. For the gradual extension of responsible government and the centralization of power in India meant that countrywide statistics about religious demography and so equally expansive notions of religious identity came to displace the political pluralism of the past.[5]

## In the provinces

The Muslim leaders most directly engaged with the politics of numbers were those who had, from the mid-nineteenth century, preached an accommodation with British rule and counselled their co-religionists to take advantage of English education, not least so as to play some role in the administration of their country. These so-called modernists, with the famous reformer Sir Syed Ahmed Khan at their head, were members of the Aligarh Movement, named after the town housing its two major institutions, the Mohammedan Anglo-Oriental College, later Aligarh Muslim University, and the Mohammedan Educational Conference, as well as a journal, *Tahzib al-Akhlaq* (Refinement of Morals). These gentlemen, minor landowners and administrative officials for the most part, with some literary figures from the same classes thrown in, viewed the founding of the Indian National Congress in 1886 with some concern. Given the party's very moderate character in that period, this was not primarily because they saw it as being radical or disloyal in any way. What worried men like Sir Syed was that as part of a single nation, Muslims could only play the role of a minority in a new, countrywide political arena, one in which Hindus would necessarily dominate, trying to prevent noxious practices like cowslaughter by the force of their numbers alone. Even the limited forms of democracy envisaged by Congress, then, struck Syed Ahmed Khan as being potentially oppressive, as they might rely upon the weight of numbers rather than negotiation and goodwill to ban such practices, to say nothing of other liberties claimed by minority groups. He also thought that this crude enforcement of majority rule would only give rise to more conflict and disagreement.[6]

Sir Syed tried initially to fight against the kind of majority rule he feared, rightly or wrongly, by stressing the importance of regional arenas and crosscutting identities based on rank rather than religion. So in a speech made at Meerut on 16 March 1888, describing northern India as a distinct country or homeland (*mulk*), he claimed that the Congress was basically a Bengali party and had little to do with the Hindus of North India, whose character and interests were similar to those of their Muslim neighbours:

The Hindus of our country should understand that while their condition is to a certain degree better than that of the Muslims, it is not so good that they can run and come out ahead of us. We are all the inhabitants of the same country. There are many Hindus who have been infiltrated by Muslim habits—such as my friend the Kayasth. Their customs and conditions are not so much more advanced than ours. Whatever will be our fate, so too will be the fate of the Hindus of this country. This is why whatever I'm saying is for the good of all the inhabitants of the country.[7]

Accusing the educated Bengali Hindus who then led the Congress of being grasping, deracinated and pusillanimous, Syed Ahmed Khan recommended leaving them to their own devices and forming, instead, a regional alliance of well-born North Indians from both religious communities:

Every people, not just Muslims, but all this country's Hindus, honored kings and brave Rajputs who worship the swords of their fathers, will they tolerate the command of the Bengali who falls from his chair upon seeing a table knife? Not a piece of this country will remain where faces other than Bengali ones will be seen at the table of command and justice. We say we are happy that only our Bengali brother should progress, but the question is, what will happen to the state of the country's administration? In your opinion, can the Rajput or fiery Pathan, who do not fear the noose, the police, or the army, live peacefully under the Bengali?[8]

Let those who live in Bengal worry themselves: they can do what they want and not do what they don't want. Neither their character nor their condition is that of our countrymen. So what's the point of the people of our country joining them?[9]

Eventually, however, Syed Ahmed Khan, who had worked all his career to bring high-ranking Hindus and Muslims together, was forced to admit that his vision of an India divided into regional cultures and polities was unlikely to succeed, and he despairingly threw in the lot of Muslims with their British rulers:

Our Hindu brothers in this country are leaving us and joining with the Bengalis. So we should join the people whom we can associate with. [...] If our Hindu brothers in this country, and the Bengalis of Bengal, and the Brahmins of Bombay, and the Hindu Madrasis of Madras want to separate from us, let them separate and don't worry about it. We can befriend the English socially. We can eat with them. Whatever expectations of improvement we have, we have from the English. The Bengalis can do nothing good for our community.[10]

It is clear from Sir Syed's speeches that by objecting to Muslims playing the role of a minority, and so of Hindus constituting a majority, he wanted to redefine these categories in non-religious ways. Thus his attempt to disaggregate both communities and form a political minority in North India based on rank instead. Of course the Congress during this period was itself made up of elites, so there was nothing unusual about Syed Ahmed Khan's focus on status in a political context where only the wellborn and well educated represented the "people." More interesting was his desire to secret the novel idea of a religious minority within an older, aristocratic version of that category, one posed against a majority defined as the common people. But even when the emergence of nationalism as a collective identity allowed the small numbers of an aristocracy to be replaced by those of the minority defined in religious and other ways, the latter also continued to be seen as an elite of some kind, which is no doubt why minorities are still routinely accused of placing themselves above majorities, however absurd such an argument might be in reality.

Sir Syed, however, struggled to separate the aristocratic from the merely religious or communal aspect of minority politics, and despite bemoaning the establishment of a countrywide Hindu identity, even if only incidentally, in parties like the Congress, he refused to do the same for Muslims. Interested primarily in his own North Indian constituency, Syed Ahmed Khan even resisted the efforts of associates like Mahdi Ali Khan, known as Nawab Mohsin-ul-Mulk, to build a countrywide Muslim organization, despite the fact that Muslim elites in cities like Bombay were eager to do so.[11] And so it took his death in 1898 to change the course of Muslim politics in India. Faced, then, with an India-wide Congress and the mushrooming of independent Muslim organizations in other parts of the country,

Syed Ahmed Khan's North Indian gentry suddenly came to seem unrepresentative of Muslim interests more broadly, as everyone from Congress, the colonial state, Muslims elsewhere in the country, and even the young men who were the first products of Sir Syed's college at Aligarh agreed. Or as *The Tribune* put it in its issue of 26 November 1901:

It is certain that there is general dissatisfaction in the community with the present condition of affairs. In some parts of India a fairly large section of Mahommedans has been hitherto content to receive their opinions on matters political ready made from Aligarh. But of late there has been a suspicion that in the things and men of Aligarh all that glitters is not gold, and consequently there has been much searching of hearts, which has naturally fluttered the dovecots at Aligarh. A Mahommedan friend of ours very felicitously but correctly character-ized the existing situation of affairs as 'the Revolt against Aligarh'. There can be no doubt that Aligarh is no longer to dominate the polit-ical opinions of Mahommedans in the different parts of the country. For the Mahommedan community this freedom from a yoke that had become very heavy and almost unbearable will itself be no small gain.[12]

And in fact the old idea of natural leadership, which had nothing to do with being validated by a constituency, died with Syed Ahmed Khan, something that was duly noted by one of his successors, Nawab Viqar-ul-Mulk, in a letter to *The Pioneer* of 16 August 1903.[13]

### Risk and representation

Given all these transformations, members of Aligarh's old and young generations convened a meeting in Lucknow on 21 Octo-ber 1901, at which they determined to found an All-India Mahommedan Political Association.[14] Reporting on this gather-ing, the *Aligarh Institute Gazette* made clear its fundamental importance. On the one hand it noted the novel membership of the meeting, which comprised ten barristers, four young aristo-

crats, three pleaders, and only two "influential gentlemen representing the learning and enlightenment of an older generation,"
namely Viqar-ul-Mulk and Masih-uz-Zaman, a former tutor to
the Nizam of Hyderabad.[15] On the other hand the *Gazette*
pointed out that all these people were from the north, and
warned that representation required much more than this:

Is it feasible or warrantable to make it an All India organization? If so,
what evidence is there to show that the two presidencies—Madras and
Bombay—Sindh, Central Provinces, and Berar are even remotely and
partially in touch with the organization? [...] the principle of representation being in the ascendant, it is advisable that Mahommedans
should learn to act on it. It should, however, be remembered that there
are certain tests which are applicable and which, as a matter of fact,
are applied by the press and critics generally to such institutions as
claim a representative character.[16]

Yet such forms of countrywide representation, as Sir Syed well
knew, had their risks, chief among them being the loss of leadership to other sorts of elites. Indeed it was probably this desire
to preserve the North Indian gentry that informed Syed Ahmed
Khan's ambivalent relations with other Muslim organizations.
But after his passing the bar was lifted, and so in 1900 the
Mohammedan Educational Conference was invited to Calcutta,
in 1901 to Madras, and to Bombay in 1903. The North Indian
gentry did not quite know what to make of this attention. In a
speech at Madras, for instance, Mohsin-ul-Mulk confessed that
he had never thought that Muslims of different regions could
come together.[17] And in 1903, at Delhi, he admitted that he had
never even thought about Sind until Muslims from that province
asked to be included in the Conference.[18] The gentlemen at
Aligarh were certainly pleased with this fame, but they still did
not consider these other Muslims as anything more than sympathetic acquaintances who at most could provide examples for
their co-religionists in North India. Thus Mohsin-ul-Mulk
addressed the merchant-princes of Bombay with these words:

O people of Bombay, having met you and seen your condition and wealth, they will reflect that although you do not rule, by God's grace you are the masters of millions of rupees [...] and when they reflect upon the reasons for your wealth, they will leave off complaining about fortune and crying over fate. Some spirit will be born in them, and they will make manly efforts toward industry and commerce.[19]

In response to a resolution on changing the Conference's rules to accommodate Muslims all over the country, Mohsin-ul-Mulk wonderingly remarked that whereas the Muslims of Calcutta and Madras had thought of the Mohammedan Educational Conference as an organ of the "Aligarh Party," and had not seen fit to demand rights in its constitution, Bombay had broken its bounds for the first time.[20] Now Mohsin-ul-Mulk's speech on commerce and industry quoted above illustrates that representation was not the only factor that brought the old politics of Sir Syed to crisis, for the provincial constituency Aligarh had created seemed to be unable even to sustain itself financially. For instance the Mohammedan Anglo-Oriental College, Syed Ahmed Khan's flagship project, moved from crisis to economic crisis. Thus when Sir Syed died in 1898, the institution had a shortfall of 150,000 rupees, and its architects and masons had suspended work because they had not been paid.[21] And such a situation was possible both because the system of donations upon which the college relied was slow, inefficient and costly, and because North Indian Muslims did not or could not generate the kind of money Aligarh required. So of the 9,000 rupees pledged for scholarships at the time of Syed Ahmed Khan's death, only 3,500 had been received by 1900.[22] Indeed conditions were serious enough for Mohsin-ul-Mulk to make these sad revelations for the first time at the 1900 session of the Mohammedan Educational Conference in Rampur. Sir Syed, he said, had not managed to raise more than 700,000 rupees in thirty years of vigorous campaigning,[23] while the scheme for the college's development into a university required a million rupees, of which only 115,000 had been collected in two and a half years.[24]

These troubles of representation and finance approached crisis in 1906, when the proposed introduction of a limited franchise for legislative bodies, what would become the Morley-Minto Reforms, provoked a debate on the competitive abilities of India's Muslims. Something had to be done, a Muslim political party had to be formed, if the young products of Aligarh were not to abandon the guidance of their elders for political opportunities elsewhere. So we have Mohsin-ul-Mulk anxiously writing to the principal of the college, W. A. J. Archbold:

You are aware that the Mahommedans already feel a little disappointed, and young educated Mahommedans seem to have a sympathy for the 'Congress'. [...] Although there is little reason to believe that any Mahommedans, except the young educated ones will join that body, there is still a general complaint on their part that we (Aligarh people) take no part in politics, and do not safeguard the political rights of Mahommedans, they say that we do not suggest any plans for preserving their rights, and particularly do nothing and care nothing for the Mahommedans beyond asking for funds to help the college. [...] I feel it is a very important matter, and if we remain silent, I am afraid, people will leave us to go their own way and act up to their own personal opinions.[25]

No doubt playing to British fears of an uncontrolled Muslim intelligentsia, Aligarh's leaders petitioned their rulers for the right to organize politically, a right they were granted in a much-publicized staging of their grievances as a minority before the viceroy, Lord Minto, on 1 October 1906.[26] This meeting, which resulted in the introduction three years later of separate electorates for Hindus and Muslims, effectively blocked Congress's representative claims. Although they were unprecedented in the constitutional history of any country, these separate electorates, which were meant to protect either community from being deprived of political representation in areas where it was a minority, clearly belonged in the world of imperialism's multiple jurisdictions. And in this way the new Muslim politics did inherit something from the old. In order to stake a claim to represent their co-religionists across the country, however, Muslim leaders had to prove themselves in a new way. Indeed the concern with representation assumed the status of a mania among them, as is clear from the very beginning of the Muslim address to Lord Minto:

Availing ourselves of the permission awarded to us, we, the undersigned nobles, jagirdars, taluqdars, lawyers, zemindars, merchants and others representing a large body of the Mahommedan subjects of His Majesty the King-Emperor in different parts of India, beg most respectfully to approach your Excellency with the following address for your favourable consideration.[27]

And to make things even more evident, here is how the viceroy began his response:

I welcome the representative character of your deputation as expressing the views and aspirations of the enlightened Muslim community in India. I feel that all you have said emanates from a representative body basing its opinions on a matured consideration of the existing political conditions of India, totally apart from the small personal or political sympathies and antipathies of scattered localities [...].[28]

These quotations make two things clear. For one thing the Muslim representatives were still natural leaders in a certain sense, men of enlightenment who were representative only in the variety of their vocations and places of origin. And for another this group was composed of aristocrats, merchants and lawyers, comprising a new Muslim elite, one that, while it was not dominated by Aligarh, had the will as well as ability to fund it and any other Muslim organization required by the new politics of representation in the Raj. The Muslims who presented a memorial to the viceroy in 1906, for example, were led by the Aga Khan, a wealthy Iranian nobleman exiled in Bombay who also happened to be the spiritual head of a Shia sub-sect with tens of thousands of members in India. It was such men who broke through the parochial politics of Aligarh and went on to lead a new kind of community under the auspices of the Muslim League, whose first president was none other than this very Aga Khan, the most unrepresentative of Indian Muslims. Not surprisingly, the Aga was immediately set the task of raising funds to make the Mohammedan Anglo-Oriental College into a university, and in doing so he launched the first India-wide campaign in Islam's modern history, giving rise to the kind of popular effusions and large-scale fundraising that set the model for Muslim politics subsequently. Given the fact that many of his spiritual followers happened to be businessmen whose cultural, social and professional dealings were overwhelmingly aligned with the Hindu trading castes they did business with, it was also natural that the Aga should himself be a generous donor to the campaign for a Hindu university in Benares, his crosscutting alliances illustrating not only the pluralistic imperative of Muslim politics in general, but also the complexity that the entry of new capital brought to it.[29]

Not coincidentally, the League's last president in colonial times was also from Bombay, and born into the very sub-sect that was led by the Aga Khan. And like his predecessor, Mohammad Ali Jinnah was also able to raise the kinds of funds from Muslim merchants and industrialists, as well as from the aristocrats allied with them, which evaded politicians even from provinces where their co-religionists were more populous. Apart from a few noblemen scattered around India, after all, it was only such trading groups based in the great port cities of Bombay, Madras and Calcutta that possessed large enough reserves of capital to finance the League. While small in number compared to Muslims elsewhere in the country, these merchant castes, whose role, like that of sectarian minorities in Muslim politics, has largely been ignored by historians of Pakistan, were

61

important enough to allow the League and its last president to be based in Bombay. The city was also headquarters to the Habib Bank, which had been set up in 1941 by a family from Jinnah's own caste and was responsible for mobilizing the League's finances. Though severely damaged by Z. A. Bhutto's nationalization policies in the 1970s, it remains Pakistan's largest bank to this day, and is now unsurprisingly managed by an organization at whose head sits the Aga Khan's successor. Many such genealogies are to be found in the unexplored history of Muslim capitalism. Yet from the very start it was evident that the capitalists based in India's port cities and their aristocratic allies in the country's interior were inclined to despair of their more numerous co-religionists in the north, whose leaders tended to be associated with Aligarh. So in an interview with *The Times of India* on 8 March 1912, the Aga Khan had the following words to say about the problem of raising funds for a Muslim university:

He remarked that unfortunately those who were most backward in supporting the University financially were those who would benefit most materially from its establishment. For instance, the Mahomedans of the Central Provinces had borne their part in the financial burden fully. In Bombay too a splendid response had been made by the local Mahomedans, and almost all the subscriptions promised, which in a majority of cases came from his own intimate friends, had been fully paid. In northern India, however, the position was less satisfactory. Little had been done by the Mahomedans of the Punjab and not much more in the United Provinces.[30]

However the Aga hastened to add that such small-mindedness was not true of aristocratic figures, often Shia like himself, from the north:

The Raja of Mahmudabad and the Raja of Jehangirabad in the United Provinces had, for instance, not only subscribed liberally, but had worked most zealously in inducing others to support the movement. In northern India as a whole, which would benefit most by the University, because it would be situated within easy reach of the boys, the smallest sacrifices had been made.[31]

Despite their derisory contribution to the advancement of the Muslim community, the Aga noted with some bitterness that his co-religionists in the north seemed intent on excluding those outside their region, including the members of Shia sub-sects like his own, from any role to play in Aligarh:

His Highness remarked that there was an increasing complaint that the trustees of the college were almost entirely elected from the United Provinces and that they included a large professional element whose members had not made very material sacrifices for the M.A.O. As an illustration of this he mentioned that Sir Adamjee Peerbhoy had contributed more than Rs. 110,000 to the funds of the college and yet not one member of the family had been placed on the Board of Trustees.[32]

From the beginning, then, the Muslim League marked its departure from the old politics of Aligarh. It was inaugurated in Dacca under the patronage of the leading prince of that city; and its first session was held in Karachi, with a prominent industrialist from Bombay, Sir Adamjee Peerbhoy, presiding. It was at this first meeting that lines were drawn between merchants and large landowners on the one hand and the North Indian gentry on the other. The former pressured the government for commercial and aristocratic causes, calling for the development of free and skilled labour, the establishment of banks, the organization of princely politics and the preservation of noble inheritances, while the latter were concerned with liberal education, professional vocations and reserved places in the civil service. Sir Adamjee's presidential address almost turned these divisions into battle-lines:

It is scarcely necessary for me to say that I have but a poor knowledge of the paths of political controversy. I am no scholar nor a man of many words. My sphere of action in this life has been cast in an entirely different direction. Since the time when nature made it possible for me to turn my hand to toil, I have laboured, and I must admit I still have much affection for the man who uses his energies in that direction. But I do not wish to be misunderstood. I do not despise those who labour in other fields. There is work for us all. Circumstances have compelled me to direct my energies into the paths of industrialism, and no higher duty could be placed upon an individual. I believe in the dignity of labour as the great Prophet did. The history of our people, the history of our heroes and of those who have carried the flag of Islam over the world has been one of strenuous and ceaseless effort. Whatever we may have lacked in recent times in purely literary accomplishments, no one can charge the Mahommedan with not doing his fair share of the world's work. In India he has shown his special aptitude in industrialism, and I believe it is along these lines that he can best exert his influence and carve for himself a high position in the Empire. I love to see the development of Mahommedan enterprise, for it is a true measure of the energy and spirit of the people and we can never be without hope so long as we can maintain the reputation we have already earned.[33]

It is difficult to imagine a speech more calculated to insult the sentiments of North India's Muslims, and Sir Adamjee's address marked the beginning of a long and unresolved struggle between these two groups for control of the League and its policies. More than economic interests, moreover, these groups often represented differing sectarian affiliations, with Shia figures like the Aga Khan, Adamjee, the Raja of Mahmudabad and the Nawab of Rampur largely responsible for financing the League and making it into a non-sectarian as well as country-wide party during its early history, in which it is normally written about only as an unrepresentative grouping of elites. The usual categorization of the League's leaders and members as being divided between an old party and a young, or between progressives and reactionaries, is in some sense irrelevant, a description retailed by congressmen like Jinnah himself, in his early days as an Indian nationalist. Derived from a similar division between moderates and extremists in the Congress, such a characterization is misleading, however accurate it might otherwise be, because it defines Muslim Leaguers by their attitude towards the British and their policies alone. But Muslim politics, like that engaged in by Dalit, Hindu nationalist and other groups, was much more informed by their opposition to the Congress.

Similarly suspect is the stereotyped account of the League representing the interests of "feudal" landowners and big capitalists, itself a standard theme of Congress polemic. For while we have seen that the party was, indeed, supported financially by an odd combination of landed aristocrats in the north and merchant castes from western India, to define such "classes" by religious affiliation, rather than the means and relations of production in a given economy, is automatically to exclude the latter from playing any primary role as categories of identification or analysis—unless the patently false argument is made that Muslim landowners and capitalists were excluded by their Hindu rivals from a share of their country's economic spoils. The moment capitalists have to be divided into "Hindu" and "Muslim" rivals in the same economy, they cease to function as a class, and it even becomes possible to break them down further into equally competitive "Bohra," "Khoja" or "Memon" factions in an absurd reduction. Merchant castes might be capitalist, but they do not necessarily constitute a capitalist class, and even if they did, it is not clear what particular advantage they might have gained by supporting the Muslim League instead of the Congress. Indeed it is interesting to note that the creation of Pakistan did not lead to the wholesale transfer of these groups there, and that the leadership of the Shia sects among them either stayed put in India, or shifted to Europe rather than making Karachi their base. In fact despite their dominance of the country's financial sector in its early years, most businessmen from such castes only appear to have moved to Pakistan in the middle of the 1950s, when its economy looked like it was more open to entrepreneurship than India's.

While they are certainly an important element of Pakistan's elite today big landowners, too, had not always supported the League in places like the Punjab until 1946, too late to shape its ideology in any appreciable way. In any case the Congress, its socialist rhetoric apart, was itself no enemy of capitalists and landowners during this period, with the Muslim League, for instance, deliberately threatening these interests by bringing in a "poor man's" budget as part of the interim government in 1946, in which Liaquat Ali Khan, a landowner himself, was minister of finance. However cynical the League's move to tax the rich and alleviate financial impositions on the poor by abolishing the famous salt tax, it demonstrates, clearly, that no unambiguous link can be drawn between class interests and party politics. Instead of taking categories like class, capitalism and even interest at face value, then, it might be more productive to ask how and to what degree they came to exist in colonial India. This work, indeed, has already started happening for Indian history, with the scholarship on Pakistan lagging, as usual, far behind.[34] As far as the League was concerned, sectarian tensions within Muslim society can even be seen as being more important to its politics than anti-Congress or anti-Hindu feeling, to say nothing of class conflict. Indeed I'd like to suggest that the Shia figures who took such a prominent role in the consolidation of a countrywide Muslim "community" under the League, were largely concerned with making a space for themselves within an Islam increasingly unified under colonial law and dominated by Sunni groups. And in this sense the minority protection sought by the League's Shia leaders had to do with their fear of a Sunni majority as much as a Hindu one, something that has been neglected in a historiography marked both by the Muslim League's "ecumenism" in conceiving of a unified Muslim community, and, to be charitable about it, the inadvertent sectarianism of ignoring its internal differences in the name of this unity.[35] But this meant that Shia populations could gravitate towards the League or reject its ecumenical appeal for exactly the same reason, in order to safeguard themselves from Sunni rather than Hindu domination.[36]

Indeed, given their minority status within the Muslim "community," and the higher than average economic and educational status their restricted social roles gave them within it, the Shia tended to enjoy better relations with Hindus than with Sunnis, as, for instance, had always been (and continues to be) the case in the region of Awadh, which was once ruled by a Shia prince. And the same goes for the Bohra and Khoja trading castes, who had in the past been persecuted by Sunni rulers like the Mughal emperor Aurangzeb, and whose economic success was largely manifested in areas where Hindus were a majority. In this way the League's Shia leaders bear comparison to their contemporaries, the Christian writers and politicians who were so influential in the development of Arab nationalism, also an "ecumenical" movement, and one whose broad regional appeal did not depend upon the specificities of state making in the Middle East. Of course these Shia figures rarely if ever mention their sectarian affiliation, even when they write glowingly about the sect itself in their historical works, but this too is a sign of their careful avoidance of any public reference to a faith which, however, is never denied either. Why should the Aga Khan, for instance, not mention Jinnah's background in a caste that owed allegiance to him, even while he praises the Qaid effusively in his memoirs? The most important precedent, politically speaking, of what I am calling Shia ecumenism is provided by the well-known pan-Islamic activist, Jamal al-Din al-Afghani, who, in the late nineteenth century, concealed his Iranian and Shia background behind a Sunni appellation.[37] I shall return to the secretive if not esoteric nature of the Shia presence in Muslim League politics in chapter six, something which is in fact constantly implied in the historiography, generally in the form of speculations about what Jinnah "really" wanted in a politics recognized as being deceptive and even duplicitous. And if I have dwelt on such details in the pages above, it is only to suggest something of the complexity that characterized the emergence of Muslim politics in its modern, institutional form, not least because this variant of it is routinely ignored in the historiography. But I want now to describe how the countrywide minority represented by the Muslim League came to be dismantled and remade as a nation only three decades later.

## Beating the census

Apart from separate electorates, Muslims (and therefore Hindus who were minorities in Muslim provinces) were granted something called weightage under the Morley-Minto Reforms. This latter was a principle according to which minorities were reserved more seats in councils and legislatures than their numbers warranted, in order to give them "effective" representation there. The important point to note is that such weightage was granted not simply to bolster insufficient numbers, but out of consideration for non-numerical factors like the historical importance of Muslims in India's political traditions and the large role they played in the army. Hindu weightages, on the contrary, were based on nothing but the demands of reciprocity. While numbers, in other words, constituted the very basis of claims to separate representation, the policy of weightage was premised upon an entirely non-numerical argument, for which the idea of the minority was both necessary but also irrelevant. Whether or not it really helped Muslims in any way, this system of protections was unprecedented and went well beyond anything the League of Nations would eventually adopt for minorities in Europe.

From the day they were introduced, separate electorates and weightage became the subjects of political debate in India as much as in Britain, and since then historians have done little more than perpetuate these controversies. However what I find interesting about them is not how effective such procedures were in representing Muslims, but how quickly they became part of a politics that questioned the very category of the minority while at the same time making use of it. For weightage was only one way of conceiving of politics beyond numbers, alongside the desire of Muslim leaders to place their community in a worldwide context within which it was Hindus who were almost, but not quite, rendered into a minority. Pan-Islamism, of course, was the standard term describing this effort to set India's Muslims in a political arena wider than their own country, though it was used to refer only to the kind of religious solidarity that might threaten the Raj. But equally, if not more important, was the attempt by Muslim politicians to think about Islam's worldwide community as a partner in Britain's equally world-encompassing empire. Indeed the two forms share the same history, since pan-Islamism was itself a modern phenomenon that took European imperialism as its model. Thus despite colonial fears of a "crescentade" that went back to the mid-nineteenth century, the first Indian movements in which Muslims showed solidarity with their co-religionists abroad only date from the twentieth century.

The possibility of Muslims joining the British to keep Hindus enslaved caused much concern to Indian nationalists throughout the colonial period, as did the reverse possibility of an Anglo-Hindu alliance against Islam. But the fantastic plans of Muslim leaders should perhaps be seen more as efforts to escape the status of minority, and in doing so to question that of the majority as well in a way that would eventually redefine politics itself in India. Initially this transcending of numbers could only occur by elaborating upon India's imperial character—whether it was seen as being fundamentally British, Muslim or indeed Hindu. Maybe the most ambitious such plan ever proposed was that detailed by the Aga Khan in his book *India in Transition*, published just as the war was coming to an end in 1918, and meant to inform discussion of the political reforms being considered for the country once peace had been declared. Though it dealt with almost every important aspect of Indian politics, what interests me about this treatise is its remarkably world-encompassing vision, one that easily outflanked even the most speculative of Congress narratives, being comparable in this respect only to the communist imagination that was itself a product of the war. Even before it had adopted the nation as its defining category, then, Muslim politics strove to escape the logic of numbers by inventing a new world for itself.

And yet it was clear that India was central to this new world, which made Muslim visions of the future as intensely patriotic as that of any Congressman, and in some ways even more ambitious of the country playing a world-historical role as a great power in her own right. The only difference between such patriotic fantasies had to do with the fact that Muslims were imagined as playing a far more prominent role in theirs than would be possible for a mere minority. Influential with Britain's governing elites when it was first published, and regularly cited by Indian writers well into the 1940s, the Aga Khan's book opens with a description of India as the only country that could be said to constitute the world in miniature, representing as it did four great civilizations, Brahmanical, Islamic, Western and Far Eastern.[38] This idea of India being the world, or at least Asia in miniature, would enjoy a long career in Muslim political thought. And its function was not only to demonstrate the country's diversity, which made any unitary form of majority politics there impossible, but also to internationalize it through and through.

As the world in miniature, India could form the basis of a sub-imperial order of her own, one the Aga Khan compared to the Monroe Doctrine that united the Americas under US domination. For he argued that the world was moving towards such large agglomerations, saying that:

It is for the Indian patriot to recognize that Persia, Afghanistan, and possibly Arabia must sooner or later come within the orbit of some

Continental Power—such as Germany, or what may grow out of the break-up of Russia—or must throw in their lot with that of the Indian Empire, with which they have so much more genuine affinity. The world forces that move small states into closer contact with powerful neighbours, though so far most visible in Europe, will inevitably make themselves felt in Asia.[39]

And so he laid out a fantastical vision in which:

looking forward a few years, at most a decade or two, we may antici-pate an economic, commercial, and intellectual India not bounded by the vast triangle of the Himalayas on the north and the Indian Ocean and Bay of Bengal on either side down to Adam's Bridge, but consist-ing of a vast agglomeration of states, principalities and countries in Asia extending from Aden to Mesopotamia, from the two shores of the Gulf to India proper, from India proper across Burma and includ-ing the Malay Peninsula; and then from Ceylon to the states of Bokhara, and from Tibet to Singapore. The aggregation might well be called the 'South Asiatic Federation', of which India would be the pivot and centre.[40]

Crucial about this vision was its commercial and indeed cap-italist focus, something only to be expected from the Bombay-based leader of a trading community. Like Sir Adamjee's speech quoted above, in other words, the Aga's narrative, while being generally Muslim was also grounded in a view of the world that did not respect religious boundaries, and that in effect even excluded the old Muslim elite of North India. Elsewhere in the book, for instance, he strongly pressed the case for German East Africa to be given over for Indian colonization (just as German South-West Africa was eventually given to the South African Union) after the war, a proposal that not only had a powerful resonance for a number of British politicians, including the Sec-retary of State for India, but that also put the Aga at the head of a largely Hindu constituency of merchants both in Bombay and cities like Dar-es-Salaam and Mombasa. Naturally the fact that many of the Aga Khan's followers were traders in East Africa made him both an interested party and a qualified expert in such a proposal, but his position was complex enough to allow for cross-cutting alliances between Hindus and Muslims in these grandiose plans for India's post-war future. Indeed the Aga attributed the proposal for German East Africa's colonization by Indians to his friend, the eminent Indian nationalist Gopal Krishna Gokhale, who had made the demand in a political testament given to the Aga Khan and published by him after the former's death.[41] And yet compared to the other imperial and international fantasies set loose by the end of the war, of which communism's truly global vision was only the most ambitious, the Aga's proposals were not in the least eccentric.

While his plan was presented as a contribution to what the Aga Khan saw as Britain's worldwide political mission, its scale also entailed India's emergence as by far the most important part of her empire. And this further meant that India required both autonomy and the greater participation of her people in their own governance—to say nothing of their rule over other peoples. So in tune with nationalists in the Congress, the Aga recommended some version of dominion status for his country, but imagined it playing a role far more extensive than anything Canada or Australia could possibly command. In any case his South Asiatic Federation had quite different issues to address, chief among them being to conceive a form of representative government that did not disenfranchise minority groups. For augmented as it would immeasurably be in a South Asiatic Federation, India's great diversity could not be encompassed within a parliamentary government on the Westminster model, and so:

In a word, for India, with her vast population, her varied provinces and races, her many sectarian differences (brought to the surface by the present search for the lines of constitutional advance), a unilateral form of free government is impossible. If we include in our survey the far greater grouping of to-morrow, to which we have given the name of the South Asiatic Federation, the idea is still more hopelessly impracticable.[42]

The Aga Khan instead recommended a federal system with Indian provinces reconstituted along racial, linguistic and cultural or religious lines, another suggestion that would come to play a crucial role in the Pakistan Movement. "In a word, the path of beneficent and growing union must be based on a federal India, with every member exercising her individual rights, her historic peculiarities and natural interests, yet protected by a common defensive system and customs union from external danger and economic exploitation by stronger forces."[43] The Aga went further and maintained that it had been the Mughal attempt to unite India as a single, absolutist state that had resulted in the oppressiveness of that dynasty's rule and the final collapse of its empire, for which he blamed the most powerful of India's Muslim rulers, thus setting a precedent for what we shall see in the next chapter was the Pakistan Movement's paradoxical dismissal of Islam's Indian history:

With Aurangzeb the policy of excessive centralization culminated. [...] Had he been content to leave the rich kingdoms of Bijapur and Golconda unannexed, it is probable that one of two things would have happened, each equally satisfactory from the point of view of Imperial consolidation. Either the Moslem dynasties of the south would have identified themselves more and more with their Hindu subjects, much as the early Nizams did, and ultimately the southern kingdoms would have been federated with the empire-nation at Delhi. The other eventuality, that of the Mahrattas under Sivaji wiping away the local dynasties, would still have meant the establishment of a powerful confederacy in the south, but with a natural and inevitable attraction toward the empire of the north. Sooner or later, they would have united for common purposes, while each kept its own internal independence and national character. [...] After careful study of Indian history from the rise of Akbar onwards, I have no hesitation in attributing the break-up of the Mogul Empire and the terrible anarchy of the eighteenth century mainly to the centralizing policy of Akbar, Jehangir, Shah Jehan, and Aurangzeb.[44]

In addition to forcing a decentralized political system upon India, the Aga Khan's South Asiatic Federation had the function of lifting Muslims out of their status as a minority, or rather of rendering both categories, majority as well as minority, irrelevant in the vast and plural sub-empire that India was meant to dominate. And about this he was quite clear, saying that "If we turn from numbers to surface of territory, the Islamic provinces of South Asia will be almost as great in extent as the India of yesterday. Hence there is little danger of the Mahomedans of India being nothing but a small minority in the coming federation."[45] Going so far as to embrace contemporary Hindu fantasies of empire in an admirably impartial way, the Aga even saw in India's world-historical mission the only real chance for resolving the country's religious rivalries:

Can anyone deny that, if the Mogul Empire had not been dissolved, or if it had been succeeded by a powerful and united Hindu Empire over the whole of India, the lands of the Persian Gulf littoral would long ago have been brought under Indian dominance? Nor can the process of Indian expansion westwards be stopped by any series of treaties or political conditions. Whatever else happens, and whatever the flag that may hereafter float over Basra and Bagdad, over Bushire and Muscat, Indian civilization, commerce, and emigration must become an increasing power in Mesopotamia, Persia, and Arabia. This process will add greatly to Mahomedan influence in India itself, while, on the other hand, by taking Hindu influences into lands hitherto regarded as the preserves of Islam, it must inevitably lead to a better understanding between the Brahmanical and Islamic peoples of the peninsula.[46]

Though it was far more expansive and capitalistic in its orientation than the visions of Syed Ahmed Khan and his followers, the Aga Khan's plan was similar to theirs in its conviction that India's minority question could only be resolved in an imperial landscape, where such numerical categories of political identity might become irrelevant. Indeed this way of thinking about the country's constitutional future, for which the British connection was not of primary importance, can also be seen in the imperialism of Hindu leaders like M. K. Gandhi, whose early career was devoted precisely to making India into the pivot for a new kind of political order whose mission would be universal in scope.[47] It is also not inconsequential that in the early days of his own career, the Aga Khan had approached the Turkish sultan on behalf of the Rothschild family among other Zionist luminaries, to ask that the Jews be given a homeland of their own within the Ottoman Empire, conceived of as a similarly pluralistic world order. Surely the Aga could not have been unaware of the comparison with his own politics, despite the huge difference in scale that was involved. This is how the Aga Khan describes this episode of his career in his memoirs, published in 1954:

Now Zionism, I may say in passing, was something of which I had had long and by no means unsympathetic experience. My friend of early and strenuous days in Bombay, Professor Haffkine, was a Zionist—as were many other brilliant and talented Russian Jews of his generation who escaped into Western Europe from the harsh and cruel conditions imposed upon them by Tsarist Russia. Haffkine, like many of the earlier Zionists, hoped that some arrangement could be made with the Turkish Sultan whereby peaceful Jewish settlement could be progressively undertaken in the Holy Land—a settlement of a limited number of Jews from Europe (mainly from the densely populated areas then under Russian rule) in agricultural and peasant holdings; the capital was to be provided by wealthier members of the Jewish community, and the land would be obtained by purchase from the Sultan's subjects.[48]

Thus the Aga's conception of Zionism in its early years was of a piece with his advocacy of Indian settlement in, and indeed colonization of, German East Africa, to say nothing of his ideas about the role that his fellow countrymen might play in a larger South Asiatic Federation. And it is in this context, too, that emerging ideas about Muslim autonomy and even resettlement within India should be considered. It is also clear that these novel visions of the future took their meaning from the new world emerging in the wake of the First World War. For the nation state was not the only political norm that had been established following the wartime destruction of three great empires, the Habsburg, Romanov and Ottoman, to say nothing of the Hohenzollern—so was the idea of an international order, whether in the form of the League of Nations or, indeed, the Communist International. Both pan-Islamism as a popular movement and the kind of hybrid, imperial-international federation that the Aga Khan desired for South Asia were in effect products of the Great War, and the Aga was not alone in seeing them as being of a piece with other forms of internationalism, including that represented by the League of Nations, in which he represented India for much of the 1930s, becoming president of the League's General Assembly in 1937. The imperial or international rather than national character of these projects is made clear in the way the Aga Khan goes on to justify early Zionism:

There were, after all, precedents for population resettlement of this kind within the Ottoman Empire, notably the Circassians—of Muslim faith, but of purely European blood—who were established with excellent results by Abdul Hamid in villages in what is today the Kingdom of Jordan. Abdul Hamid could well have done with the friendship and alliance of world Jewry, and on the broader ground of principle, there is every natural reason for the Jews and the Arabs, two Semitic peoples with a great deal in common, to be close friends rather than the bitter enemies which unfortunately for both sides the events of the past thirty years or so have made them.[49]

Imperial though it was, the Aga's endorsement of Zionism was by that very token linked, as well, to New World and Enlightenment notions of a politics delinked from blood and soil, since the American states, after all, had also been founded within empires. So he goes on to recount the proposals of his Zionist associate and France's Chief Rabbi, Zadok Kahn, commenting in a footnote how his own name, Khan, was mistaken as a Jewish one by Americans, and that he was once identified as the brother of Otto Kahn of New York's Metropolitan Opera House:

Rabbi Kahn prepared a statement of his and his friends' ideas on Jewish settlement in Palestine. It was an elaborate plan for colonization on a scale and in a manner which would have helped and strengthened Turkey; and one of its most logical claims to consideration was that the Ottoman Empire was not a national state but was multi-national and multi-racial. With the Rabbi's proposal I made my approaches to Abdul Hamid through Munir Pasha, the Turkish Ambassador in Paris, and then through Izzet Bey, the Sultan's confidential secretary. However, the scheme, good or bad as it may have been, was turned down by the Sultan, and I heard no more of it. I must say its rejection has always seemed to me one of Abdul Hamid's greatest blunders.[50]

In addition to such status as he enjoyed as a Muslim leader in India, the Aga Khan's position as a petitioner to the sultan was buttressed by the fact that many thousands of his Syrian followers were Ottoman subjects, over whom the Aga Khan might well have wanted to exercise more sway. And so his thoughts on the future of that empire were by no means entirely abstract or disinterested. Given his far-flung interests and influence, to say nothing of his heterodoxy, the Aga was untypical of his co-religionists in the subcontinent, and yet he was perhaps also the one best placed to elaborate the kind of international vision that went into shaping Muslim politics in India. This imperial-international vision, moreover, continued to have a life in Jewish thought well beyond the First World War and the destruction of the Ottoman Empire. So Hannah Arendt, in an article of 1943, recommended inserting a Jewish homeland within a new kind of imperial or post-imperial order, the British Commonwealth, which, like Gandhi two decades earlier, she saw as providing a context for politics where majorities and minorities would no longer exist:

The Jewish people could then achieve political status as a *people* with equal rights within all regions belonging to the British Commonwealth. The same holds true for Arabs. In Palestine both Jews and Arabs would enjoy equal rights as members of a larger system that ensures the national interests of each. And the question of who should rule over whom would then have become meaningless. Without requiring a national state of their own, the Jews would have the same political status as all other members of the Commonwealth, whereby Palestine would be given a special status as a Jewish homeland.[51]

As always, Arendt was certain that such a Commonwealth could only assume reality if India joined it, thus making Palestine's inclusion possible, because the white dominions alone would have been unable to constitute such a world-historical experiment in freedom.[52] In the absence of India, she imagined another kind of commonwealth within which Palestine might find a place, a Mediterranean federation constituted by Spain, France, Italy and their former colonial possessions.[53] Chimerical as they may seem today, these plans were by no means the fantasies of colonial "reactionaries" like the Aga Khan alone, but possessed an international salience, particularly among minority populations like the Jews. For like the leadership of the Muslim League, even the most fervently nationalist of Zionist politicians continued to think in terms of imperial alliances, especially with Britain, until the eve of their respective countries' independence. While she was critical of Zionism in many ways, therefore, Arendt serves here as one of the most intelligent analysts of its hidden history, for which nationalism was a problem as much as it was a promise. And the same may be said for Muslim visions of Palestine's future as a Muslim territory, with the poet and philosopher Mohammad Iqbal, for instance, who would in future come to be known as Pakistan's spiritual father, condemning even the idea of an Arab state in the Holy Land. This is what he had to say in a statement of 27 July 1937 that was read out at a public meeting sponsored by the Muslim League in Lahore:

Experience has made it abundantly clear that the political integrity of the peoples of the Near East lies in the immediate reunion of the Turks and the Arabs. [...] The Arabs, whose religious consciousness gave birth to Islam (which united the various races of Asia with remarkable success), must never forget the consequences arising out of their deserting the Turks in their hour of trial. [...] The possibilities of the Palestine problem may eventually compel them seriously to consider their position as members of that Anglo-French institution miscalled the League of Nations and to explore practical means for the formation of an Eastern League of Nations.[54]

Curious about these new ways of imagining politics, then, was the fact that they managed to connect the imperial past to an international future while leaving out the nation state as a mere relic of tradition, though one that all knew would continue to cause them much difficulty. While it might be thought only natural given the precarious religious position of the Shia sub-sect he led in the Muslim world, for instance, the Aga's identification with the "Jewish Question" in Europe was deliberately phrased in the more general terms of Islam. And he returned to this identification frequently, as in a 1935 letter to the Punjabi politician Fazl-i-Husain, in which the Aga noted that India's Muslims occupied a role "similar to the Jews in Europe or the Parsees and Christians in India."[55] And of course Parsi thinkers and politicians from the nineteenth century had themselves identified with the Jews as an international minority.[56] But by the 1930s the Aga Khan was worrying about the fate of India's Muslims in the context of what he saw as British decline and the rise of Hindu nationalism, writing to Fazl-i-Husain that "they would descend to the position of the Jews in Germany at present."[57] By the time the war had begun, this identification of India's Muslims with Europe's Jews had become so generalized that the British journalist Patrick Lacey could compare India under Congress to Europe under the Nazis in his book *Fascist India*, a copy of which he sent to Jinnah with his compliments.[58] It was the drawing to a close of imperialism, then, that served to curtail the political imagination of these minority groups, Jews and Muslims both, forcing them into a most ambiguous form of nationalism.

*Dream and reality*

Those who might have doubted if there was anything real about the Aga Khan's imperial vision when *India in Transition* was first published in 1918 would have had to revise their opinions the year after. For 1919 saw the improbable cause of the Caliphate in distant Turkey give rise to Muslim mobilization on a mass scale for the first time in India's history.[59] The Khilafat Movement, as it was known, emerged as a protest against British attempts to despoil the defeated Ottoman Empire of her Middle Eastern possessions, these being seen as essential to the status of the caliph, the titular authority that the Turkish sultan claimed over Muslims around the world. Comparable to the Holy Roman Empire that had also come to an end with the war, the Caliphate had never before attracted much attention in India, and the sudden dedication of Muslims to its preservation there has continued to confound historical explanation. But in one of the more lucid passages of his book the Aga Khan, who was instrumental in defending the Turkish claims in his own loyal way, had already guessed at the reasons for this feeling, writing that:

the Indian Mahomedan, instead of holding but the outposts of Islam in the east, sees around him nothing but Moslem societies in a far greater state of decay than his own. The banner of the Prophet is no longer in strong hands in North Africa or Persia, and Turkey has become a political enemy of England and a satrapy of Germany. Under these circumstances, he necessarily looks upon India more and more as the hope of his political freedom and as the centre that may still raise the other Mahomedan countries to a higher standard of civilization.[60]

India, in other words, had after the war come to occupy, in the view of many Muslims, a central position in world politics, one that allowed her to agitate for causes abroad even at the cost of sacrificing much in the way of time, effort and resources. Thus Indian Muslims during the Khilafat Movement donated large amounts of money for the Turks, dispatched medical missions to the Middle East and lobbied Britain to take a more favourable line in her Levantine policy. Much to his disgust, the significant sums that had been raised by the Aga for a Muslim university at Aligarh were also, by popular acclaim, given to the Turks. It is important to recognize how the Muslims in this extraordinary movement pressed their claims as British subjects, demanding that their views be taken into consideration both because of their numbers, and due to the very significant role they had played in the Indian army that had defeated the Turks and fought the Germans during the war. These claims to citizenship sought to do nothing less than democratize the British Empire, and in the very terms that the Aga Khan and Gandhi had each in his own way proposed. And so whatever his political calculations, it was only natural for the Mahatma to join the Khilafat Movement, and indeed to become its leader. For no merely Indian movement could have allowed her leaders to play such a role on the world's stage, speaking on behalf of tens of millions beyond the borders of the subcontinent, and even sending a delegation to the Paris Peace Conference. But remarkable though it undoubtedly was, we might also see in Khilafat one of the many attempts to remake the world in the wake of the war, when for a while anything seemed possible in a political geography defined by the fall of three empires and the establishment of a communist state on the remains of one.

With Gandhi's encouragement, Khilafat became a major plank of the Congress platform, bringing together Hindus and Muslims in the first and last truly national mobilization of colonial times. The Muslim League was relegated to a shadowy existence during this period, when the Prophet's followers joined Congress in their thousands, demanding, in the name of Gandhi's non-violence, India's freedom as a part of a nation which had as an important goal the protection of Islam, as of other peoples around the world who were threatened by colonial powers. In yet another example of the new role that Muslim capitalists in the port cities were playing in politics, the Central Khilafat Committee was based in Bombay under the presidency of Seth Chotani, a wealthy Gujarati mill-owner from a cognate community to Jinnah and the Aga Khan's. Jinnah himself, however, who had been an important Congress leader until this time, resigned from the party in opposition to the course that it was taking under the Mahatma's leadership, though he had to wait until the disastrous end of the Khilafat Movement to have his views more widely heard. For in 1922, much to the fury of Muslim and other Indian leaders, Gandhi had called off his campaign of non-cooperation in response to violence breaking out among Congress supporters. And in 1924 the Caliphate itself was abolished by a revivified Turkish state, which used as a pretext to do so the "foreign" interference of Indian Muslims, who were after all British subjects. The Assembly in Ankara was particularly enraged by a public letter written by none other than the Aga Khan, together with a fellow Shia from Calcutta, the eminent jurist and historian Syed Ameer Ali, asking it to retain the Caliphate for the sake of Muslim unity.[61] The fact that both men were members of a sect that did not recognize the legitimacy of this Caliphate said a great deal about the ecumenical or non-sectarian character that Islam was taking in Indian politics, to which I shall return in chapter six, but it did not help matters much in Ankara.

With the end of the Khilafat the imperial-international phase of Muslim politics also came to a close, with schemes to diversify India's political culture now turning inwards and attempting the reorganization and finally the redistribution of the country. For the sake of those who see it as being wholly irrational, however, we should also note that pan-Islamist politics was the only one to achieve a Hindu-Muslim understanding, however temporary it might have been, for communal riots proliferated exponentially in its aftermath. Those like Jinnah who had resisted its seductions saw pan-Islamism of this type as representing a dangerous political error, with the Qaid thinking it reduced Muslims to a purely religious group. Quite apart from losing whatever education and professional advancement they had gained by forsaking government jobs and universities in responding to Gandhi's call for non-cooperation, in this view Muslims were also abandoning their distinct political status, based on their quest for adequate representation in government, by agitating for theological causes abroad. Indeed the journalist Z. A. Suleri, in his 1945 book about the Qaid, *My Leader*, contended that the Khilafat Movement had been a catastrophe for India's Muslims, for its mass mobilization not only brought what he considered retrograde elements like Muslim divines into political life, but in adopting a religious idiom it also acknowledged that the community of believers was nothing more than a minority. Suleri therefore describes Gandhi "butchering" Muslim souls by supporting the Khilafat only in order to draw his hapless victims into the "fold of Hindudom" once that cause had evaporated.[62]

For Jinnah, then, Muslim politics in British India was based not on religious sentiments or claims but rather the opposite. For in fact Muslims were both too numerous, and since the Morley-Minto Reforms of 1909, were also too distinct a group constitutionally to exist merely as a religious community. This was so particularly because Muslims, while being a numerical minority in the subcontinent as a whole, were also a majority in large parts of it and thus existed as an indubitably political entity in their own right and not simply a religious one. Thus in a statement of 1939 to *The Manchester Guardian*, the Qaid argued that:

The Congress insistence that they, and they alone, represent the peoples of India is not only without any foundation, but is highly detrimental to the progress and advancement of India. They know that they do not represent the whole of India—not even all the Hindus, and certainly not the Muslims, who are often wrongly described as a minority in the ordinary sense as understood in the west. They are in a majority in the north-west and in Bengal, all along the corridor stretching from Karachi to Calcutta. That part of the Indian continent alone has double the population of Great Britain and is more than ten times in area.[63]

It was of course possible to come to an arrangement whereby Muslims might be persuaded to relinquish separate electorates, which the Qaid himself had never favoured, but not to deprive them of this constitutional status, theoretically according to some legitimate conception of democracy, but in fact by the majority's will alone. Jinnah's rejection of religious politics was therefore prompted not by a generalized advocacy of secularism, but instead motivated by a very specific demographic and constitutional situation. He had left the Congress because he was opposed to Gandhi's introduction of religious concerns into its politics not for Hindus so much as for Muslims. As we have already seen in Z. A. Suleri's description of the Khilafat Movement above, Jinnah was opposing not merely the Hindu nature of Gandhi's politics, but also its appeal to Muslims as a merely religious group.

We should not be misled in this respect by the accusations Jinnah later made of Congress's Hindu character, which he conceived for the most part in terms of a national rather than a strictly religious interest. Indeed these almost obsessive reiterations of Congress's rule as a Hindu Raj seem to point in a different direction: that Gandhi's methods would make Muslims more religious and therefore, in Jinnah's eyes, less political than they were already. Gandhi was dangerous because he might seduce Muslims into a religious madness, as he had done during the Khilafat Movement, and in doing so destroy their advancement in every field of life by persuading them to abandon their distinct political status and join the Congress in the guise of a religious minority. A Hindu Raj would therefore be established not by making Hindus more religious, since the presence or absence of religiosity among a political majority was irrelevant to its power, but by making Muslims more religious in a way that threatened their political future precisely by confining them to the demographically and constitutionally powerless, degraded and impossible position of a religious minority. Impossible because the existence of Muslim majority provinces in India meant that Muslims already existed as a politically distinct entity or, to put it in words that Jinnah would use from 1940, Pakistan already existed in colonial India.

Yet in all this Jinnah was doing nothing more than returning to one of the chief claims made by the kind of imperial vision we have seen outlined by the Aga Khan, for by denying the status of minority to Muslims he was at the same time denying that Hindus were a majority as well. Indeed, this claim had become crucial for the League's politics from the 1930s, despite frequent lapses back into the language of majority discrimination and minority protections. So in 1931, at the second Round Table Conference held in London to work out a constitutional framework among India's various parties, the Muslim, Dalit, Indian Christian, Anglo-Indian and European delegates came together in a minorities pact that they claimed represented nearly half of the country's population, thus demolishing the idea that India possessed a Hindu majority. Gandhi, who was the sole delegate from the Congress, denied the representative character of his counterparts, and the conference disbanded without reaching an agreement of any sort. I shall return to this event in chapter five, when discussing the role of caste in Muslim politics, and will close this chapter by pointing out the consequences that the Qaid drew from this situation in assessing the nature and possibility of democratic politics in India.

In its modern incarnation as a demand for representative government, we have seen that Muslim politics in British India started by fighting the category of minority, one that both a colonial sociology of knowledge and the introduction of a limited franchise had forced upon them. And even when they had accepted this category, Muslim politicians strove to displace it in various ways, primarily by emphasizing the plural jurisdictions and ethnographic plenitude of an imperial order, one they sought, in addition, to expand into a specifically Indian internationalism. This in turn led to a denial of both majorities and minorities as categories appropriate to Indian society. Whatever its motivations, such a claim is an extraordinary one, not least because it allowed Indian Muslims to rethink some of the foundational concepts of modern politics. So from a crude notion of Hindu domination, those associated with the Muslim League turned to thinking in a more sophisticated way about the nature of communal rivalry. Democracy, contended the Qaid, depended upon the existence of changing and therefore political majorities and minorities, but India's largely illiterate and superstitious population, divided into an infinite variety of castes and communities, could not produce the kind of public opinion that was required for such a politics.[64] In this situation, then, democracy would only make for permanent or communal rather than political majorities and minorities.[65]

We shall see in chapter five that Jinnah's arguments were followed very closely by a number of non-Muslim politicians, including the Dalit leader Dr Ambedkar, making the League's position representative of a wider set of debates. But while the Qaid's references to illiteracy and superstition were rather crass and played quite deliberately to colonial prejudices, the poet and philosopher Mohammad Iqbal invoked these themes in a more refined way, asking in his presidential address to the All-India Muslim Conference in 1932 whether "the gamble of elections, retinues of party leaders and hollow pageants of parliaments will suit a country of peasants for whom the money economy of modern democracy is absolutely incomprehensible [...]. Educated urban India demands democracy."[66] According to Iqbal, then, the kind of democracy espoused by the Congress worked to the advantage of the urban and educated classes that dominated the party, because its freedoms of political interest, representation and contract were characteristic of a money economy that was foreign to India's peasant majority. In the 1930s and '40s when they were made, such statements also became part of the widespread criticism of parliamentary democracy that characterized a period dominated by the rise of fascism and communism. And so we find Jinnah too, in a speech of 1941 to the Muslim University Union at Aligarh, quoting H. G. Wells and Salvador de Madariaga to show how democracy was breaking down in a Europe ruled by new aristocracies and leisure classes.[67] But unlike countries like Britain, which at least possessed a composite ruling class, India with its many vertical hierarchies couldn't even rely upon the diluted form of democracy that this offered.[68]

Paradoxically, then, it was precisely because Hinduism with its castes was not a real majority, and Islam with its massive numbers and regional concentrations was not a true minority, that they could lay permanent hold of these categories and so dominate electoral politics by fear and violence alone. The only way to create variable and so democratic majorities and minorities organized around a changing set of issues was to raise one community into a merely demographic majority and reduce the other to a similar kind of minority. And Jinnah thought this had to be done by dividing the country in some way, whether by an internal redistribution of provinces and powers or, as eventually was to be the case, a partition into two sovereign states. Once he made the demand for Pakistan in 1940, therefore, the Qaid would insist on describing her freedom as being a double one, since it would at the same time guarantee the freedom of India as well. In other words he saw himself as the liberator of two countries, which he thought should be able to enjoy the best of relations once they had been rendered fit for democracy in this peculiar way. This point was made very clearly in a book with a foreword by the Qaid:

Obviously, a country can be more efficiently governed if it has to face the opposition of a minority scattered over a wide distance than a minority concentrated in compact parts and capable of threatening its very existence. With the separation of the Muslim predominant areas of the north-west and the east, the proportion of Hindus will rise from 70 per cent at present to 90 per cent in the rest of India, while the Muslim minority will be reduced from 25 per cent to 10 per cent.[69]

Perhaps we should hesitate before dismissing this desire to rid India of its excess Muslim population and reduce it to a minority as mere rhetoric. For it may be possible to say that insofar as Jinnah was right, he ended up sacrificing Pakistan for India's liberty as a nation state by doing exactly the reverse of what he said in a speech of 1941 in Cawnpore where, "Speaking about the fate of Muslims in the non-Pakistan zone, Mr Jinnah said that in order to liberate seven *crores* [70 million] of Muslims where they were a majority he was willing to perform the last ceremony of martyrdom if necessary and let two *crores* [20 million] of Muslims be smashed!"[70]

3

# A PEOPLE WITHOUT HISTORY

When on 15 August 1947 Britain's empire was broken in two, the Indian Union emerged from its division claiming to inherit the better part of a country that had both fallen and been formed under colonial rule. But Pakistan did so with the claim of having made a radical and unprecedented beginning, of having inherited nothing from the past, not even from the past of Islam by which it justified its existence. Indeed this founding was recognized by Muslim nationalists as being so extraordinary as to be world-historical in nature. So Mohammad Ali Jinnah, in his presidential address to the Constituent Assembly of Pakistan, expected no disagreement when he said that:

the whole world is wondering at this unprecedented cyclonic revolution which has brought about the plan of creating and establishing two independent sovereign dominions in this subcontinent. As it is, it has been unprecedented; there is no parallel in the history of the world. This mighty subcontinent with all kinds of inhabitants has been brought under a plan which is titanic, unknown, unparalleled.[1]

The difference between Jinnah's address and its counterpart, Jawaharlal Nehru's famous "tryst with destiny" speech made to India's Constituent Assembly a few days later, could not be more striking, dominated as the latter was by the theme of historical recovery. Also important is the fact that while Jinnah mentioned both of the empire's successor states when speaking of Pakistan's freedom, which indeed he did repeatedly during this period, Nehru referred to that country only in an indirect and glancing way, when acknowledging that India's independence had not been achieved in "full measure." Rather than simply illustrating the former's bad faith or the latter's ill grace, I will argue here that such ways of thinking about sovereignty are deeply embedded in each country's respective nationalism, one relying on the language of historical continuity and its betrayal by Pakistan, while the other depends upon rejecting the past, and in so doing acknowledging both states as being coeval in their utter novelty.

Pakistan's radical beginning obviously had nothing to do with the juridical and administrative machinery of the new state, all of which had been inherited from British India, and whose links with this past were fully acknowledged. What, then, did the notion of an unprecedented beginning mean for the Muslim League, which had brought Pakistan into being? I want to argue in this chapter that it had something to do with the fact that the Muslims of British India, as advocates of the Congress never tired of pointing out, were a minority unevenly dispersed throughout the country, divided linguistically and ethnically, as well as by habit, sect and class. So for a congressman like Jawaharlal Nehru, in his *Discovery of India*, India's Muslims could only be united as Indians, by the country's natural unities and historical continuities, which meant that the very elements of nature and history that united Muslims also made them a religious minority and not a nation.[2] And since Nehru was right, Muslims could only become a nation by rejecting what both nature and history had given them.

## Nationalism against itself

We saw in the first chapter how supporters of the Muslim League rejected being defined by geography, even as they claimed a territory of their own. Here I will be concerned with the way in which Muslim nationalists exhibited a similar ambivalence as far as history was concerned, which led them to conceive of a novel and remarkably abstract form of political unity premised upon a paradoxical rejection of the past. In a pamphlet published in 1946 for the Pakistan Literature Series, for example, the historian Ishtiaq Husain Qureshi begins in a conventional enough way by stressing the unchanging unity of Muslim life:

The homogeneity of all Islamic peoples is a most striking feature of the influence of Islam; a common idealism has not only affected their outlook on life; it has fashioned its very pattern. Islam does not divide life into watertight compartments; it claims the entire allegiance of its followers. Hence it is all-pervading in character and affects all aspects of human activity. As a consequence, the uniformity of all Muslim peoples is far more striking than their diversity.[3]

He then goes on to describe the development of a specifically Indian Muslim culture, one that made for a set of complex and fruitful relations with the country's Hindu majority, though without compromising its purely Islamic element or, indeed, the integrity of Hinduism either. This common culture, claims Qureshi, was destroyed not so much by British imperialism, but the impetus it gave to Hindu revivalism, which counselled the repudiation of India's unity for an accommodation with colonialism, in order to take sole and even monopolistic advantage of whatever fruits it had to offer in the way of jobs, education and influence. "Thus the bridges which the Muslim had taken seven hundred years to build were burnt and in their place was left the deep, dark gulf."[4] We are told that it was their abandonment by Hindus who, in addition to outnumbering Muslims, had come to dominate them politically, economically and socially, that finally led to the emergence of an exclusively Islamic culture. "Hindu revivalism has left them in possession of all the distinctive characteristics of a separate nation."[5]

Now it is one thing to exculpate Muslims of destroying India's unity, as those in the Indian National Congress were forever accusing them of doing, by blaming her division on Hindus instead. But it is not clear why the League's supporters should have sought to defend themselves in this way, since they could easily stick to received narratives like that of a country which had never been united before the British. Indeed, to defend themselves from accusations of separatism by attributing the emergence of Muslim nationalism to its enemies is nothing short of extraordinary, though it echoes the related idea of Zionism being a product of anti-Semitism. And yet we see such an equation being made over and over again by League stalwarts such as Choudhry Khaliquzzaman, who like many others attributes even the name of Pakistan to its foes. Though it was the invention of Rahmat Ali in the early 1930s, the word Pakistan had never been taken seriously by Muslim politicians, and Khaliquzzaman, following similar statements by no less a figure than Mohammad Ali Jinnah, argues that it was only foisted upon the League by the scare-mongering reactions of Hindu newspapers to the Lahore Resolution of 1940, in which the first demand for a separate or autonomous state was put forward:

The next morning the Hindu press came out with big headlines 'Pakistan Resolution Passed', although the word was not used by anyone in the speeches nor in the body of the resolution. The nationalist press supplied to the Muslim masses a concentrated slogan which immediately conveyed to them the idea of a state. It would have taken long for the Muslim leaders to explain the Lahore Resolution and convey its real meaning and significance to them. Years of labour of the Muslim leaders to propagate its full import among the masses was shortened by the Hindu press in naming the resolution the 'Pakistan Resolution'.[6]

Whatever the truth of such statements, what is interesting about them is the resort to a national history that can only manifest itself in a form of self-abnegation. Like Qureshi before him, then, Khaliquzzaman begins his memoirs by asserting the historical continuity of Hindu and Muslim distinctions in a typically nationalist manner:

Geography is subject to change, either by natural causes or human action or both; but not so history, which is immutable, pursuing nations and peoples through the ages like a shadow, often dim and blurred but always traceable in their social, religious and political make-up. Hindu-Muslim relations have suffered from this historical fatality.[7]

Having rendered the very national distinctions he wants to propound utterly ambiguous by describing their role as a kind of historical curse, Khaliquzzaman, again like Qureshi before him, goes on to claim that it was Muslims who were responsible for India's unity:

It is a great irony that the Muslims, who had endeavoured for centuries to unify India and made untold sacrifices for the cause, even to the last days of Emperor Aurangzeb's life in 1707, were themselves forced by circumstances, so little of their own making, to seek the partition of the country.[8]

Qureshi was writing in the very different circumstances of colonial India, when the denial of Muslim responsibility for their own nationalism might have made some propagandistic sense. But why should Khaliquzzaman, writing years after Pakistan's founding, feel the need to offer his readers such a qualified, grudging and even guilty endorsement of India's partition? Whatever might have been the personal motives involved, Khaliquzzaman's account is entirely typical of Muslim nationalism, whose narratives had always been dominated by a strange contradiction between the nation's hoary past on the one hand and its very recent achievement on the other. So in his autobiography Khaliquzzaman is eager to point out the numerous instances when he thinks the Congress threw away the chance of attaining a united country, thus making Pakistan out to be an unwanted and even accidental consequence of Indian politics. Indeed Khaliquzzaman is so insistent on making Hindus rather than Muslims responsible for Pakistan that he attributes its creation more to Nehru's mistakes than Jinnah's intentions:

If he, on the proper occasion, had broken through the iron curtain around him, including some number of petty-minded Hindu socialists or communists and a few Ulema posing as nationalists, with his influence in Congress, on Gandhiji and on Muslim India he might have been able to have [sic] averted the crisis.[9]

And yet by referring to the "iron curtain" that an unlikely combination of communists and Muslim divines had set between Nehru and the League, Khaliquzzaman invokes the internationalist and ideological language that, as we saw in the first chapter, defined Muslim nationalism, thus making it clear that his vision of a united India can by no means be considered a "national" one in any standard way. In fact his regret seems to be that neither India nor Pakistan ended up at the centre of an international or ideological political order, even going so far as to agree with his Bengali compatriot Husain Shaheed Suhrawardy, another important politician in the League, who "doubted the utility of the two-nation theory which to my mind also had never paid any dividends to us. But after the partition it proved positively injurious to the Muslims of India, and on a long-view basis for Muslims everywhere."[10]

I shall return later in this chapter to the meaning that such a paradoxical rejection of the Muslim nation, together with its history, has for the Pakistan Movement, a rejection that I will argue is embedded in its ideology and goes beyond the particular disenchantment of men like Suhrawardy or Khaliquzzaman. For this rejection reappears in the writing of Pakistani politicians in different guises. So Mohammad Ayub Khan, the leader most associated with "nation building" in Pakistan, initiating as he did large irrigation projects and the construction of a new capital city, could still note approvingly in his diary on 25 June 1969 that "Ayub Khuhro came to lunch. He started off by saying that we are not a nation and united for democracy. Even the Quaid-e-Azam told him in 1947 that freedom had come much too early, before our people were ready to hold it."[11] While Ayub Khan's reflections on his people's lack of nationality served to justify military rule, none of the various forms of regret voiced by such men ever leads to a desire for the reunification of India and Pakistan in any form, not even in some impossibly remote future. In other words, unlike the case of many other partitioned countries, most famously Germany, but also Korea, Vietnam, Cyprus or Yemen, there has never been any movement to unify Pakistan and India except as part of a trade bloc or security umbrella, one made necessary by their sheer contiguity and having nothing to do with the shared history that links both countries. And this means that despite its half-suppressed rhetoric of guilt and regret, the equivocal narrative of Pakistani history possesses its own integrity and cannot simply be seen as expressing some weary acquiescence to a set of unfortunate circumstances.

If men like Qureshi or Khaliquzzaman entertained an ambiguous view of their country's history, Pakistan's founder possessed an even more radical perspective on its past. For Mohammad Ali Jinnah was entirely disdainful of India's Muslim history, and refused to trace his nation's development from it. The Qaid-e-Azam's speeches are littered with statements disparaging the supposed glory of the Muslim past. He was, for example, reported as saying to students at the Anglo-Arabic College that:

It would be no use indulging in tall talk like saying that Muslims had ruled over this country for centuries in the past, and had a right to rule even now. What was required was industry, sustained effort and a sense of duty and responsibility. That was the way to lay the foundation of a nation.[12]

More than this, Jinnah reviled the achievements of Muslim rulers in the past by describing them as imperialists no different from the British. So the League's president had the following words to say to his critics after the promulgation of the Lahore Resolution in 1940:

What, however, is most astounding is Mr Rajagopalachariar's talk when he says: 'Indeed, not even Tippu Sultan or Hyder Ali or Aurangzeb or Akbar, all of whom lived during days when differences seemed more deep-rooted than now, imagined that India was anything but one and indivisible. These great men might have differed from one another in many respects, but they agreed in looking upon this precious land and this great nation as one and essentially indivisible.' Yes, naturally they did so as conquerors and parental rulers. Is this the kind of government Mr Rajagopalachariar does still envisage? And did the Hindus of those days willingly accept the rule of these 'great men'?[13]

It might well be the case that coming as he did from a Gujarati trading caste with a background in Hinduism, Jinnah had scant respect for the largely North Indian histories that preoccupied a Qureshi or a Khaliquzzaman. But his contempt for the Muslim past was also part of a general logic and moved beyond the polemics of party politics. For one thing such a dismissal of history was shared by a number of Pakistan's supporters, with F. K. Khan Durrani, for instance, writing in *The Meaning of Pakistan* that:

the Muslim Empire in India was Muslim only in the sense that the man who wore the crown professed to be a Muslim. Through the whole length of their rule in India Muslims never developed the sense of nationhood [...] So we had two peoples, Hindus and Muslims, living side by side in equal servitude to an imperial despotism, and both devoid of any national feeling or national ambition.[14]

Whatever their stance towards it, then, Muslim Leaguers tended to dissociate their nationalism from the past, tying it instead to a colonial history of more recent vintage. But Jinnah's dislike of history went further than this, since for him the past separating Hindus from Muslims was, at the same time, one that bound them together. Here is how the Qaid described this situation in his presidential address to the Lahore session of the All-India Muslim League in 1940:

The Hindus and Muslims belong to two different religious philosophies, social customs, literatures. They neither intermarry nor interdine together and, indeed, they belong to two different civilizations which are based mainly on conflicting ideas and conceptions. Their aspects on life and of life are different. It is quite clear that Hindus and Musalmans derive their inspiration from different sources of history. They have different epics, different heroes, and different episodes. Very often the hero of one is a foe of the other and, likewise, their victories and defeats overlap.[15]

The first thing to note about this celebrated description of the famous "two-nation theory" is how perfunctory it is. And in fact Jinnah never expanded upon his definition of it, always hurrying through such lists, in which history was included as one of a number of formulaic differences between India's two major religions. More interesting than this list itself is the fact that it identifies the shared or "overlapping" history of Muslims and Hindus as being fundamental to their differences. In other words it was because the hero of one was very often the foe of another that these communities had become rivals in each other's historical imagination. And so the Qaid saw his task as being to uncouple these communities that had become too intertwined in history. And this provided another reason why he wanted to free the Muslim nation from its own past, if only to create the possibility of a new relationship with its Hindu counterpart. This new possibility, I have already suggested, he imagined in terms of a social contract, in which all that had been inherited from the past could be abandoned so as to begin afresh. The British Raj, therefore, had to be seen as a state of nature, though Jinnah does not seem to have used this phrase, with India and Pakistan emerging from it as if born for the first time, in a negotiated settlement that the

Qaid frequently said was unprecedented in the history of nations. Jinnah was incensed by Congress's claims to have inherited a preexisting India, and even resentful that it would use this historical name, preferring instead the homophonous ones Hindustan and Pakistan, neither of which possessed any modern or constitutional history of their own. In his 1944 talks with Gandhi, therefore, Jinnah felt it necessary to stress that "Ours is a case of division and carving out two independent sovereign states by way of settlement between two major nations, Hindus and Muslims, and not of severance or secession from any existing union which is non-existent in India."[16]

Naturally the idea that Indians and Pakistanis could exit history altogether was an extraordinary one, and by the time partition and independence arrived, Jinnah found that he was unable to hold back the violent past he had wanted to set aside in order to come to what he repeatedly called an "honourable" settlement with Congress. His frequent demands during this period that Hindus and Muslims should "forget" or "bury" the past and start anew were entirely in keeping with the Qaid's anti-historical thinking, but had themselves begun to sound anachronistic by the time he was making them, as in his statement upon leaving India for the last time on 7 August 1947, in which he said:

I bid farewell to the citizens of Delhi, amongst whom I have many friends of all communities and I earnestly appeal to everyone to live in this great and historic city with peace. The past must be buried and let us start afresh as two independent sovereign states of Hindustan and Pakistan.[17]

The large-scale brutality unleashed by partition finally put an end to the Qaid's vision of making the idea of a social contract into a reality for the first time, though he continued trying to rescue it by increasingly desperate appeals, like that delivered over Radio Pakistan on 30 October 1947:

I am speaking to you under deep distress and with a heavy heart. We have, undoubtedly, achieved Pakistan and that too without bloody war and practically peacefully by moral and intellectual force and with the power of the pen, which is no less mighty than the sword, and so our righteous cause has triumphed. Are we now to besmear and tarnish this greatest achievement for which there is no parallel in the whole history of the world by resorting to frenzy, savagery and butchery?[18]

Yet this approach to the past hadn't always been so bizarre and unrealistic, not only because it was entirely in keeping with the lawyer's profession to which Jinnah belonged, but also due to the distinct advantages it possessed. It is perhaps no accident that the only book Jinnah recommended to his followers, John Morley's essay *On Compromise*, should contain an attack on the "Historic Method," which the future Secretary of State for India described as resulting in the sort of obfuscation that prevented the making of clear judgements:

In the last century men asked of a belief or a story, 'Is it true?' We now ask, 'How did men come to take it for true?' In short the relations among social phenomena, which now engage most attention, are relations of original source, rather than those of actual consistency in theory and actual fitness in practice.[19]

Given his distrust of Hindu as well as Muslim narratives about the past, which were premised upon the search for historical instances of one group oppressing the other, we can see why Jinnah might not have been enamoured of at least one version of the "historic method." But Morley's words tell us that this dislike could also possess a moral and political rationale of a more general kind, since he thought that the historical imagination, by finding everything interesting and yet belonging only to its time, prevented the recognition and development of principles that might guide both one's thinking and action in the present. For *On Compromise*, despite what its title appears to promise, is a book concerned with the upholding of principles. And yet it is precisely because such principles are unvarying and unhistorical that they allow one to escape the past and create a new future, without it becoming simply the product of some random desire. Jinnah laboured hard to lift the language of Indian politics out of the swamp of history, giving the Muslim past in particular only his most perfunctory attention. And his object in doing so was, we have seen, to make a social contract possible between Congress and League, something that required the nominalization of identity in purely juridical terms. Instead of invoking the rich past, whether violent or harmonious, of Muslims and Hindus in India, the Qaid was interested in turning these religious categories into legal persons defined by their demographic attributes of wealth, education, number and power. The only history that mattered for Jinnah was the contractual or rather constitutional past that bound these juridical figures together in British India.

*Signing the social contract*

In order to settle the differences between Hindus and Muslims on the basis of a contract, Jinnah had not only to excise any "national" history from their relationship, but in doing so also to despoil each community of what we might call its existential weight. Reduced to legal personalities, then, India's two great religious communities could be made to shift shape in the most radical way so as to come to a principled agreement in which the rights of each were secured. The most important such shift in the Qaid's politics had to do with the category of the nation, which we know was deprived of much of its conventional ballast in the Muslim League. The idea that India's Muslims were a nation, I have argued, came to be adopted by the League less than a decade before Pakistan's creation, and its popularity in the party cannot be traced back before 1937, when elections were held that for the first time allowed Indians to take over the running of provincial governments. The League went into these elections claiming, as it had always done, to defend the rights of Muslims conceived as a minority, and it did so, at Jinnah's insistence, by coming to an informal agreement with Congress. So the Muslim League's platform was brought as close to that of the Congress as possible, and the two parties also tended not to compete with each other for Muslim seats.

The election results gave Congress large majorities in the provinces where Muslims were a minority, the Muslim majority provinces voting for regional parties with which Congress and the League both sought to ally. But if the Muslim League wasn't able to form a single provincial government, it had nevertheless swept the seats reserved for Muslims in the Hindu majority provinces, and thus sought to enter into coalitions with the Congress there. The latter was under no compulsion to do so given the extent of its mandate, and the Congress president, Jawaharlal Nehru, worried about the divided governments this might create, given the importance he placed in a single command structure that would be required to work for independence. These concerns about the British using the perquisites of office to lure Indians of all persuasions into investing in the colonial state, and of being able to turn one party against the other in a coalition government, led Nehru to refuse an alliance with the League. He was, however, willing to accept in government those of its members who signed the Congress pledge and therefore repudiated their own party.

Jinnah saw things very differently, accusing the Congress of trying to destroy all political differences and opposition the moment it had secured power, for the party's inclusion of Muslims in its own ranks did not compensate for the fact that the Muslim electorate had in these provinces voted overwhelmingly for the League. The actual representatives of the community, in other words, were rejected by Congress for token Muslims, while those elected on the League's ticket were being seduced into abandoning their party in order, said Jinnah, to make Congress into a "totalitarian" organization that, in claiming to represent all Indians, did not hesitate to absorb or eliminate all dissent in the greatest betrayal of democracy imaginable. So in a statement to *The Manchester Guardian* he made it clear that:

since the inauguration of the new provincial constitutions, it has been established beyond doubt, particularly by the way in which the Congress High Command has pursued its policies and programmes, that the sole aim and object of the Congress is to annihilate every other organisation in the country, and to set itself up as a fascist and authoritarian organisation of the worst type.[20]

But within a decade the League was able to win over Muslims where they were a majority, as well as keeping those in minority provinces with it, thus demolishing Congress claims to represent the whole of India.

Focussing on the aftermath of the 1937 elections as a defining moment for Muslim nationalism, historians have busied themselves in justifying one or the other side in the debate over the League being brought into government. What interests me is the fact that Jinnah responded to this "betrayal" on the grounds of principle alone, defending the necessity of political pluralism over and over again. Thus he went on to attack Congress governments in the provinces primarily by accusing them of such breaches of principle, which he summarized in a 1940 article for the London journal *Time and Tide* by saying that "In the six Hindu provinces a '*kulturkampf*' was inaugurated. Attempts were made to have 'Bande Mataram', the Congress party song, recognized as the national anthem; the party flag recognized as the national flag, and the real national language Urdu supplanted by Hindi."[21] Seen by Congress as largely symbolic, these criticisms were nevertheless addressed, if perhaps unevenly and too late, by altering the song, pulling down the flag from government buildings and accommodating Urdu, with Indian nationalists asking if:

these charges were of such a serious import as to justify the outcry that the Congress was planning dark and sinister designs for the enslavement of the Muslim community. After all, flags and songs, howsoever intimately woven into the sentiments of a people, are not such formidable things as to dig an unbridgeable gulf between the Congress and the League.[22]

Eventually Jinnah would bring charges of discrimination and even atrocity against the Congress governments, though with so little proof that he continued relying upon *"kulturkampf"* as his main accusation. And while many of his contemporaries, like the historians who came after, treated such arguments as constituting merely a set of polemical manoeuvres, I want to argue that Muslim politics was based precisely upon such matters of principle, governed as I have said it was by ideas to which interests had to conform. So the historian Beni Prasad, writing in 1941, already noted the curious role that principle and logical consistency seemed to play in Indian politics at this time, characterizing both of its great parties, but the League in particular, about whose claims he says "It is not the merits of the demand or the refusal that call for attention here; it is the tendency to stand on abstract claims that is noteworthy. The same mentality is responsible for the presentation of political or communal claims in all their logical completeness."[23] Perhaps it was the long and purely theoretical gestation of this politics, in the decades of colonial rule when Indians had no part in their own government, which made for this curious abstraction. Whatever the case, it was precisely this kind of politics detached from any language of history that, after 1937 allowed Jinnah to reject the category of minority which had for so long defined Muslims socially as well as politically. The people he sought to lead, therefore, were now suddenly to be called a nation, not because the Qaid-e-Azam had finally come to accept a reality he had long denied, but in order to extricate Muslims from an untenable constitutional position, one that actively prevented the negotiation of a social contract by making the minority forever dependent upon a majority's goodwill. And since this did not appear to be forthcoming, Jinnah advocated instead the idea that whatever the demographic differences between Hindus and Muslims, the fact that they were both nations meant that constitutional parity was crucial for any settlement between them.

If the colonial state, in other words, was nothing but a "state of nature," then neither majorities nor minorities existed, since such categories could only have meaning in a nation state. We have already seen in the last chapter how the denial of these categories came to be central in Muslim politics, but its transformation into a new kind of political demand was left to Jinnah. The settlement between Hindus and Muslims, then, had to be conceived of as one between two nations, if only because this would allow it to take the form of a social contract. To envision the country's partition and freedom as an inheritance from the Raj, thought Jinnah, reduced this unprecedented event to a mere squabbling after the spoils of empire while at the same time denying the break with history that a social contract implied. So in a statement of 1940 to the *Daily Mail*, he excoriated the idea of historical succession as embodied in Congress proposals for a constituent assembly:

Mr Gandhi continues to ignore realities. He demands independence—there is no objection. He demands self-determination, again there is no objection. But how does he seek to fulfil all these unexceptionable ideals? Despite what he says, he asks the British Government to bring them about. He proposes that a representative assembly of Indians be summoned to evolve a constitution, which will include the fullest satisfaction of legitimate minorities. Who is to produce this assembly? And, when it has reached its conclusions, assisted by the highest and most impartial tribunal human ingenuity can conceive, who is to implement its findings? There exists at the moment no other sanction in Mr Gandhi's mind than the British power. Likewise does Mr Gandhi imagine that the legitimate minorities are to rely on his word, or a party's word, as guarantor of the fullest satisfaction of the legitimate minorities' question. Experience of Congress rule in the provinces does not impel the Muslims to rely on that. Moreover, it is unthinkable that the social contract, which must be the basis of an agreed constitution, can ever be the subject of judicial decision by even the highest impartial tribunal.[24]

Instead of being tied to a language of historical and territorial integrity, therefore, nationality for Jinnah was a purely constitutional category, one crucial to the making of a social contract. This was already clear in his address to the Lucknow session of the All-India Muslim League in October 1937, in which Jinnah characteristically invoked the international politics of communism and fascism, as well as the issue of Palestine, to explain his position by describing Indian politics as, in effect, manifesting all the characteristics of a "state of nature":

No settlement with the majority is possible, as no Hindu leader speaking with any authority shows any concern or genuine desire for it. Honourable settlement can only be achieved between equals, and unless the two parties learn to respect and fear each other, there is no solid ground for any settlement. Offers of peace by the weaker party always mean confession of weakness, and an invitation to aggression. Appeals to patriotism, justice and fair play and for goodwill fall flat. It does not require political wisdom to realise that all safeguards and settlements would be a scrap of paper, unless they are backed up by power. Politics means power and not relying only on cries of justice and fair play or goodwill. Look at the nations of the world, and look at what is happening every day. See what has happened to Abyssinia, look what is happening to China and Spain, and not to say of the tragedy of Palestine to which I shall refer later.[25]

The nation, in other words, was little more than a negation of the minority, and had no positive content of its own. And its emptiness, or rather fixation on the present, continues to haunt the concept of nationality in Pakistan, whose contradictions I shall explore in the following chapters. But instead of seeing its development merely as a political ploy, it is important to recognize how the Qaid's views about nationality were shaped by the collapse of the international system itself in the 1930s, which allowed him to think about a new kind of politics, one I have argued was founded upon strangely old-fashioned principles and ideas regarding a social contract that derived at least in part from the thought of the European seventeenth century, some of which was instantiated in the New World during the Enlightenment. One of the consequences of this new politics was its ability to hold on to the principle of parity in contract without requiring the nation to exist in any substantive sense as a sovereign polity, so that as late as 1946 the League could agree to a loosely federated India under the Cabinet Mission Plan, or State Paper as it was also known, which was eventually scuttled by Congress, allowing Choudhry Khaliquzzaman to say that "Congress had thrown away the chance of keeping India undivided and Muslims can say with great pride that, even under great pressure from their people, they had agreed to retain the unity of India under the State Paper."[26]

Similarly, after years of mobilizing for Pakistan on the basis of the "two-nation theory," Jinnah could tell the many millions of Muslims who were to remain behind in India that they were once again to become a "sub-national" minority there, while in his famous presidential address to Pakistan's constituent assembly on 11 August 1947, he could speak about Hindus, Muslims and others in the new country forming part of a single nation.[27] Indeed in a revealing slip the Qaid even referred to the 400 million people of India and Pakistan combined as a single nation,[28] this reference, I want to contend, following very easily from his negative or purely juridical conception of nationality, which rejected the inflexible prose of history for a variable legal status in the present. Thus in the same breath that he proclaimed India's Muslims to be a nation after 1937, Jinnah could also bemoan their lack of such an identity and counsel them to achieve it by copying the Hindus, who he thought had achieved the kind of political integrity to qualify as one. During his presidential address in December 1938 to the annual session of the

All-India Muslim League at Patna, for instance, the Qaid made it clear that for him nationality simply meant a political unity of very recent origin, one that was voluntary rather than inherited and based upon common interests of a constitutional kind:

To-day you find—apart from the fact whether the Congress's claims are right or wrong—to-day you find that the Hindus have to a very large degree acquired that essential quality—moral, cultural and political consciousness, and it has become the national consciousness of the Hindus. This is the force behind them. That is the force I want the Muslims to acquire. When you have acquired that, believe me, I have no doubt in my mind, you will realise what you want. The counting of heads may be a very good thing, but it is not the final arbiter of the destiny of nations. You have yet to develop a national self and national individuality.[29]

Like Jinnah, his great rival Gandhi was also highly critical of history, which he, too, wanted to escape, though for somewhat different reasons. I would like to close this section, then, with a summary of the Mahatma's views about the past, which in some respects agree in an almost uncanny way with those of the Qaid-e-Azam. The empire which had shaped both men, of course, was legitimized in historical terms, for at their most generous its supporters claimed to be holding India for the benefit of her people, who had not yet attained the political maturity to rule themselves. British imperialism, then, was conceived as a vast pedagogical project, one in which a backward country was tutored by a more advanced one in order that it might achieve the kind of freedom that only history could give it. Informed as it was by the language of progress, evolution and development through time, imperialism was a thoroughly modern enterprise, and for good or ill its logic thrives today in the practice of development as well as regime change and humanitarian intervention. Unlike some among his compatriots, who accepted the argument upon which imperial legitimacy rested while questioning Britain's good faith in upholding it, the Mahatma saw historical knowledge itself as a form of violence and wanted as little to do with it as possible. Perhaps the first of his many statements on the violence of history is to be found in *Hind Swaraj*, the manifesto on Indian home rule published in 1909.[30]

Gandhi pointed out in this text that history as commonly conceived was nothing but a narrative of conflict to whose violence alone did historians attribute any real change, regardless of whether this was to be praised or condemned. Yet societies could only sustain and reproduce themselves, he argued, in non-violent ways, by quotidian and unexceptionable practices that didn't deserve the name of history. For it was not the violence either exercised or prevented by law and the state that provided the parameters for non-violence but rather the reverse. When he referred to the long centuries of Hindu-Muslim cohabitation in India, therefore, Gandhi tended not to cite any historical instances of such harmonious relations, but simply to point out that as in the present, the adherents of India's two great religions could not have survived for so long, nor indeed flourished, without the kind of quotidian relationships that could not themselves be described as historical. Instead of trying to expand the reach of historical knowledge by including everyday life within its ambit, in other words, the Mahatma insisted upon describing the historical record as providing both an account of violence and its justification. After all, since narratives of persecution and revenge, of peace and war, stood on the same historical footing and indeed overlapped one with the other, as Jinnah might have said, none was innocent of violence. And by this token non-violence was not merely unable to provide a subject for history, it was incapable almost by definition of possessing a history.

By suggesting that non-violence had no history, Gandhi did not mean that it was entirely removed from the world of violence. On the contrary he held that violence was present in every aspect of life, from eating to giving birth, so that even reflexive processes like blinking or digestion, which preserved life, also ended up wearing down the body and finally destroying it. Non-violence therefore could not possibly imply the more or less successful avoidance of violence, something that the Mahatma would in any case have considered cowardly, but rather entailed an engagement with it. Violence had to be seduced from itself and converted into its opposite by acts of love and practices of sacrifice. And this had to be done not by posing one historical account against another but instead by disregarding such narratives altogether. Only by refusing to situate present-day moral and political action within an historical account that could only constrain it, thought Gandhi, might new possibilities for the future emerge. Non-violence, in other words, worked by breaking up narrative histories and thus freeing human action, though it did so not by opening up some dazzling new future for it, as did the utopias retailed by the ideological movements of the day, but rather by focussing exclusively on the present as a site for moral action.

## Lost to the universal

If supporters of the Muslim League could be so ambivalent about their history as to question the very idea of the nation for whose freedom they were fighting, this was because the Pakistan Movement was heir to a tradition of anti-nationalist thinking, one that we have seen originated late in the nineteenth century but drew upon the widespread disenchantment with Woodrow Wilson's notion of self-determination in the wake of the First World War. For as Beni Prasad put it in his 1941 book *The Hindu-Muslim Questions*:

It was perhaps inevitable that the controversy over group adjustments in India should be influenced by similar debates in Europe. A militant nationalism created serious minority problems there in the nineteenth century by encouraging a policy of suppression and assimilation on the one hand and by reviving racial or nationalist feeling on the other. The post-war attempt to protect minorities took the form of international and constitutional guarantees of civil rights and for a while evoked a sympathetic response in India but it broke down within a few years.[31]

The rise of transnational ideological movements like communism and fascism in the inter-war period, and the collapse of the international order itself during the Second World War, only intensified this suspicion that the nation state was neither indispensable nor inevitable for modern politics. As it turns out, the greatest critic of nationalism in India was also the man known as the spiritual father of Pakistan. By the time he died in 1938, nearly ten years before that country's founding, Mohammad Iqbal had been recognized as India's most important Muslim thinker. Hugely popular among all classes of people, his poetry was declaimed in the streets of cities like Lahore, and his apparent support for Muslim nationalism gave the League an intellectual credibility it would otherwise have lacked.

We have seen in the previous chapter how Muslim efforts to avoid being defined as a minority resulted in a politics that was often directed along international lines, though in a way that tracked Britain's world empire so closely as to make it unclear whether it was pan-Islamism or British imperialism that provided one a model for the other. Before the First World War, Iqbal's anti-nationalism was also internationalist in character, and it too adopted the British Empire as a model for the working out of democracy as a purely human destiny. So in "Islam as a Moral and Political Idea," an essay published in the *Hindustan Review* in 1909, he wrote:

The membership of Islam as a community is not determined by birth, locality or naturalisation; it consists in the identity of belief. The expression 'Indian Muhammadan', however convenient it may be, is a contradiction in terms, since Islam in its essence is above all conditions of time and space. Nationality with us is a pure idea; it has no geographical basis. But inasmuch as the average man demands a material centre of nationality, the Muslim looks for it in the holy town of

Mecca, so that the basis of Muslim nationality combines the real and the ideal, the concrete and the abstract.[32]

But this ideal, suggested Iqbal, could also be seen operating in the British Empire:

since it is one aspect of our own political ideal that is being slowly worked out in it. England, in fact, is doing one of our own great duties, which unfavourable circumstances did not permit us to perform. It is not the number of Muhammadans which it protects, but the spirit of the British Empire that makes it the greatest Muhammadan Empire in the world.[33]

Iqbal's political imagination, it will immediately be recognized, is nothing if not historical. Yet its detailed and loving embrace of the past does not in the least make for a national history, only a universal one in which Islam itself can become nothing more than a precedent for a rival tradition. So in his *Stray Reflections* of 1910 Iqbal could write that "As a political force we are perhaps no longer required; but we are, I believe, still indispensable to the world as the only testimony to the absolute unity of God. Our value among nations, then, is purely evidential."[34] We shall see shortly how this very "Jewish" theme, at least of the pre-Zionist period, is recognized as such by Iqbal in other parts of his work. What is interesting about his rejection of Islam's political history was the simultaneous turn to events from the life of the Prophet, when that religion could be studied in its republican or pre-imperial phase. I want to argue that this retrieval of Islam's origins did not indicate a properly historical inquiry, and even less an historical identification for Iqbal. For like other Muslim thinkers of the time, he was concerned with Muhammad's life more as a constitutional model for a future society freed from its grandiose past, of the kind that Periclean Athens or republican Rome played in the West, than as a site of historical analysis or imagination. The Prophet's life, we shall see, was not to become some alternative vision of nationalism's historical romance. As an admirer of the French philosopher Henri Bergson, Iqbal looked askance at what he termed "serial time," seen as a kind of space, a continuum in which individuals and groups might be placed, and spoke instead of time as a form of "pure duration" that was only predicable of historical subjects and did not define them.[35] And this meant that the origins of Islam belonged not merely to the past but could also be posited in the future, constituting a destiny rather than a moment in serial time. Indeed he even thought that this notion of time was linked to a specifically Semitic view of the world, and when he met Bergson in Paris in 1932 Iqbal, in referring to the former's Jewish background, spoke of the Semitic spiritual affinity that he had for his work.[36]

In addition to rejecting a national history, which, after all, could only be written in serial time, Iqbal also dismissed geography as a basis for political life, favouring instead a foundation made up of ideas alone, which he lauds insofar as they are universal in scope. In fact he was severely critical of space as a category, preferring, like Bergson, to see it as a dynamic structure of events instead.[37] In other words he tried to dismantle space itself in philosophical terms, for to Iqbal this entity simply indicated one form that the "idolatry" of race, geography and indeed matter took. Islam, therefore, constituted nothing more than an example of a non-material claim to universality, though like previous attempts made by the Greeks and Romans to create a world state on this principle, the Arab conquests also proved to be a failure. For as Iqbal put it in his essay "Political Thought in Islam," published a year later in the *Hindustan Review*:

The life of early Muslims was a life of conquest. The whole energy was devoted to political expansion which tends to concentrate political power in fewer hands; and thus serves as an unconscious handmaid of despotism. Democracy does not seem to be quite willing to get on with empire—a lesson which the modern English imperialists might well take to heart.[38]

Nevertheless, he thought that such an ideal was still capable of realization, since:

The life of modern political communities finds expression, to a great extent, in common institutions, law and government; and the various sociological circles, so to speak, are continually expanding to touch one another. Further, it is not incompatible with the sovereignty of individual states, since its structure will be determined not by physical force, but by the spiritual force of a common ideal.[39]

By the end of the First World War, Iqbal had become a stern critic of imperialism, and now considered communism to be Islam's greatest rival in the establishment of a universal polity based upon a common or ideological understanding of the world. His arguments against nationalism, too, had come to be couched in vaguely Marxist terms, with the nation state, being itself a mythical form of collective ownership, seen as representing the apotheosis of private property in social life. Nevertheless, he thought that communism, by transferring all property to the state, actually made it an even more oppressive presence in society, thus smuggling back into everyday life the very forms of alienation that it criticized in private ownership. Iqbal maintained that territorial belonging, in the populist form it assumed with the nation state, destroyed or at the very least enfeebled all ethical or idealistic imperatives in political life, making for an international regime of parochial and so continuously warring interests. In other words he argued that the "interests" to which historians routinely attribute all actions and ideas were themselves the products of history, and could not have existed before the establishment of property as the foundation of social order. For it was only in such an order that interests could even be conceived in terms of the ownership of some substance, whether in the form of land, rights or indeed religion. Interests, after all, had meaning only in general terms, as defined by historical categories like class or any other form of identity, and did not possess a natural or individual reality.

For Iqbal, then, moral ideals were as real as any interests in a society not regulated by private property, as India he thought was still for the most part not. And his politics was therefore dedicated to preventing the disappearance, or rather powerlessness of such ideals, which would lead in India to the kind of conflict and exploitation that Iqbal saw in modern Europe. This condition he thought was brought into being there by the Protestant Reformation, whose individualization of religion and revolt against the universality of the Roman Catholic Church ushered the nation state into history. And within the modern state religion now occupied the fading realm of spirit as opposed to the ever-expanding world of matter, a purely metaphysical dualism that Iqbal argued was itself inherited from Christianity, saying in his presidential address of 29 December 1930 to the Muslim League in Allahabad that:

If you begin with the conception of religion as complete other-worldliness, then what has happened to Christianity in Europe is perfectly natural. The universal ethics of Jesus is displaced by national systems of ethics and polity. The conclusion to which Europe is consequently driven is that religion is a private affair of the individual and has nothing to do with what is called man's temporal life.[40]

Nationalism represented, therefore, the metaphysical domination of matter over spirit, rather than some merely functional division between social spheres. And by vesting itself in land, race, language or religion, all seen as forms of collective property, nationalism sought to efface both the moral idea and its purely human universality from politics. All of this posed a problem for Muslims especially, whose principle of solidarity, Iqbal thought, was based on the universality of an idea that demanded some manifestation in society. In India, furthermore, where they happened to be in a minority, Muslim forms of solidarity could only be threatened with extinction by nationalism. For of all their co-religionists the world over, the Prophet's dispersed and scattered Indian followers were the only ones to be united on the basis of an idea alone. Or as Iqbal said in his presidential address to the League in 1930:

It cannot be denied that Islam, regarded as an ethical ideal plus a certain kind of polity—by which expression I mean a social structure regulated by a legal system and animated by a specific ethical ideal—has been the chief formative factor in the life history of the Muslims of India. It has furnished those basic emotions and loyalties which gradually unify scattered individuals and groups and finally transform them into a well-defined people. Indeed it is no exaggeration to say that India is perhaps the only country in the world where Islam as a society is almost entirely due to the working of Islam as a culture inspired by a specific ethical ideal.[41]

It was because India's Muslims represented the Islamic principle of solidarity more than their co-religionists elsewhere that Iqbal considered their fate to be that of Muslims the world over. Indeed, echoing in some respects the world-historical perspective that we saw expounded by the Aga Khan in the previous chapter, he spoke in the same address of India being Asia in miniature, with the working out of a solution to the problem of nationalism there serving as an example for the continent, if not the world as a whole. And this meant, he told his audience, that:

We have a duty towards India where we are destined to live and die. We have a duty towards Asia, especially Muslim Asia. And since 70 million Muslims in a single country constitute a far more valuable asset to Islam than all the countries of Muslim Asia put together, we must look at the Indian problem not only from the Muslim point of view but also from the standpoint of the Indian Muslim as such.[42]

But this patriotic if not quite nationalist position, of seeing the world as India writ large, also entailed conceiving of Muslims in this world as a minority, as indeed they were from a purely demographic point of view.

And it is from this world perspective that Iqbal can compare the fate of Muslims to that of Jews, his attempt to escape the status of a national minority by turning to the world outside, therefore, resulting in a much more fearful vision of virtue outnumbered. So in his *Stray Reflections*, Iqbal followed up one of his typical repudiations of the nation state as an idolatrous political form destructive of Muslim solidarity by noting that "From what I have said above on Islam and patriotism it follows that our solidarity as a community rests on our hold on the religious principle. The moment this hold is loosened we are nowhere. Probably the fate of the Jews will befall us."[43] This line of argument is pursued more elaborately in his long Persian poem of 1918 called *Rumuz-e Bekhudi* (Mysteries of Selflessness), in which Iqbal invokes the Jews' fate in diaspora first as an example of endurance that Muslims might have to follow:

> *Ibrat az ahwal-e israil gir*
> *Garm-o sard ruzgar-e u nagar*
> *Sakhti-ye jan-e nazar-e u nagar*
> *Khun-e giran sir ast dar ragha-ye u*
> *Sang-e sad dahliz-o yek sima-ye u*
> *Panjah-e gardun chu angurish fashard*
> *Yadgar-e Musa-o Harun namard*
> *Az nawa-ye atishinish raft suz*
> *Lekin dar sineh dam darad hanuz*
> *Zankeh chun jamiatish az ham shikast*
> *Juz barah-e raftagan mahmal nisbat*

> Take warning from the Israelitish case;
> Consider well their variable fate,
> Now hot, now cold; regard the obduracy,
> The hardness of their spare and tenuous soul.
> Sluggishly flows the blood within their veins,
> Their furrowed brow sore smitten on the stones
> Of porticoes a hundred. Though heaven's grip
> Hath pressed and squeezed their grape, the memory
> Of Moses and of Aaron liveth yet;
> And though their ardent song hath lost its flame,
> Still palpitates the breath within their breast.
> For when the fabric of their nationhood

Was rent asunder, still they laboured on
To keep the highroad of their forefathers.[44]

But secondly, this fate also served as a warning for Muslims, who like the Jews were bound by an idea, monotheism, that was uniquely powerful while at the same time being vulnerable to the seductions of polytheism in the form of attachments to different lands and languages:

*Ibrati ay muslim-e rowshan zamir*
*Az amal-e ummat-e Musa bagir*
*Dad chun an qawm markaz ra za dast*
*Rishtah-e jamiat-e millat shikast*
*An keh balid andar aghosh-e rasal*
*Juzv-e u danandah-e asrar-e kul*
*Dahr sayli bar bana gushish kashid*
*Zindagi khun gasht va az chashmish chakid*
*Raft nam az risheha-ye tak-e u*
*Bid-e makhbun ham narawid khak-e u*
*Az gil-e ghurbat zaban gum kardahi*
*Hamnawa hamashiyan gum kardahi*
*Sham' murd-o noha-khwan parwaneh-ish*
*Musht-e khakam larzad az afsaneh-ish*

Take heed once again,
Enlightened Muslim, by the tragic fate
Of Moses's people, who, when they gave up
Their focus from their grasp, the thread was snapped
That bound their congregation each to each.
That nation, nurtured up upon the breast
Of God's apostles, and whereof the part
Was privy to the secrets of the whole,
Suddenly smitten by the hand of Time
Poured out its lifeblood in slow agony.
The tendrils of its vine are withered now,
Nor even any willow weeping grows
More from its soil; exile has robbed its tongue
Of common speech; dead the lamenting moth—
My poor dust trembles at the history.[45]

117

It is entirely in keeping with the nature of Muslim politics in this period that Iqbal's verses on the Jews, which are only some of several similar scattered throughout his work, should be so close to Zionist sentiments as to easily be mistaken for them. For even Iqbal's rejection of nationalism does not contradict the world-historical role that Zionism would attribute to its homeland. The fate of India's Muslims, then, like that of Jews around the world, was intimately tied to the future of monotheism itself as a global fact, and in this way to the political future of humanity as a whole. All of which made the question of nationalism in India much more important than one defined merely by her domestic politics. Despite or perhaps because of their much-contested position as a minority, in other words, India's Muslims were able to look upon themselves from a world-historical perspective that diverged significantly from any vision retailed by the Congress, bringing to the politics of nationalism a set of ideas whose dimensions were so great they risked overwhelming its categories altogether. Not that men like Iqbal were unable to deal with the everyday reality of such a politics. In his Allahabad speech, for instance, the "Poet of the East" pinned his hopes to what he saw as the anti-national spirit of Indian society in general:

'Man', says Renan, 'is enslaved neither by his race, nor by his religion, nor by the course of rivers, nor by the direction of mountain ranges. A great aggregation of men, sane of mind and warm of heart, creates a moral consciousness which is called a nation.' Such a formation is quite possible, though it involves the long and arduous process of practically remaking men and furnishing them with a fresh emotional equipment. It might have been a fact in India if the teachings of Kabir and the Divine Faith of Akbar had seized the imagination of the masses of this country. Experience, however, shows that the various caste-units and religious units in India have shown no inclination to sink their respective individualities in a larger whole. Each group is intensely jealous of its collective existence. The formation of the kind of moral consciousness which constitutes the essence of a nation in Renan's sense demands a price which the peoples of India are not prepared to pay.[46]

Nevertheless, Iqbal feared the destructive forces that he thought nationalism had unleashed in India, and which he considered even more fatal to Hinduism, held together as it was by the complex structure of caste, than they were to Islam. And it was in order to defend themselves against such forces that Iqbal advised Muslims to support the League, either by insisting on the autonomy they already possessed in the form of separate electorates and other protections guaranteed by the multiple jurisdictions of the Raj, or by seeking another kind of unity in territorial adjustments that would create Muslim provinces within an Indian federation. Historians have done little more than follow Indian or Pakistani nationalists in arguing if Iqbal's conception of territorial autonomy can be seen as a precursor to the subcontinent's partition, but what is of real interest in his always ambiguous pronouncements on the subject are Iqbal's reasons for making the demand. By giving Muslims the political and economic power to organize and administer their own societies, such autonomy, he thought, would allow them to remake Islam itself, or rather address the challenge that modernity posed it. In his Allahabad address, then, Iqbal puts his demand like this:

I therefore demand the formation of a consolidated Muslim State in the best interest of India and Islam. For India it means security and peace resulting from an internal balance of power; for Islam an opportunity to rid itself of the stamp that Arabian imperialism was forced to give it, to mobilize its law, its education, its culture, and to bring them into closer contact with its own original spirit and with the spirit of modern times.[47]

It will be noted that the Muslim territories of Iqbal's imagination had nothing of the national about them, and were indeed dedicated to the rejection of history as much as to its recovery. And in this way these lands, together with their inhabitants, constituted nothing more than instances of Islam as a form of the universal idea. It is not surprising, therefore, that Iqbal should have seen communism alone as Islam's competitor in this paradoxical enterprise. So in his epic poem of 1932, *Javid Namah* (Book of Eternity), Iqbal has the famous pan-Islamist Afghani address the Russian people as potential successors of the Muslims, who broke up the empires of antiquity only to create one of their own. On the one hand, then, he is afraid that God's favour will be lifted from these Muslims to be given to the Bolsheviks:

*Zikr-e haq az ummatan amad ghani*
*Az zaman-o az makan amad ghani*
*Zikr-e haq az zikr-e har zakir judast*
*Ihtiyaj-e rum-o sham u ra kujast*
*Haq agar az pish-e ma bar daradish*
*Pish-e qawm-e digari baguzaradish*
*Az musalman dideh-am taqlid-o zann*
*Har zaman janam ba-larzad dar badan*

God's remembrance requires not nations,
It transcends the bounds of time and space.
God's remembrance is apart from the remembrance of every remembrancer—
what need has it of Greek or Syrian?
If God should remove it from us
He can if He will transfer it to another people.
I have seen the blind conformity and opinionatedness of Moslems
and every moment my soul trembles in my body;
I fear for the day when it shall be denied to them,
and its fire shall be kindled in quite other hearts.[48]

But on the other hand Iqbal is keen to invite the communists to complete the work of Islam by joining with the struggles of colonized Asian peoples and identifying with their non-Western history, for he thought that Marxism's focus on European thought could only provincialize and turn it into an accomplice of imperialism:

*Tu ke tarh-e digari andakhti*
*Dil za dastur-e kuhan pardakhti*
*Hamchu ma islamiyan andar jahan*
*Qaysariyyat ra shikasti astakhwan*

## A PEOPLE WITHOUT HISTORY

*Ta bar afruzi chiraghi dar zamir*
*Ibrati az sarguzasht-e ma bagir*
*Pa-ye khud mahkam guzar andar nabard*
*Gird-e in Lat-o Hubal digar magard*
*Millati mikhahad in dunya-e pir*
*Anke bashad ham bashir-o ham nazir!*
*Baz miyayi su-ye aqwam-e sharq*
*Basteh ayyam-e tu ba ayyam-e sharq*
*Tu ba-jan afgandahi suz-e digar*
*Dar zamir-e tu shab-o ruzi digar!*
*Kuhneh shud afrang ra ain-o din*
*Su-ye an dayr-e kuhan digar mabin*
*Kardehi kar-e khudawandan tamam*
*Baguzar az la janib-e illa khiram*
*Dar guzar az la agar juyandahi*
*Ta rah-e asbat giri zindahi*
*Ay ke mikhwahi nizam-e alami*
*Justehi u ra asas-e mahkami?*

You who have set forth another way
Dissociated your heart from the ancient usage
In the world like us Muslims
Have broken the very bones of empire
So that you might illumine yourselves
Take warning from our history
Set your foot firmly in the battle
Circle no longer about this Lat and this Hubal
This decrepit world needs a community
To be both herald and warner!
So turn again to the peoples of the East
For your battles are tied up with the battles of the East
You who have lit another fire of the spirit
In your souls resides another kind of night and day!
The law and faith of Europe have grown old
Do not look to that ancient cloister again
You have finished up the work of lordship
Now pass from the negation of 'no' into the affirmation of 'but'
Pass onwards of 'no' if you are a seeker

So you might follow the path of living affirmation.
You who desire world dominion
Have you found for it a sure foundation?[49]

The negation and affirmation Iqbal refers to in the quotation above are taken from the first line of the Islamic credo "no god but God." Iqbal often cited it as an example of his view that negation was the principle of movement in Islam, and had to precede affirmation, by stressing the paradoxical way in which the credo can be read as a denial of the very deity who is then to be accepted. And in the next chapter I want to explore the important role that negation plays within Muslim nationalism.

4

# THE FANATIC'S REWARD

We have seen in previous chapters how Muslim nationalists rejected history, geography and even demography as the foundations of their political life, opting instead for an abstract idea of belonging together. But what could such an idea mean in the practice of Indian politics? I want to reflect here upon the ambiguous implications of such a practice, beginning with how this idea defined the Pakistan Movement, like Zionism or New World settlements, as in some ways a product of the Enlightenment. Perhaps the best way to start, then, would be to say something about what I mean by Enlightenment politics. And fortunately I can do so by reference to Islam, which, like the Athenian agora, Roman republic or Chinese empire, provided the Age of Reason with one of its mirrors.

Voltaire's tragedy *Le Fanatisme ou Mahomet le Prophète* (Fanaticism, or Mahomet the Prophet) was considered a masterpiece in its day, and seen by audiences in places like London and Baltimore to represent struggles as different as those between French revolution and English freedom or American liberty and British tyranny.[1] And in Paris itself the play was soon withdrawn from the stage as it was seen by some to be a veiled denunciation of the Catholic Church, despite or perhaps because it was dedicated to the pope. While the ostensible plot of *Le Fanatisme* remained the career of the Prophet Muhammad, Voltaire's tragedy was judged by his contemporaries as being, in addition, a commentary on modern politics by a major intellectual of the Enlightenment. In fact it can be read as an attempt at self-criticism by one of reason's great defenders. The great thinkers of the Enlightenment often saw Islam as being a more reasonable religion than Christianity, with writers like Gibbon, for example, extolling its virtues in his *Decline and Fall of the Roman Empire*. Indeed, Voltaire too had described its ideals and early history in this fashion, which is why his portrayal of the Prophet as a fanatic and impostor has puzzled some scholars. But I don't think there is any contradiction here, since for him *Le Fanatisme* represented the dark side of a politics of reason.

The play takes place in Mecca on the verge of its conquest by Mahomet, whose great enemy is the elderly Zopire, leader of the city's senate and defender of its traditional gods and customs. In the battles they had fought before, Zopire killed Mahomet's son, while the Prophet captured the old man's own children, a son and daughter whom he thought dead. But Palmire and Séïde had in fact been brought up in Mahomet's camp, knowing neither their paternity nor relationship with one another, and meant to be used in future to exact the Prophet's revenge. Having grown up, the brother and sister had fallen in love, something that should have played into Mahomet's designs but did not, since he had in the meantime fallen in love with Palmire himself. At the heart of Voltaire's narrative, then, is a contradiction between the reason of politics and its passion, and it is entirely unclear to which one the term fanaticism can be applied. Even the play's title, "Fanaticism or Mahomet the Prophet," simultaneously connects its hero with fanaticism and separates him from it.

## The politics of an idea

Having been captured by Zopire before the action begins, Palmire is kept in his house and treated with great courtesy by her unknowing father. During their conversation in act I scene II, Zopire commiserates with her on a life spent amidst the tumult of military camps and the horrors of the desert, which he describes as an errant homeland abandoned to troubles. But Palmire replies that her homeland lies where her heart is, and goes on to say that without parents and a natal home, she and her lover lacked the pride of birth, and were therefore able to cherish their equality among strangers, with faith in God as their only compass:

Zopire:

*Ainsi de Mahomet vous regrettez les fers,*
*Ce tumulte des camps, ces horreurs des deserts,*
*Cette patrie errante au trouble abandonee.*

And so you miss Mahomet's fetters,
The tumult of camps, the horrors of the desert,
This errant homeland abandoned to troubles.

Palmire:

*La patrie est aux lieux où l'âme est enchâinée.*
The homeland is that place to which the heart is chained.

[...]

*Nous ne connaisons point l'orgueil de la naissance;*
*Sans parents, sans patrie, esclaves dès l'enfance,*
*Dans notre égalité nous chérissons nos fers;*
*Tout nous est étranger, hors le Dieu que je sers.*

We know nothing of the pride of birth;
Without parents, without a fatherland, slaves since childhood,
In our equality we cherish our fetters;
All is foreign to us, apart from the God I serve.[2]

Already, then, we can recognize some of the themes described in earlier chapters, including an opposition between the particularity of place and the universality of the idea, with its necessarily homeless vision of freedom and equality. This opposition is treated in more detail in scene IV, when Zopire converses with Mahomet's lieutenant Omar, who has come to ransom Palmire and offer Zopire a place of honour in Mecca if he surrenders it to the Prophet. Zopire asks Omar if he doesn't blush to serve a leader of such low birth, and in response receives a lecture on the equality of all men, a principle that Mahomet intends to make into historical reality, thus becoming the only master Omar is willing to accept. Apart from the ominous but still vague link drawn between the mastery of one and the equality of all, which was seen in the period as a characteristic of despotism, the monotheistic ideals that Islam represents against Meccan idolatry are entirely in keeping with the Enlightenment's narrative of individual virtue triumphing over the hereditary privilege of birth, land and history:

Zopire:

*Ne rougissez-vous point de servir un tel maître?*
*Ne l'avez-vous pas vu, sans honneur et sans biens,*
*Ramper au dernier rang des derniers citoyens?*
*Qu'alors il était loin de tant de renommée!*

Don't you even blush to serve such a master?
Haven't you seen him, without honour and wealth,
Set in the lowest rank of the lowest citizens?
When he was far from such fame!

Omar:

*Ne sais-tu pas encore, homme faible et superbe,*
*Que l'insecte insensible, enseveli sous l'herbe,*
*Et l'aigle impérieux, qui plane au haut du ciel,*
*Rentrent dans le néant aux yeux de l'Éternel?*
*Les mortels sont égaux; ce n'est point la naissance,*
*C'est la seule vertu qui fait leur différance.*
*Il est de ces esprits favorisés des cieux,*
*Qui sont tout par eux-mêmes, et rien par leurs aïeux.*
*Tel est l'homme en un mot que j'ai choisi pour maître;*

*Lui seul dans l'univers a mérité de l'être.*
*Tout mortel à sa loi doit un jour obéir,*
*Et j'ai donné l'exemple aux siècles à venir.*

Do you still not know, feeble and superb man,
That the insensible insect under the grass,
And the imperious eagle, which floats high in the sky,
Return to nothing in the eyes of eternity?
Human beings are equal; there is nothing in birth,
It is only virtue that makes them different.
He is among those spirits favoured by the heavens,
Who are entirely self-made, owing nothing to their ancestors.
In a word this is the kind of man whom I've chosen for a master;
He alone in the universe merits the position.
Every human being must obey his law one day,
And I have given an example for the centuries to come.[3]

In act II scene V, we see a famous dialogue between Mahomet and Zopire, which Voltaire's great rival Jean-Jacques Rousseau described as one between virtue and genius.[4] Refusing to be persuaded by his new god, Zopire accuses Mahomet of sowing dissention among the people of his home town, at which the Prophet confesses to his own disbelief in this deity, telling Zopire that his ambition is in fact to raise Arabia to an undreamt of height by uniting it under an idea alone. Islam will destroy all that is petty, stupid and weak to elevate men and make heroes of them, with the conquest of the world itself as their goal. Men being what they are, unfortunately, they have to be subjected first in order to become illustrious. Given that he is conversing with the chief of a senate, Mahomet in this dialogue may well represent the Roman Empire as opposed to the Republic. Likewise, the name Palmire evokes the ancient Syrian kingdom of Palmyra, whose celebrated queen Zenobia was defeated by the Romans in the third century. But Zenobia herself in turn evokes one of the Prophet's wives, Zaynab, who according to Muslim tradition had been married to his adopted son Zayd, and divorced from him to marry Muhammad once he had seen and

127

fallen in love with her.[5] The similarity of names and even narratives linking all these figures demonstrates that Voltaire was familiar enough with Islam's early history, so that the fanciful elements he included in *Le Fanatisme* have nothing to do with ignorance or even malice, but were instead informed both by the requirements of drama as well as by properly philosophical questions. For example the play's extended meditation on the useful or white lie, which was seen by Enlightenment thinkers as being characteristic of the "benevolent despotism" some of them supported as much as the "infamy" they despised. Important about this scene, in other words, is its fundamental ambiguity:

Zopire:

*Ton nom seul parmi nous divise les familles,*
*Les époux, les parents, les mères et les filles;*
*Et la trêve pour toi n'est qu'un moyen nouveau,*
*Pour venir dans nos coeurs enfoncer le couteau.*
*La discorde civile est partout sur ta trace;*
*Assemblage inouï de mensonge et d'audace,*
*Tyran de ton pays, est-ce ainsi qu'en ce lieu*
*Tu viens donner la paix, et m'annoncer un Dieu?*

Your name alone divides families among us,
Spouses, parents, mothers and daughters;
And the truce for you is nothing but a new means,
To push a knife deeper into our hearts.
Civil discord lies everywhere in your wake;
An incredible assemblage of lies and audacity,
Tyrant of your country, is it in this way that
You come to give peace, and announce a god to me?

Mahomet:

*Je suis ambitieux; tout homme l'est sans doute;*
*Mais jamais roi, pontife, ou chef, ou citoyen,*
*Ne conçut un projet aussi grand que le mien.*
*Chaque people à son tour a brillé sur la terre,*
*Par les lois, part les arts, et surtout par la guerre*
*Le temps de l'Arabie est à la fin venu.*

I am ambitious; every man doubtless is;
But never has a king, pontiff, or chief, or citizen,
Conceived of a project as great as mine.
Every people has in its turn shone on earth,
By laws, by the arts, and above all by war
Finally Arabia's time has come.

[...]

*Ne me reproche point de tromper ma patrie;*
*Je détruis sa faiblesse et son idolâtrie.*
*Sous un roi, sous un dieu, je viens la réunir;*
*Et pour la render illustre, il la faut asservir.*

Don't reproach me for deceiving my homeland;
I destroy its weakness and idolatry.
Under one king, under one god, I come to reunite it;
And to render it illustrious, it must be subjected.

[...]

*Oui; je connais ton people, il a besoin d'erreur;*
*Ou véritable ou faux, mon culte est nécessaire.*
*Que t'ont produit tes dieux? Quel bein t'ont-ils pu faire?*
*Quels lauriers vois-tu croître au pied de leurs autels?*
*Ta secte obscure et basse avilit les mortels,*
*Énerve le courage, et rend l'homme stupide*
*La mienne élève l'âme, et la rend intrépide.*
*Ma loi fait des héros.*

Yes; I know your people, it has need of error;
True or false, my cult is necessary.
What have your gods produced? What good have they done you?
What laurels do you see gathered at the foot of their altars?
Your obscure and low sect degrades human beings,
Enervates their courage, and makes man stupid
Mine elevates the heart, and makes it intrepid.
My law makes heroes.[6]

These dialogues are, of course, set pieces in which philosophical arguments are deployed against one another. And from what
we have seen so far, it should be evident that the virtuous if also

hierarchical particularity of pagan Mecca is evenly balanced with the genius of Mahomet's egalitarian universality. For despite the need to fool people for their own good, with the minimum of superstition that Islam represented in the Enlightenment's imagination, the Prophet is in no doubt that he stands for the future. But this makes of his fanaticism a thoroughly modern phenomenon, particularly since Mahomet himself does not believe in his own God, and neither, indeed, does Omar, his confidant. It is thus not evident who exactly the fanatic is, here, with Rousseau claiming the identity for Omar, who followed the Prophet despite recognizing his deception.[7] Only the people believe, in particular Palmire and Séïde, with Omar suggesting to the Prophet that the latter be used to murder his own father, and then be killed as a punishment, thus ridding Mahomet of a rival at the same time. The plot then becomes convoluted, with Séïde, having been administered a slow poison, sent to assassinate Zopire, which he finally does after many misgivings, only to find out from the man who had brought him up under the Prophet's instructions that he has become a parricide as well as his sister's incestuous lover. With both brother and sister now apprised of the truth, Séïde goes to rouse the Meccan people, but just as they are about to turn against a defenceless Mahomet and Omar, he collapses as the poison takes its effect, thus convincing all that the Prophet and his new God have punished this impious act. Palmire, despairing of breaking the people's superstition, then stabs herself with her brother's sword and dies, to Mahomet's great anguish.

The important Enlightenment tropes of superstition and its cynical manipulation are obviously in full evidence here, but Voltaire is also concerned with the inability of reason to escape the limitations of the very particularity it wants to destroy, if only in order to fulfil the universality of an idea. So Mahomet is forever wondering why human beings must either be fought or fooled to be convinced of an idea which might well be true and even to their own advantage, as he does in act V scene I, exclaiming *"Faut-il toujours combattre, ou tromper les humains?"* (Is it always necessary either to fight or fool human beings?)[8] But while the inability of reason to transcend the particular leads inevitably to violence, the opposite is also true, with reason exacting a heavy price from its own votaries, who are incapable of abandoning it for the momentary pleasures of particularity. For as Omar's decision to stand by Mahomet, when it looks like they will be killed by the Meccan mob, illustrates, reason here is the reverse of mere ambition and opportunism, since both men are willing to die for a cause whose God they have no faith in. Surely, therefore, Rousseau was right to describe Omar as the play's true fanatic, because he was willing to risk his life for an idea that took precedence over any particular interest. Indeed, Mahomet is a tragic hero not only because his dedication to the universality of reason is betrayed by the passion he feels for Palmire, but precisely due to the fact that he is unable to compromise the empire of reason for his love, which he must sacrifice at the cost of his future happiness. For in his closing monologue in act V, scene IV, the Prophet admits that he defies in vain the traits of personality he knows must be subdued, and yet is able only to fool others but not himself:

> *Je brave en vain les traits don't je me sens frapper.*
> *J'ai trompé les mortels, et ne puis me tromper.*

> In vain do I battle the traits that I know harm me.
> I have deceived men, and yet am unable to fool myself.[9]

The reason that Mahomet thought he could control, then, ends up controlling him instead, and it is this that makes the Prophet into a tragic hero as much as a fanatic in the peculiarly modern sense that word was coming to have. For by the time the French Revolution had translated a number of Enlightenment principles into historical realities, it had become clear to European thinkers that fanaticism was simply another name for reason's own violence. Certainly Rousseau was convinced that Voltaire's Mahomet was a self-portrait of the Enlightenment, since his essay criticizes the period's theatre for the very unmediated universality and abstraction that the Prophet represents. Like Mahomet himself, Voltaire's theatre, and the Enlightenment's politics of the idea in general, was essentially a form of imposture that destroyed all particularity, for:

if theatrical imitations draw forth more tears than would the presence of the objects imitated, it is less because the emotions are feebler and do not reach the level of pain [...] than because they are pure and without mixture of anxiety for ourselves. In giving our tears to these fictions, we have satisfied all the rights of humanity without having to give anything more of ourselves; whereas unfortunate people in person would require attention from us, relief, consolation, and work, which would involve us in their pains and would require at least the sacrifice of our indolence, from all of which we are quite content to be exempt. It could be said that our heart closes itself for fear of being touched at our expense.[10]

After condemning the abstract sentiments of love or indeed hate that are inculcated by the Enlightenment, especially in its theatre of instruction, Rousseau urges that its fanaticism be destroyed not by reasoning but force, recommending the banning of theatrical performances altogether. It is not simply the portrayal of tragic heroes like Mahomet as men of genius that Rousseau objects to, in other words, but Enlightenment forms of representation and instruction in general, in which he recognizes the origins of fanaticism. More explicitly political versions of this argument soon became common, with Edmund Burke's famous *Reflections on the Revolution in France*, for instance, taking the part of Zopire against Mahomet by lauding the inherited virtues of custom, tradition and unequal rights to property over the fanaticism unleashed by a revolutionary reason detached from all such particularities.[11] And already the fanaticism of reason was being given the name of Islam, so that when

Hegel came to describe that religion, he could draw upon a tradition in which it stood in for the purely abstract universality of the idea that was, in modern European history, instantiated by France's revolutionary terror; "*La religion et la terreur* was the principle in this case, as with Robespierre, *la liberté et la terreur*."[12] It was because Islam represented not the past but the future, therefore, that Hegel includes it in the "German World," seen as the most recent phase in the career of reason, in his *Philosophy of History*, where the Muslim religion is placed between Catholicism and Protestantism.[13] And the universal idea of Islam, whose untrammelled freedom he admiringly criticizes in the *Lectures*, reappears in far more sombre colours under the title "Absolute Freedom and Terror" in Hegel's *Phenomenology of Spirit*.[14]

The idea, then, required grounding in particularity; or rather it needed to be mediated by things like property, custom, religion and country if it was not to remain a source of constant and violent upheavals. For having been given the name Islam, the idea's abstract universality could now become manifest in every kind of modern movement, from revolutionary terror to communism.[15] When this abstract idea was adopted by the Pakistan Movement, therefore, it indicated not the Muslim League's return to Islam so much as its adoption of a distinct form of modern politics tied, in the twentieth century, to ideological states. But of course Muslim nationalism's repudiation of mediation in the form of geography, history or even property, as we saw with Iqbal in the previous chapter, was a very different thing compared to that exercised by communism. And it is this difference to which I now want to turn.

*A leap of faith*

The Muslim League's ideology, I have suggested, was of a piece with Enlightenment thought, especially in its revolutionary aspect, whose politics of the pure idea was fanatical because its

133

abstract logic was capable of sweeping away all that was given to a people by nature and history. But Enlightenment thought was also perversely religious, demanding the consent of its votaries in a manner so pure as to became a kind of conversion, supposedly unmediated by any inclination apart from the idea itself. Indeed this is how we have seen it operate in Voltaire's *Le Fanatisme*, where reason can be compared to religion because it too is founded on an idea and nothing more. It might even be said that fanaticism and the act of conversion it entails, rather than representing the Enlightenment's kinship with religion, are actually native elements projected onto religious thought as if by way of self-criticism. Whatever the case, fanaticism and conversion together contribute to the unique power as well as the weakness of Enlightenment thinking, whether or not they are ever instantiated in political life.

For Jinnah and the Muslim League, the idea of Pakistan was defined, in the curiously religious terminology of the Enlightenment, primarily by the word faith. For this obsessively invoked word implied precisely a politics of uprooting oneself from the elements of time and place that were already given to Muslims, and that served only to make them a backward minority in every respect: politically, intellectually, culturally and economically. Faith meant transcending those inherited traditions that Indian leaders like Gandhi would enshrine at the heart of modern politics, in order to build a nation and achieve a state on the basis of a popular will that was cut off from nature and history both. This is why faith was such an important, even crucial word for Jinnah, indeed the second term in his motto for the League: "Unity, Faith, Discipline." So in a radio broadcast to the Australian people in 1948, Pakistan's first governor-general described his new country in the following way:

West Pakistan is separated from East Pakistan by about a thousand miles of the territory of India. The first question a student from abroad should ask himself is—how can this be? How can there be unity of government between areas so widely separated? I can answer this question in one word. It is 'faith': faith in Almighty God, in ourselves and in our destiny.[16]

Extraordinary as this statement is, it had become a commonplace by the time Jinnah uttered it. For as M. A. H. Ispahani, Jinnah's lieutenant in Calcutta, put it in his memoir of Pakistan's founder:

It was a common saying of the Qaid that if one has faith in what he undertakes and in what he does, he puts into the job his best endeavour and when success attends him, his joy is great and is mixed with thankfulness. He would often say, 'Have faith and you will triumph.'[17]

Despite Jinnah's invocation of God in the quotation above, his use of the word faith rarely mentioned the deity except in a subordinate fashion, and referred instead to Muslim self-confidence and self-reliance in a secular or non-religious way, which was perhaps why it has always been translated into Urdu as *yaqin* or "certitude" rather than by the more religious term *iman* or "belief." For the Qaid thought that those Muslims who acceded to the Congress had lost faith in themselves, since they could only play the role in Indian political life that their population, distribution and constitutional history entitled them to if they rejected the status of a minority. For as he said in a speech to the Muslim University Union at Aligarh in 1942, "Nowhere in the world would 100 million people be regarded as a minority."[18] Indeed, anything else would mean not only their betrayal of the community, but also of India herself, since Muslims were incapable of acting as a minority they were in fact not without also doing violence to its "national life." So in his presidential address at the Lucknow session of the League in October 1937, even before the demand for Pakistan had been made, Jinnah had the following words to say about the loss of Muslim faith:

I have pointed out before that a section of Musalmans is divided, that there is a group that stands with its face turned towards the British. If they have not learnt by now of the bitter consequences they will never learn. God only helps those who help themselves. There is another group which turns towards the Congress, and they do so because they have lost faith in themselves. I want the Musalmans to believe in themselves and take their destiny in their own hands. We want men of faith and resolution who have the courage and determination and who would fight single-handedly for their convictions, though at the moment the whole world may be against them. [...] The Congressite Musalmans are making a great mistake when they preach unconditional surrender. It is the height of defeatist mentality to throw ourselves on the mercy and goodwill of others, and the highest act of perfidy to the Musalman community; and if that policy is adopted, let me tell you, the community will seal its doom and will cease to play its rightful part in the national life of the country and the government. Only one thing can save the Musalmans and energise them to regain their lost ground. They must first recapture their lost souls and stand by their lofty position and principles which form the basis of their great unity and which bind them in one body politic.[19]

While he was condemning only the "Congressite Musalmans" for losing their faith in his Lucknow speech, Jinnah was in fact equally disparaging of Muslims in general, as is evident in his correspondence and conversation as reported by others. His secretary, K. H. Khurshid, for example, recalls a number of instances in his memoirs when the Qaid inveighed against the Muslim character, or rather lack of it, an opinion he was not above putting into writing, as in a 1945 letter to Ispahani describing how:

Corruption is a curse in India and among Muslims, especially the so-called educated and intelligentsia. Unfortunately, it is this class that is selfish and intellectually corrupt. No doubt, this disease is common, but among this particular class of Muslims, it is rampant. All this is due to the demoralised and degenerated state to which we are reduced and for want of character.[20]

Muslims, in other words, had be rescued from themselves as much as from any "Hindu Raj," since their degradation was due to the fact that they were not being true to the political obligation their status laid upon them. So when in 1938 Subhas Chandra Bose, a sometime president of the Congress, repudiated the League's claim to represent India's Muslims by mentioning both those who supported his own party and others outside the Muslim League, the Qaid could respond by pointing out the principle involved in his claim of representation. Their insignificant numbers apart, he wrote, these Congress Muslims could not represent their community because "as members of the Congress they have disabled themselves from representing, or speaking on behalf of the Muslim community. Were it not so, the whole claim of the Congress [...] regarding its national character, would fall to the ground."[21]

Jinnah's contempt of the Muslim majority was also entirely in keeping with his origins in a western Indian trading caste, with its largely Hindu background and culture, and his secretary writes that "He thought one of the reasons why the Muslims of Bombay had made great advances in the fields of commerce and education compared to the Muslims in other parts of India was that they realized the value of money, thanks to their business traditions."[22] Indeed, given the fact that Jinnah had very few Muslim friends, his views of the community he sought to lead indicated a notion of representation that was not premised upon his identification with them. I shall return to this important point in the paragraphs below, and want to maintain here that these sociological explanations apart, it is clear how the Qaid's demand, that Muslims forsake all the apparent "realities" of Indian political life for a belief in their destiny, was as relevant in a "nationalist" as a "separatist" context. Crucial to it was simply the reliance on "faith" as nothing but a groundless principle. It is no coincidence, therefore, that Khurshid's memoir of his leader begins with an epigraph from, of all texts, the New Testament: "I have fought the good fight, I have finished the race, I have kept the faith."[23] Similarly, the journalist Z. A. Suleri, in his 1945 book *My Leader*, was himself being faithful to the Qaid's teachings when describing his success at wooing Muslims away from Khilafat and thus Congress in terms of giving them back their lost faith in themselves:

If I were asked to say what has Jinnah done to the Mussalmans, I would answer the question in just eight words. HE HAS GIVEN THEM BACK THEIR LOST FAITH. That is all he has done. It was their loss of faith which drove the Mussalmans into the fold of Hindudom and it is their newly acquired faith which has brought them back from the brink of ruination. [...] Mark the word *faith*. History has no instance to quote of a people ever becoming triumphant on the score of numbers. It is always faith—the idea of something to live for and die for—that sustains a people in the darkest hour of struggle and ultimately leads them to victory.[24]

As was always the case with Muslim nationalism, faith in the quotation above is defined both as the making of one's own destiny and as the abandonment of the facts of demography. Faith, in other words, is the belief in and remaking of oneself almost out of nothing, so that Indian politics ceases to be about majorities and minorities to become a politics of the pure will. Suleri goes on to illustrate faith as a reliance on will alone, a will that transcends even the demographic reality of a people, by referring to the hard-won victory of the British and the Russians over Nazi Germany, in the process also illustrating this faith's decidedly non-religious and yet completely mystical character. Moreover he thinks that the only leader with whom Jinnah can be compared is Lenin, whose ideology, of course, was also defined by a rejection of history and even geography for world revolution.[25] Naturally this faith did rest on something given both demographically and constitutionally, in this case a Muslim population, but this something was for Jinnah given only as an accident. And this accident of birth had to be swallowed up by a politics of the pure idea to such a degree as to disappear altogether. Unlike Gandhi, who made a personal and political life out of remembering and deploying the traditions he had inherited, Jinnah made his politics out of forgetting and abandoning all that he was born with for an artifice of rationality.

Repudiating faith in any external object or goal, including God, to focus so furiously on oneself, implies that Muslim nationalism was, among other things, a project of self-making premised upon the transcendence of all that was given. And in this way it was religious in the peculiarly secular sense I have already described as being characteristic of the Enlightenment. For Jinnah, this self-making without reference to any given political goal was embodied in the idea of principled action in general. Indeed the Qaid's legalistic obsession with statements of principle was such as to vitiate his own politics. So during their 1944 talks, Jinnah insisted upon Gandhi accepting the "two-nation theory" enunciated in the Muslim League's Lahore Resolution, even though the Mahatma was willing to discuss the division of India without such an acknowledgement, which Congress could not grant without renouncing its national character and in fact placing the Muslims who were to remain in India at considerable risk. But Jinnah, in his interlocutor's view, allowed the talks to fail precisely by insisting on this purely theoretical point of principle:

You keep on saying that I should accept certain theses which you call the basis and fundamental principles of the Lahore Resolution, while I have been contending that the best way for us who differ in our approach to the problem is to give body to the demand as it stands in the resolution and work it out to our mutual satisfaction. [...] And I cannot accept the Lahore Resolution as you want me to, especially when you seek to introduce into its interpretation theories and claims which I cannot accept and which I cannot ever hope to induce India to accept.[26]

While Jinnah's apparently pedantic insistence on such points of principle was and is even today often taken as a sign either of defensive negotiation or an unwillingness to come to terms, I think it should be considered important in its own right. For principle lay at the heart of the Qaid's political thought, possessing therefore a conceptual rather than merely tactical significance. Now John Morley's essay *On Compromise*, which, as I have already mentioned, was the only text the Qaid recommended to his followers, is in fact a disquisition precisely on principle, and in a speech broadcast on the festival of Id in November 1939, he said about it that:

I usually dislike recommending books to young people, but I think you all ought to read that book not only once but over and over again. There is a good chapter in it on the limits of compromise, and the lesson it teaches regarding the pursuit of truth and the limitations on our actions in practice are worth pondering over.[27]

Morley is concerned in this essay with what he takes to be an English ideal of compromise that, in its rejection of the kind of "fanaticism" seen as marking French politics and thought, ends up vitiating all principled acts and attitudes there:

The interesting question in connection with compromise obviously turns upon the placing of the boundary that divides wise suspense in forming opinions, wise reserve in expressing them, and wise tardiness in trying to realize them, from unavowed disingenuousness and self-illusion, from voluntary dissimulation, and from indolence and pusillanimity.[28]

These words could easily have been used by Jinnah to describe what he thought of as the quandary faced by Muslims torn between Congress and the League. Morley goes on to blame the revolutionary excesses of the French in bringing principle into disrepute, thus gesturing precisely to the Enlightenment's politics of the idea that I have analyzed above. His task, then, is to rescue a politics of principle from one of indefensible compromise, in the process raising the same question that we have seen Voltaire does in *Le Fanatisme*, of whether people can be fooled for their own good. It should come as no surprise, then, to discover that Morley had already written a book about Voltaire, as indeed about his great critic, Edmund Burke:

We have been considering the position of those who would fain divide the community into two great castes; the one of thoughtful and instructed persons using their minds freely, but guarding their conclusions in strict reserve; the other of the illiterate or unreflecting, who should have certain opinions and practices taught them, not because they are true or really what their votaries are made to believe them to be, but because the intellectual superiors of the community think the inculcation of such a belief useful in all cases save their own.[29]

With its use of terms like "caste," "community" and even the "illiterate," this passage too bears an uncanny resemblance to the prose of Indian politics, both at the time and since, so it would not be surprising for Jinnah to identify with it in all kinds of ways. And given his own frequent statements, of which we have already seen some examples, of how the illiteracy, ignorance and ingrained superstitions of the vast mass of Indians disqualified them from European-style democracy, we can imagine Jinnah having an equivocal attitude towards the problem Morley describes. For *On Compromise* rejects such manoeuvres, which are exemplified in the text by Ernest Renan, whose essay on nationalism we have seen was frequently cited in the League, as being disingenuous at best, and recommends instead a politics of the most principled kind. It thus did nothing less than rid such principles even of that mediation or particularity represented by the instrumentality Morley condemns. Indeed the only compromise of this sort that he will allow, interestingly enough, has to do with pretending a religious conformity one does not in fact practice:

Now, however great the pain inflicted by the avowal of unbelief, it seems to the present writer that one relationship in life, and one only, justifies us in being silent where otherwise it would be right to speak. This relationship is that between child and parents.[30]

Though it is probably a reference to Morley's own quarrel with his father over religion, this is a remarkable statement, and well worth discussing in connection with Jinnah's own attitude towards Islam. For it strikes me that *On Compromise* represents the closest thing to his political philosophy, unlikely text though it is to perform such a function. The Qaid's frequent references to it may even be read as an invitation for Muslims to think about the problems he was dealing with at a purely theoretical level, though none of them seems ever to have done so. Despite his criticism of French fanaticism, Morley is far more inclined to its politics of principle than he would like to admit, which he justifies as a necessary corrective to modern, democratic notions of truth that are increasingly, he thinks, defined merely by their belonging to a majority:

It is not their fanaticism, still less is it their theology, which makes the great Puritan chiefs of England and the stern Covenanters of Scotland so heroic in our sight. It is the fact that they sought truth and ensured it, not thinking of the practicable nor cautiously counting majorities and minorities, but each man pondering and searching so 'as ever in the great Taskmaster's eye'.[31]

It is very difficult, given this invocation of majorities and minorities, not to come to the conclusion that *On Compromise* represents the only serious theoretical statement of Jinnah's political ideal. And that this had to do with a deep suspicion of the way in which parliamentary or demographic categories corrupted truth, vitiated principles and led to the reign of the status quo that Morley describes as being just as bad as any religious dogma:

The modern emancipation will profit us very little if the *status quo* is to be fastened round our necks with the despotic authority of a heavenly dispensation, and if in the stead of ancient scriptures we are to accept the plenary inspiration of majorities.[32]

Unsurprisingly, the last part of *On Compromise* discusses technical ways in which minorities can be represented in political life, with Morley relying upon John Stuart Mill's work and, though he does not refer to it directly, *Considerations on Representative Government* in particular. In this text, Mill is concerned with the loss of democracy entailed in majority rule, where minorities are not represented, and he suggests an ingenious way in which non-territorial constituencies might be created that allow a minority dispersed across the country, especially one made up of an intellectual elite, to group its scattered forces by ignoring territorial constituencies and elect its representatives on the basis of the idea uniting them.[33] And so we again see the ghosts of Mahomet and Omar reappear, representing as they do in Voltaire the votaries of reason forced to stoop to chicanery to gain their ends among a benighted population. Mill would prevent such a situation from ever arising by redrawing territorial constituencies, or rather suspending them altogether on occasion. And Morley, let us remember, was the author of separate electorates as Secretary of State for India, whose intention was also to offset if not do away with such territorial constituencies in order to give adequate representation to a minority. The extraordinary similarity between this anti-territorial view, and Jinnah's own criticism of majority-defined territory as a basis for representation, especially in a "superstitious" society, should be evident, though of course Mill's project was a rather different one from the Qaid's, who does not, for his part, refer to the great liberal thinker much. Like Morley himself, then, Jinnah appears in some respects to be a curious mixture of liberal politics and radical thought—or is it the reverse?

## Devil's advocate

Having abandoned history, geography and numbers as foundations for a Muslim nationality, I have been arguing, Jinnah and his followers were occupied with self-making as a form of transcendence. The narcissistic potential of this procedure was very great, but even more interesting was its self-conscious flirtation with the demonic. For nothing in the traditional Muslim imagination represented Satan more than pride in one's own power and even virtue. And so the story of Lucifer's refusal to bow before Adam at God's command has been the subject of Muslim reflection for centuries, with some thinkers seeing in this sign of demonic pride a perverse form of obedience as well, since the fallen angel was only being faithful in refusing obeisance to any but God. So was Adam in some sense divine? We shall soon see how this mystical tradition of thinking about the relationship between man and God was resuscitated and transformed in Muslim politics, but what interests me for the moment is the way in which the Qaid came to figure as Satan in the Pakistan Movement.

His opponents in the Congress had always seen Jinnah as being possessed of demonic qualities, with Nehru, for instance, repeatedly making the point that his power depended entirely upon the ability to refuse and negate, as, for instance in *The Discovery of India*, where Jinnah is described as "a strangely negative person whose appropriate symbol might well be a 'no'. Hence all attempts to understand his positive aspect fail and one cannot come to grips with it."[34] And this is to say nothing about the Qaid's famous pride, arrogance and indeed rudeness, which made him the kind of leader more feared than loved by his followers. His closest associates, for instance, addressed Jinnah by title rather than name, as even their private and very deferential correspondence demonstrates. So his lifelong friend and true intimate, the Congress poetess and politician Sarojini Naidu, was not being particularly original in comparing Jinnah to Lucifer in a conversation with Lord Wavell in 1946.[35] This image, however, was also taken up by the Qaid's own followers, with Z. A. Suleri opening the first chapter of his book like this:

"Jinnah Sahib is vain..."
"India's political enemy Number One..."

"Bull in [*sic*] China Shop..."

"He wants to become the Dictator of India..."

"Prouder than the proudest of Pharos [*sic*]..."

"Would to God, he is [*sic*] silent forever..."

"...the most insufferable man."

"Disruptor of India..."

"He is an egoist who would own no equal..."

"...he would let India go to hell for the sake of his communal ambition..."

"Most unrelenting in his fanaticism..."

"To him a Muslim is ever more precious than a thousand Hindus..."

"Arrogant and uncompromising..."

"An essentially bad man..."

Precisely this 'proudest of Pharos" [*sic*], this 'most insufferable man', this 'fanatic', this 'egoist', this 'India's political enemy Number One', this 'arrogant and uncompromising', this 'Disruptor of India', this 'essentially bad man' *is* MY LEADER. I stand by him; I will follow him; I will lay down my life for him.[36]

What Suleri goes on to argue is that Jinnah's arrogance has given Muslims back their own pride and faith in themselves. And it is worth dwelling on the curious form of representation that such a relationship involved, since we have already seen that the Qaid hardly identified himself with his co-religionists in any conventional sense, and even seems to have disliked or had contempt for them. Indeed Jinnah appears to have represented Muslims as a lawyer does his clients, investing himself in the justice of their cause as a matter of principle rather than because he included himself among them. But this was not simply a personal attitude and had to do with the way in which Muslim politics had developed in India since the nineteenth century.

We have already seen in chapter two that Jinnah's rise to eminence was made possible by the increasingly parochial politics of the once dominant Muslim gentry in northern India, and by the political emergence on a country-wide scale of Muslim groups in other parts of the land. Jinnah himself was from one of these new groups, the merchants of Gujarat and Bombay, and his achievement was to bring them together with gentry, aristocrats and professional men from other regions, to lead the first popular party in India's Muslim history. How appropriate it then was that this most unrepresentative Muslim, in his background, appearance and manner, should come to lead a party in which no group could claim to represent any other. It was the disparate character of the Muslim League, in other words, that Jinnah's political style, his satanic solitude, addressed in the most original way. For might not his dandyism and anglicized demeanour have counterposed a self-fashioned and wilful sense of Muslim individuality to some impossible Muslimhood made up of common characteristics like belief, ritual or everyday practices? Jinnah, then, represented neither the Muslim past nor present, but perhaps, in the man's very departure from his community's various norms, nothing more than the future that was being imagined for it.

In one respect Jinnah's satanic character, depending as it did on what Nehru described as his politics of negation, made him quite different from and indeed more devilish than the Devil himself. And this had to do with his refusal to tempt anyone—just as he was famously beyond all temptation. Jinnah certainly advocated the cause of Pakistan, but without ever painting it in the bright colours of utopia, as congressmen were always doing for their vision of India. No doubt Muslim League propaganda came to develop its own rhetoric of a glorious if thoroughly ambiguous future, but Jinnah only ever spoke of Pakistan in terms of dry principles. So we often hear of those who were convinced by the mesmeric force of his personality suddenly losing faith in Jinnah's arguments once they were no longer in his presence.[37] In fact, Jinnah himself admitted to being stirred by the seductions of Congress rhetoric, and so like Ulysses he not only chained himself to the mast of his political principles in order to resist the siren song of Indian nationalism, but had to ensure than his associates were protected from its temptations as well.[38] During their talks of 1944, for example, Jinnah indignantly refused to allow Gandhi to address the League's working committee, since both the Mahatma and he seem to have realized the effect of Congress's temptations upon even the highest officials of the Muslim League.[39] And indeed Jinnah had regularly to rein in his men when they appeared to be leaning too closely in Congress's direction.

Certainly the Qaid's followers were not unaware of his dangerously demonic style, and we even have a remarkable description of their half-frightened response when he happened to actually mention the Devil favourably in a 1938 speech to the annual session of the League in Patna, forcing him to retreat from the comparison and turn to God instead:

I am sure even if there were a few amongst Muslims who had thought in the past that the Muslims might gain their ends by alliance with British imperialism, they have now been thoroughly disillusioned. I say the Muslim League is not going to be an ally of anyone, but would be the ally of even the Devil if need be in the interest of Muslims.

(A pin-drop silence suddenly appeared to seize the House at this stage).

Mr Jinnah paused for a moment and then continued:

It is not because we are in love with imperialism; but in politics one has to play one's game as on the chessboard. I say that the Muslims and the Muslim League have only one ally and that ally is the Muslim nation, and one and only one to whom they look for help is God. (Applause).[40]

Given that its enemies frequently accused the League of being a tool of British imperialism, and since it did in fact support the Raj against Congress every now and then, I doubt it was the Qaid's invocation of Britain that stunned his audience into silence in the quotation above. Rather it might have been his rhetorical alliance with the Devil that struck them as being a bit too apt. Yet if the demonic character of Jinnah's leadership were confined to him it would only be interesting from a biographical point of view, but in fact Satan had already become a heroic figure for Muslims in the enormously popular poetry of Mohammad Iqbal, representing therefore a new kind of political ideal for a free-floating and self-possessed nation that rejected its grounding in nature or history.

As early as 1909, in the essay "Islam as a Moral and Political Ideal," published in the *Hindustan Review*, Iqbal had written:

I hope I shall not be offending the reader when I say that I have a certain amount of admiration for the Devil. By refusing to prostrate himself before Adam whom he honestly believed to be his inferior, he revealed a high sense of self-respect, a trait of character, which, in my opinion, ought to redeem him from his spiritual deformity, just as the beautiful eyes of the toad redeem him from his physical repulsiveness.[41]

In subsequent years Iqbal would go on to praise Satan's tragic independence of mind as a model for Muslims, using almost the same words as Jinnah did when speaking about this virtue in his presidential address of 1932 to the All-India Muslim Conference in Lahore, during which he said "Nothing can be achieved without a firm faith in the independence of one's own inner life. This faith alone keeps a people's eye fixed on their goal and saves them from perpetual vacillation."[42] Steadfastness of purpose is the commonest demand in political life, and what makes it so interesting here is the fact that it is dissociated from any given foundation, including even religion itself, which is why Satan could become a Muslim ideal. So in one of his "Stray Thoughts" published in the *New Era* of August 1917, Iqbal could say that "At least in one respect sin is better than piety. There is an imaginative element in the former which is lacking in the latter."[43]

Unlike his rather conventional praise for Muslim heroes down the ages, Iqbal's verses on Satan cut to the heart of his philosophy, in which man is meant to partner and even compete with God. In his *Jawab-e Shikwa* (Complaint's Answer) of 1913, for example, God ends up resigning to mankind the stylus and tablet upon which destiny is written, while the prelude to *Javid Namah* ends with the angels singing about man's challenge to God as constituting the final act of his freedom:

> *Furugh-e musht-e khak az nuryan afzun shawad ruzi*
> *Zameen az kawkab-e taqdir-e u gardun shawad ruzi*
> *Khayal-e u ki az sayl-e hawadis parvarish girad*
> *Za girdab-e sipahr-e nilgun birun shawad ruzi*
> *Yeki dar mani-e adam nagar az ma che pursi*
> *Hunuz andar tabiat mikhalad mawzun shawad ruzi*
> *Chunan mawzun shawad in pish pa uftadah mazmuni*
> *Ki yazdan ra dil az tasir-e u pur khun shawad ruzi*

The lustre of a handful of earth one day shall outshine the creatures of light; earth through the star of his destiny one day shall be transformed into heaven.

His imagination, which is nourished by the torrent of vicissitudes, one day shall soar out of the whirlpool of the azure sky.
Consider one moment the meaning of Man; what thing do you ask of us?
Now he is pricking into nature, one day he will be modulated perfectly, so perfectly modulated will this precious subject be that even the heart of God will bleed one day at the impact of it![44]

While such verses can be taken as being atheistic and are deliberately provocative in a way acceptable to the literary tradition of Persian and Urdu, they were probably meant to indicate what Iqbal thought was a higher stage of religion, where man recognized his own divinity and God came to exist through him rather than the reverse.[45] But it is interesting to note that in his Urdu poem *Jibreel-o Iblis* (Gabriel and the Devil), Iqbal uses the same image that ends the verses above, of a prick, but this time one entering the heart of God rather than nature, to describe the work of Satan, seen as an equally heroic figure there. The poem itself is composed as a dialogue between the archangel Gabriel and the fallen angel who has become Satan. Gabriel asks if his former companion can't return to paradise by seeking God's forgiveness, only to be told that Satan's exile on earth has intoxicated him, making the silence and eternal stillness of heaven tedious by comparison. The Devil then tells Gabriel that he has a far more exalted role now than when he was an angel, exclaiming that it was his blood, after all, that gave colour to the story of Adam, and ending the poem with the following lines:

> *Main khatakta hun dil-e yazdan men kante ki tarah*
> *Tu faqat Allah-hu! Allah-hu! Allah-hu!*

> I prick into the deity's heart like a thorn
> All you can do is sing hosannas to his name[46]

Satan's rejection of paradise represented for Iqbal the power of negation as a principle of movement, one that he described most often in the fairly traditional images of stars in eternal motion, ships that never found a shore, lovers who pined in endless separation and mystics who refused union with the divine. All these familiar negations in Urdu and Persian poetry produced beauty and made life into a boundless journey. And the negation of a national homeland was only one instance of this desire for the infinite, which Iqbal described repeatedly, as in the following couplets from *Javid Namah*:

> *Rahrave ku danad asrar-e safar*
> *Tarsad az manzil za rahzan bishtar*

> The traveller who knows the secrets of journeying
> Fears the destination more than the highwayman

> *Ishq dar hijr-o visal asudah nist*
> *Be jamal-e layizal asudah nist!*

> Love does not reside in separation or union
> For there is no residing without beauty eternal

> *Ibtida pish-e butan uftadagi*
> *Inteha az dilbaran azadagi!*

> In the beginning falling down before idols
> In the end freedom from all beloveds

*Ishq be parwa-o hardam dar rahil*
*Dar makan-o lamakan ibn-e asbil!*

Love cares not and is always on the move
A journeyman in place and non-place

*Kesh-e ma manand-e mawj-e tez gam*
*Ikhtiyar-e jadah-o tark-e maqam!*

Our custom is like the swiftening wave
A willing for the road, an abandonment of the lodging[47]

It should by now be evident how the negation and abandonment of all that is given constituted, in Iqbal's work, a philosophical vision of life in general, one that provided an expansive and layered context for particular themes in Muslim nationalism. And though it was no doubt linked to the specific history of Muslim minority politics in India, this vision also possessed its own integrity, and cannot be reduced to such sociological facts, making Iqbal, for instance, a hugely popular poet among Muslims outside India. Indeed, Iqbal's vision was so expansive and his distrust of the nation state so deep that, like many others in the League, he too had a most ambiguous attitude towards ideas such as a Muslim State. Though he died a couple of years before the Muslim League adopted Pakistan as its goal, therefore, Iqbal, who was claimed as an early proponent of the idea, seems ultimately to have rejected it. Not only did he praise Motilal and Jawaharlal Nehru in the *Javid Nama* as "keen-sighted Brahmins" imbued with the desire for India's freedom, the poet of Muslim nationalism also repudiated Pakistan in his correspondence with the historian Edward Thompson, who had invited him to deliver the Rhodes Lectures at Oxford, writing in a letter dated 4 March 1933 that "Pakistan is not my scheme. The one that I suggested in my address is the creation of a Muslim province—i.e. a province having an overwhelming population of Muslims—in the north-west of India. This new province will be, according to my scheme, a part of the proposed Indian Federation."[48] We should be clear that this denial was by no means a vote of support for Indian nationalism, but instead an example of longstanding efforts on the part of India's Muslims to refashion India into a what we have seen Rajendra Prasad call a "unnational" country. This world-encompassing vision of a non-national future, however, by the same token made for a "fanatical" politics, and I want to close this chapter with an egregiously violent instance of it.

## Amsterdam for Lahore

In his book *The Returns of Zionism*, Gabriel Piterberg writes about how Gershom Scholem, the founding figure of studies on Jewish mysticism, wrote what he calls a proleptic history of Zionism by identifying its myth of return in the past of Judaism's heretical tradition.[49] Scholem's major work was focussed on the extraordinary story of Sabbatai Sevi, a seventeenth-century Ottoman Jew who claimed to be the Messiah, giving rise to a wide-ranging following. At the behest of worried rabbinical authorities Sevi was eventually arrested and forced to become Muslim.[50] But this repudiation of Judaism was itself seen by many of his followers as demonstrating the truth of Sevi's mission, since he could only save his people by sinning against his religion and thus spiritualizing it as an internal force rather than a set of outward observances. Putting aside the complex theology behind this assertion, what interests Piterberg is not only Scholem's desire to read back the messianic element of Zionism into the Jewish past, but to do so precisely by breaking the hold of rabbinical Judaism, which he thought had normalized exile and degenerated into a set of ritual prescriptions. And yet despite his concern with heresy, Scholem ended up, says Piterberg, the spokesman for Zionism as a new form of Jewish orthodoxy. A similar tale might be told about Mohammad Iqbal, who incidentally had the same academic supervisor at Munich's Ludwig Maximilian University as Scholem, though separated by a gap of more than a decade. Fritz Hommel, a Semitic expert, also seems to have played little role in the intellectual development of either of his more illustrious students. Iqbal is today accepted as an impeccably orthodox Muslim, as indeed he more or less was in his own practices, though his ideas, we have seen, draw from very heterodox and mystical traditions indeed. In some ways Scholem's notion of an apostate messiah fits rather well with Iqbal's idea of a heroic Satan. For both men saw in traditional religion an obstacle that had to be removed if a new society was to emerge, one that was faithful to its revolutionary origins.

But what is particularly striking about these men is how they managed to make a norm out of heresy by attacking the heterodoxy of others. In Scholem's case the enemy was exilic Judaism itself as a norm, and in Iqbal's it was a traditional theory of Muslim authority that in the twentieth century came, above all, to be identified with a supposedly "deviant" community called the Ahmadis. What makes the comparison so fruitful, however, is the fact that in his attacks on the Ahmadis, Iqbal himself takes recourse to exilic Judaism, with which he compares Indian Islam, thus returning to the fearful identification with it that we have already seen manifested in the previous chapter. Founded in nineteenth-century Punjab by Mirza Ghulam Ahmad, this group quickly became known for its proselytizing zeal and willingness to engage in polemics with Hindu revivalists, Christian missionaries and others. Indeed, Iqbal had once even praised them as examples of Islam's modern revival. Outwardly indistinguishable from the most orthodox of Sunnis, the Ahmadis were soon marked in Iqbal's eyes by one belief in particular, their attribution of prophetic status to Mirza Ghulam Ahmad. Now this sort of attribution, along with other claims of supernatural favour made by the Mirza, were part of a long messianic tradition in Islam, one that had sometimes produced controversy but never the kind of public obloquy and eventually mass violence that the Ahmadis were soon subject to. So apart from the role that mass communication and mobilization in the twentieth century played in expanding this controversy, what made it conceptually different from previous religious altercations?

Soon after Pakistan was established, religious organizations like the Jamat-e Islami launched an agitation against the Ahmadis that resulted in extensive riots and eventually a judicial declaration that they were not Muslim, and so could neither call themselves by that name nor, indeed, invoke God and the Prophet in Islamic fashion or even have their places of worship look like mosques. This anxiety to stop people from appearing or behaving like Muslims is not only novel, but also interesting because it suggests that Islam can easily be usurped by others and become a kind of simulacrum seducing true believers from their religion. In an essay on anti-Ahmadi discourse in Pakistan, the anthropologist Naveeda Khan has made the point that the judgements against them have drawn upon the law of patents and copyright, arguing that an "original" Islam had to be protected from false imitations or the distinction might itself be lost.[51] Islam, in other words, was legally defined as the intellectual property of its believers. Apart from illustrating the rather modern character of this controversy, which in this sense only follows the precedent set by the Ahmadis' own "modernization" of religious debate, noteworthy about it is the reliance on inner belief as a criterion of veracity, since outward appearances were no longer trustworthy. Given the fact that Sunni tradition had always been concerned with outward conformity rather than inner belief as a criterion of orthodoxy, this turn to the latter was itself curiously heretical in character, for such an emphasis on the esoteric had always been associated with mystical and sectarian groups in the past. I would like to argue, however, that this focus on an invisible doctrine had something to do with the importance of ungrounded ideas and unmediated principles in Muslim nationalism.

The judicially authorized persecution of the Ahmadis in Pakistan has opened the door to increasingly murderous attacks on all other "deviant" groups there, especially the Shia, to say nothing about the oppression of those, like Hindus and Christians, who make no claim on Islam. And though Iqbal would no doubt have been horrified by this situation, it is his reasoning on the Ahmadi issue that has come to define these various forms of intolerance. Indeed, during his own lifetime Nehru had pointed out that as far as heretics went, the Aga Khan and his Shia sub-sect were no less "extreme" than the Ahmadis, as if to warn Iqbal that targeting one group could end up in a more general denunciation, as indeed has been the case in Pakistan. But Iqbal, in an open letter responding to Nehru, defended the Aga on rather formalistic grounds, while at the same time regretting the errors of his sect. For Iqbal, then, it was not the highly visible missionary efforts of this largely middle class group that posed a problem, nor was it so much Mirza Ghulam Ahmad's declaration of other Muslims as being unbelievers, though he didn't much like that either. Crucial rather was their supposed denial, at a purely doctrinal level, of Muhammad as the final prophet.[52]

Of course the finality of prophecy is an important part of Muslim belief, though as I have suggested, it had never stopped kings, saints and others from claiming to share in or inherit Muhammad's mission throughout Islam's history. But I will argue that Iqbal's defence of this finality is in some ways far more heretical than Mirza Ghulam Ahmad's alleged repudiation of it. The man claimed as Pakistan's spiritual father saw Muhammad as standing with one foot in the ancient world and the other in the modern. The Prophet belonged, he thought, to the ancient world insofar as he was the recipient of revelation, whose "psychic energy" Iqbal described as "a mode of economizing individual thought and choice by providing ready-made judgments, choices, and ways of action."[53] But Muhammad was a modern man insofar as he put an end to this occult form of knowledge, both by disclaiming any miraculous abilities and by announcing the end of prophecy with himself. By stopping all access to divine knowledge in its occult form, then, the Prophet freed mankind from such "leading strings" and for the first time made of it history's unique actor.[54] And we have already seen how Iqbal celebrates the rise of man's "maturity" with Islam by describing God resigning the stylus and tablet of destiny to him, as well as in contemplating man's partnership and indeed rivalry with the deity.

The idea of divine partnership was in fact one of the great themes of Iqbal's thought, whose "heretical" origins he made clear in his thesis *The Development of Metaphysics in Persia*, which placed the origins of Muslim philosophy in Zoroastrianism and saw its ultimate fulfilment in Bahaism. In this text Iqbal attributed the most fulsome enunciation of such a partnership to the ancestor of Bahaism, Mirza Ali Muhammad Bab, who pointed out that "The Quranic verse, that 'God is the best of creators', implies that there are other self-manifesting beings like God."[55] Though he would omit his source in future discussions of this theme, itself a classic mode of mystical and heretical writing, Iqbal continued making use of the Bab's favoured interpretation of this verse from the Quran to the end of his career, which suggests that his self-proclaimed orthodoxy needs to be approached with a great deal of suspicion. Indeed, given the fact that the Babis and later Bahais represented a similar "threat" to Shia Iran as the Ahmadis did to Sunni India, and at the same time, it is curious how well-disposed Iqbal continued to be towards them, despite being clear that they were no longer Muslim in any strong sense. Iqbal lauded in particular the female Babi martyr Qurratul-Ayn in his poetry, and in this followed the example of many Indian Muslims, for whom she was a great heroine whose name became a popular one for girl children. In some sense, then, Iqbal was interested in the figure of the god-man, prefigured most strikingly by Jesus as God become man, but also in the messianic figures of Judaism and Islam, though he used the old mystical term of the "perfect man" (*insan-i kamil*) for him. Indeed there are many places in his verse where Iqbal speaks of man becoming like God, otherwise an unpardonable sin in Islam, verses which, unlike the Christian emphasis on incarnation, assume the ascent of man to divinity rather than God's descent into humanity. The Ahmadis, then, were dangerous because they would drag man back into the mists of occult wisdom while at the same time refusing to let him assume divinity by reserving this attribute for Mirza Ghulam Ahmad alone.

Stripping the Mirza of his divine attributes, then, had nothing to do with reserving these for Muhammad, since the Prophet, too, was increasingly seen by many Muslims, reformers as well as revivalists, as being a mere mortal. Iqbal's views about prophecy, in other words, might have been idiosyncratic in one sense, but were commonplace in another, since his conception of prophetic finality also emphasized the human element in Islam. Being deprived of miracles and other signs of grace, however, did not lessen Muhammad in the eyes of his followers, but rather the contrary, as he could now become a model for them in a new, even "secular" way. Indeed, once the Prophet had become merely human he suddenly became vulnerable to attack, and thus required the defence of Muslims as in some sense their property, as the Pakistani court forbidding the Ahmadis from calling themselves Muslim in fact argued. So while Iqbal could treat God in a rather cavalier fashion in his poetry, accusing Him (or Her) of infidelity, he would tolerate no such playful dealings as far as Muhammad was concerned, and this is true even of Muslims who protest against insults to the Prophet today, for whom God is never in need of their defence.[56] In *Jawab-e Shikwa*, for instance, after man is offered the stylus and tablet of destiny, God tells him that keeping faith with Muhammad is the only requirement of Islam. For the Prophet, as we have seen, is the founder of humanity as history's true actor, representing therefore the vanishing moment of particularity out of which Islam's universality emerges, and it is this which calls for his protection, whereas God requires none. And Iqbal took this peculiar faith in a "disenchanted" messenger so seriously as to praise the Muslim assassin of a Hindu publisher who had printed a scurrilous and immensely controversial attack on Muhammad in 1927, and, it is rumoured, even serve as a pallbearer at Ilm-ud-Din's (or Ilam Din's) funeral after his judicial execution in 1929.

It is a curious defence of orthodoxy that Iqbal mounts against the Ahmadis, in other words, premised as it is on a certain vision of Nietzsche's thesis about the "death of God," given the fact that the German philosopher was one of his favourite writers. But why did a small if persistent group like the Ahmadis in the Punjab pose such a threat to Iqbal's world-historical vision of Islam? Because having been divested of all materiality to become a pure idea it was uniquely vulnerable to disruption. The very quality that made Islam universal and gave it power, in other words, also imperilled it and required of Muslims a touchy and even aggressive defensiveness. So in an article on "Qadianis and Orthodox Muslims" in 1934, Iqbal wrote that:

Islam repudiates the race idea altogether and founds itself on the religious idea alone. Since Islam bases itself on the religious idea alone, a basis which is wholly spiritual and consequently far more ethereal than blood relationship, Muslim society is naturally much more sensitive to forces which it considers harmful to its integrity.[57]

Rather than having anything to do with old-fashioned religious disputation, in other words, this is the kind of doctrinal struggle that characterised twentieth-century ideologies, and communism in particular, with its show trials and excommunications, whose meaning cannot be exhausted by sociological factors and bureaucratic politics alone.

And it is the unique vulnerability of a community built on an idea alone that Iqbal goes on to describe in entirely Jewish terms. But rather than take the part of Judaism's heretical tradition, as Gershom Scholem did, Iqbal sides with rabbinical Judaism instead, thus secreting his own heterodox position at the heart of orthodoxy in a truly mystical way. So he can write about Ahmadism that:

> Its idea of a jealous God with an inexhaustible store of earthquakes and plagues for its opponents; its conception of the prophet as a sooth-sayer; its idea of the continuity of the spirit of the messiah, are so abso-lutely Jewish that the movement can easily be regarded as a return to early Judaism. The idea of the continuity of the spirit of the messiah belongs more to Jewish mysticism than to positive Judaism.[58]

Indeed, he even compares the rise of Ahmadism in colonial India to the emergence of Christianity as a Jewish heresy in Roman Judaea, both representing, in Nietzsche's sense, "slave moralities" that accept and religiously legitimize tyranny:

> This country of religious communities where the future of each com-munity rests entirely upon its solidarity, is ruled by a Western people who cannot but adopt a policy of non-interference in religion. This lib-eral and indispensable policy in a country like India has led to most unfortunate results. In so far as Islam is concerned, it is no exaggera-tion to say that the solidarity of the Muslim community in India under the British is far less safe than the solidarity of the Jewish community was in the days of Jesus under the Romans. Any religious adventurer in India can set up any claim and carve out a new community for his own exploitation. This liberal state of ours does not care a fig for the integrity of the parent community, provided the adventurer assures it of his loyalty and his followers are regular in the payment of taxes due to the state.[59]

Iqbal elaborated his argument about Ahmadism providing, as he saw it, a religious basis for colonial rule in his article respond-ing to Nehru, in which he described the group's refutation of holy war and accommodation with the state as being, if not unusual and even expedient in politics, then at least novel in its reliance upon occult knowledge, saying that "the function of Ahmadism in the history of Muslim religious thought is to furnish a revelational basis for India's present political subjugation."[60] But the strangest comparison he draws in this extended meditation on Jewish mysticism is between Mirza Ghulam Ahmad and the philosopher Spinoza who, Iqbal nevertheless hastens to say, was far superior to the founder of Ahmadism. Quoting from Will Durant's *The Story of Philosophy*, Iqbal writes:

Furthermore, religious unanimity seemed to the elders their sole means of preserving the little Jewish group in Amsterdam from disintegration, and almost the last means of preserving the unity, and so ensuring the survival of the scattered Jews of the world. If they had had their own state, their own civil law, their own establishment of secular force and power, to compel internal cohesion and external respect, they might have been more tolerant; but their religion was to them their patriotism as well as their faith; the synagogue was their centre of social and political life as well as of ritual and worship; and the Bible whose veracity Spinoza had impugned was the 'portable fatherland' of their people; under these circumstances they thought heresy was treason, and toleration suicide.[61]

While the difference between Jews in diaspora and Indian Muslims might seem very great, for Iqbal their similarity was based upon either community's dependence on an ideal or, as he would say, "ethereal" form of solidarity, which made both groups vulnerable and strong at the same time. And so Iqbal could conclude his train of thought by saying that "Similarly the Indian Muslims are right in regarding the Qadiani movement, which declares the entire world of Islam as *kafir* and socially boycotts them, to be far more dangerous to the collective life of Islam in India than the metaphysics of Spinoza to the collective life of the Jews."[62] Iqbal, in other words, managed in his anti-Ahmadi writings to adopt an orthodox mien in a specifically rabbinical way, while at the same time upholding a radically mystical vision of Islam. But this had to be compensated for by the most rigorous conservatism, since the "portable fatherland" of Islam, too, otherwise risked destruction in a world context where Muslims were increasingly seen, as in India, to be nothing more than a minority. And so the very radicalism of Iqbal's thought impels him towards a conservative protection of Muslim practice in a gesture that can be seen as paradoxical if not a sign of bad faith.

5

# TO SET INDIA FREE

While it probably derives from the name of a South Indian caste, the word pariah entered into European languages as early as the eighteenth century, where it came to refer to outcastes or "Untouchables," now known in India as "Dalits," in general. But it was soon extended to describe any ostracized figure, both human and animal, like a pariah dog, with all these senses of the word returning to India and lodging themselves in the imaginations of those who know English there. What is interesting about the word's history, then, has been its worldwide dissemination and transformation into a conceptual category, especially in social and political life, thus allowing the particular exclusion of caste to be generalized as a uniquely degrading form of oppression. One social relationship that was, in the nineteenth century, marked by the term pariah, happened to be that defined by anti-Semitism within declining empires and new national states. And this link between Indian outcastes and European Jews was by no means confined to the latter's imagination, with Gandhi, for example, frequently describing them as the "Untouchables of Christianity," just as he described Indians as having themselves become "Pariahs of the Empire" at least in part for tolerating the sin of untouchability.

While the Mahatma's comparison of Jews and Dalits was not a very accurate one, he did recognise that the pariah could serve as a distinct yet universal figure of oppression. The term still has a certain currency in our own day, though for the most part negatively, in forms like "pariah state," where ostracism is seen as a value to be encouraged. For since the Holocaust became an important historical theme from the 1960s, the pariah has been replaced by the figure of the Jew it had once described, a figure whose fate in fascist Europe has now been universalized as a potential for every group under threat. Indeed, Holocaust studies has even provided the model for recent scholarship on the large-scale violence that accompanied the partition of India, thus reversing the conceptual trajectory of the word pariah, by allowing Indian scholars to return to Europe for models of analysis and interpretation. While the recognition of the outcaste as a universal figure, moreover, had served to launch a certain kind of politics among Jews and Dalits both, the fear of genocide can only signal its end in a kind of apocalypse. The difference between these two figures of universality, in other words, is very great indeed.

Drawing on an Indian comparison to describe the new kind of persecution they faced as a minority group within Europe's emerging nationalities, Jewish intellectuals in the nineteenth and early twentieth centuries were in some sense universalizing their predicament and resisting the particularity to which their enemies would reduce them. And in doing so, as Gabriel Piterberg argues in *The Returns of Zionism*, they were also presented with an existential and political choice.[1] Should European Jews erase their particularity by assimilation, which of course includes Zionism as another form of "normalization," or should they instead acknowledge it as part of a universal struggle against oppression? Following the French journalist Bernard Lazare and the philosopher Hannah Arendt, Piterberg contends that the latter is a far more productive choice, one that entails the refusal either to be identified merely as a minority posing a question for the nation state, or, in another gesture of the parvenu, to reconstitute oneself as a majority in its own state. In an essay of 1944 called "The Jew as Pariah: A Hidden Tradition," Arendt wrote about the conceptual status of the pariah as a world-historical figure intractable to the politics of assimilation, minority rights or nationalism:

That the status of the Jews in Europe has been not only that of an oppressed people but also of what Max Weber has called a 'pariah people' is a fact most clearly appreciated by those who have had practical experience of just how ambiguous is the freedom which emancipation has ensured, and how treacherous the promise of equality which assimilation has held out. In their own position as social outcasts such men reflect the political status of their entire people. It is therefore not surprising that out of their personal experience Jewish poets, writers, and artists should have been able to evolve the concept of the pariah as a human type—a concept of supreme importance for the evaluation of mankind in our day and one which has exerted upon the gentile world an influence in strange contrast to the spiritual and political ineffectiveness which has been the fate of these men among their own brethren.[2]

Aamir Mufti, in his book *Enlightenment in the Colony*, explores the implications of this choice to be a "conscious pariah" internationally, by looking at the way in which a number of Muslim intellectuals in colonial India responded to the emergence of similar national majorities there from the end of the nineteenth century.[3] He foregrounds in particular how these men resisted being identified as members of a minority in India and, eventually, as part of a majority in Pakistan. My own project here, of course, has to do with those who rejected not only the status of minority, but that of pariah as well, though I would argue that the nation states produced out of this repudiation were by no means intended to be copies of Europe's majority-defined polities. Nevertheless, pariah status has dogged both

Israel and Pakistan, especially in recent times, when one is vilified by those on the left as representing a form of "apartheid," while the other is condemned by those on the right as a "terrorist" or "rogue" state. How then did Muslim nationalism engage with the figure of the pariah in the society of its origin?

Rarely dealt with in the historiography on Pakistan, this question is important because religious politics in colonial India was never dualistic, with Hindus and Muslims always triangulated by a third category. For both Congress and the League, as well as for the rival bands of historians who follow each party, this third figure has always been identified with the British state, seen as having operated either deliberately or inadvertently according to a policy of "divide and rule." But I want to argue in this chapter that Indian politics during this period was triangulated by caste as a category that, far more crucially than class and other social or economic distinctions, threatened to undo both majority and minority in a fashion that might have redefined Indian society in radical new ways.[4] Indeed, caste has served as a mediating figure in Hindu-Muslim relations from their modern emergence during the Indian Mutiny of 1857, when it was the threat supposedly uttered by an "Untouchable," of British attempts to destroy the caste and religious integrity of Hindus and Muslims by violating their dietary taboos, that provided the revolt's mythical charter and allowed them to unite against the East India Company.[5] Obscured by the Manichaean narrative of religious enmity, then, was another politics without which the Pakistan Movement cannot be understood.

## The vanishing mediator

When describing his earliest memories of caste in a speech delivered in Ahmedabad to the Suppressed Classes Conference in 1921, Gandhi recalled that "While at school I would often happen to touch the Untouchables, and as I never would conceal the fact from my parents, my mother would tell me that the short-est cut to purification after the unholy touch was to cancel the touch by touching any Mussulman passing by."[6] It is not clear whether the pollution would thereby be passed on to the Mus-lim, or like a charge of electricity be grounded in him, but in either case it is evident that Muslims could serve as mediators between high and low caste Hindus, as they were in some sense part of another system of social relations. In other words Mus-lims both made caste relations possible and, as we shall see, endangered them by threatening to separate one kind of Hindu from another. The problem posed by Muslim mediation recurs in writings of this time, and the Mahatma himself would describe the most direct instances of it, for example in another issue of his journal *Young India*, published on 5 May 1927 and quoted by his great foe, the Dalit leader B. R. Ambedkar. Gan-dhi begins by citing a letter from an "Untouchable" man describ-ing how a woman of his caste who had just given birth in the Mahatma's own home region of Kathiawar found it difficult to get a doctor to attend to her, and when one did come he behaved in the following way:

'He came, we took out the woman who had a baby only two days old. Then the doctor gave his thermometer to a Musalman who gave it to me. I applied the thermometer and then returned it to the Musalman who gave it to the doctor.'

What shall one say about the inhumanity of the doctor who being an educated man refused to apply the thermometer except through the medium of a Musalman to purify it, and who treated an ailing woman lying in for two days worse than a dog or a cat?[7]

In this passage the Mahatma describes the role of the Muslim as being to purify some object polluted by a Dalit, thus making of him a kind of neutralizing element like fire, water, or indeed, given the medical procedure involved, a sterile medium. How-ever polluting the Muslim himself might be, in other words, with his water and cooked food being impermissible to a high caste

Hindu, he could function as a purifying or mediating element making possible the relations of others. But this made Muslims into the only truly universal element in Indian society, able to circulate among all its constituent parts and put each in touch with the others. And it was precisely this role, when translated from the ritual dimension to the political, which made Muslims into such a threat for caste Hindus, at least once these latter had been constituted as part of a national majority. For the service performed by Muslims in a caste society suddenly came to seem a threat with the rise of political representation, when their mediation could be redefined as a way of interrupting or dividing the social relations between Hindus themselves. And so throughout the twentieth century high caste Hindu organizations were haunted by the fear that their religious majority would be destroyed if low caste groups were to convert to Islam or, less importantly, to Christianity, a fear that was never too far from the many efforts undertaken by such organizations to "uplift" Dalits and cleanse Hinduism itself of caste discrimination. And indeed, starting in the 1920s, both Hindu and Muslim missionaries began imitating their Christian predecessors, so as to convert communities of indeterminate religious affiliation and thus augment their respective numbers.

Naturally, this situation provided Dalits and other low caste Indians with new political opportunities as well as threatening them with the risk of being submerged within some larger community in a subordinate way, thus illustrating how fragile the categories of majority and minority really were, and how generalized the fears of being swamped by larger numbers. In some sense, then, the Muslim League's intermittent criticism of these categories, and attempts to avoid them altogether, had a certain political truth about it. And so the sheer violence between majority and minority groups which, in different parts of India, could each be represented by Hindus and Muslims, or, in a few areas, by Christians and Sikhs, might have resulted from the inability of these categories to assume a political reality. In fact this violence may have produced majorities and minorities rather than itself being their product. Whatever the importance of proselytizing movements and religious revivalism in this three-way struggle, however, of most significance in the world of political institutions was the fact that the Muslim League, which eventually became the largest party in opposition to the Congress, came to represent the model for anti-Congress politics among everyone else. Even when they did not ally with it, in other words, groups as hostile to the League as the Hindu Mahasabha faithfully copied many of its arguments and demands, and were especially quick to mirror Muslim fears of assimilation, thus identifying with the status of a minority that was instantiated primarily by the Prophet's followers. But what is noteworthy here is how low caste politics interacted with the League, taking up both its early defence of minority rights and representation, and its later demand for separate zones and even an independent state.

The provincial politics of the so-called Aligarh Movement, we saw in chapter two, was dedicated to protecting the Muslim gentry of northern India and, if possible, associating them with their high caste Hindu neighbours, with Syed Ahmed Khan and his associates taking little notice of low caste Hindus or Muslims, and at most recommending a course of "reform" that placed them under the continued tutelage of their betters. So at a speech to the Islamic Association of Rae Bareilly in 1883 Sir Syed, who was otherwise a great advocate of modern education for Muslims, suggested that the children of his poor and, one assumes, low caste co-religionist, should only be given a traditional education at the doorsteps of the gentry and aristocracy, saying:

I would be very happy if during my lifetime I could see this dead method again revived, and see sitting in the doorway of every gentleman and noble a teacher who would teach the common boys of the neighborhood from the same books which our ancestors used to teach them. [...] You should make such efforts that these boys should know how to read and write, and learn as much arithmetic as is necessary in everyday life. And they should be made to read such short essays as would inform them of the requirements of prayer and fasting that come up in daily life, and the straightforward rules of the Muslim faith.[8]

With the founding of the Muslim League, however, and the increasing dominance of a politics of numbers, as representative institutions were slowly introduced into India, low caste groups and minorities of other sorts as well had now to be taken into account. And the first time these groups came together in a serious way was during the Round Table Conferences of the 1930s that brought on board Indian interests of various kinds with the purpose of getting them to agree to a future constitution for the country. None of the three conferences held in London was able to reach any agreement, and the British government had eventually to put forward a "communal award" unilaterally, which with some alterations was finally embodied in the Government of India Act of 1935, that still forms the basis of both India's and Pakistan's constitutions. Despite their apparent failures, however, Indian debates at the Round Table Conferences not only shaped the 1935 Act, which remains probably the most important piece of legislation for contemporary South Asia, they also allowed for the possibility of a minorities alliance on a country-wide basis.

The Minorities Pact between Muslims, Dalits (or Depressed Classes as they were known), Indian Christians, Anglo-Indians and Europeans that was agreed to by their representatives at the second Round Table Conference, claimed to represent nearly half of India's population, thus reducing caste Hindus to a mere plurality rather than a majority. Gandhi, who spoke for the Congress at this conference, was willing to grant Muslim demands for separate electorates, but refused to do so for Dalits, ostensibly because he thought that leaders like Ambedkar did not in fact represent them, and also because such a recognition of their autonomy would completely fragment Indian politics by setting the precedent for any group to claim protections and electorates. And this, he thought, could only strengthen the hand of the British in ruling over an India forever divided from within. The fear of setting a precedent for internal fragmentation, leading to the perpetuation of colonial rule, was in fact the primary argument that Congress deployed against all its Indian rivals, including the Muslims, communists and Hindu nationalists. But scholars studying this event have focussed mostly on Gandhi's refusal to divide the Hindu community and destroy its majority.

When the Communal Award was given, and the Depressed Classes received separate electorates, Gandhi went on a famous fast to the death, in order, he said, to convince Hindus to eradicate caste discrimination. Creating as it did a huge commotion all over the country, the Mahatma's fast eventually compelled Ambedkar to come to an agreement with him called the Poona Pact, in which he relinquished separate electorates for Dalits in exchange for reserved seats in councils and legislatures that would still, however, mostly be in the control of caste Hindu voters. In later years Ambedkar would always complain that he had been forced to parley with Gandhi, whose death would have unleashed a wave of violence against the "Untouchables," but at the time he was loud in defending the Poona Pact against caste Hindus who started questioning it shortly after it had been agreed.[9] Was it the consequences of Gandhi's possible death that compelled Ambedkar to treat with him, or the possibility that the Mahatma would be able to demonstrate his own command over the Depressed Classes, unjust or coerced though it may have been? Given Ambedkar's signal failure in electoral politics, something that might well have been due to the way in which the franchise was defined in India, we should at least consider the latter option. But whatever the case, the Poona Pact marked the first and probably most serious defeat of a tentative politics that might have demolished the categories of majority as well as minority, not only for India, but in the constitutional framework of any modern state. For like Jinnah the Dalit leader was well aware that neither of these "communities" could be described as a majority or a minority of any political kind, writing to A. V. Alexander, one of the members of the Cabinet Mission sent to India to negotiate a constitutional arrangement for her freedom after the war on 14 May 1946:

To my mind, it is only right to say that the Hindus and the Muslims are today mentally incompetent to decide upon the destiny of this country. Both Hindus and Muslims are just crowds. It must be within your experience that a crowd is less moved by material profit than by a passion collectively shared. It is easier to persuade a mass of men to sacrifice itself collectively than to act upon a cool assessment of advantages. A crowd easily loses all sense of profit and loss. It is moved by motives which may be high or low, genial or barbarous, compassionate or cruel, but is always above or below reason. The common sense of each is lost in the emotion of all. It is easier to persuade a crowd to commit suicide than to accept a legacy.[10]

In a single passage, then, Ambedkar was able to account for the sublime character of Gandhi's non-violence as well as the base cruelties that also marked the behaviour of his followers, who in turn were seen as being no different from those of the Muslim League. In noting how the actions of Hindus and Muslims as political constituencies could not be defined by economic theories of "profit and loss," Ambedkar recognized the commercial basis upon which the category of interest rested. For the apparently universal form of self-interest that is presumed in Hobbesian theories of political action, in which it is the fear of death that makes a social contract possible, cannot legitimately be extended to interest as a more general or less existentially freighted category. And if interest in the latter sense is not in fact universal, but depends upon commercial ideas of contract, then, of course, it could not be predicated of most Indians, and especially not the country's two great religious communities. Figures like Gandhi and Iqbal had realized that interest, and its corollary, contract, could not be universalized in any society without completely destroying the bonds of friendship or family that made each one possible, and so they tried to build a new set of relations between Indians in explicitly non-contractual ways.[11] Ambedkar, however, was clearly suspicious of the violence these religious and other forms of sociability might entail and, like Jinnah, was far keener to turn them into interests, though he seemed to think that religious groups were not amenable to the logic of contract. How then, was Ambedkar's politics different from the one he so succinctly describes above?

## Fear of falling

Ambedkar would have known that the Muslim League, upon which any such scheme as the Minorities Pact must depend, was fairly opportunistic about it and, as we shall see, he often spoke bitterly about the League's lack of commitment to the freedom of other minorities. The responses we have from Muslim leaders are certainly ambivalent enough. Mohammad Iqbal for instance, in a statement of 1933 explaining the attitude of Muslim delegates to the Round Table Conferences, said that:

Mr Gandhi's second and most unrighteous condition was that Muslims should not support the special claims of Untouchables, particularly their claim to special representation. It was pointed out to him that it did not lie in the mouth of Muslims to oppose those very claims on the part of the Untouchables which they were advancing for themselves and that if Mr Gandhi could arrive at a mutual understanding with the Untouchables the Muslims would certainly not stand in their way. Mr Gandhi, however, insisted on this condition. [...] In this sense perhaps the greatest anti-national leader in India of to-day is Mr Gandhi, who has made it a life-mission to prevent the fusion of Untouchables with other communities and to retain them in the fold of Hinduism without any real fusion even between them and the caste Hindus.[12]

While he might well have been committed to the Dalit cause, in other words, Iqbal was not above using the breakdown of the Minorities Pact as a stick with which to beat the Mahatma. Three years later, in a speech in the Legislative Assembly on the Report of the Joint Parliamentary Committee on Indian Constitutional Reforms, Jinnah referred to the Poona Pact in a similar way, but this time approvingly and as a precedent for regulating the negotiations between Congress and the League. For Congress at this time was maintaining, as it did until the end of colonial rule, that in order to avoid the possibility of India's fragmentation and the consequent perpetuation of imperialism, Hindus and Muslims should achieve her freedom first and come to an agreement over protections and partitions later, something that Jinnah, of course, saw as merely a ploy to crush Muslims under a Hindu raj:

Then my Honourable friend laid down the proposition; acquisition first and distribution afterwards. There is a great fallacy, if I may say so, most respectfully, in that statement. This is not a question of acquisition and distribution. It is not that we are acquiring some land, it is not that we are going to enter upon a venture and then we share or distribute the spoils. But, may I know, if that proposition is correct, why did Mahatma Gandhi fast to death and come to an agreement with the sanction and concurrence of all leaders from India and arrive at the Poona Pact as regards the Depressed Classes? (Hear, hear). Why were they not told, acquisition first and distribution afterwards? (Hear, hear). Mahatma Gandhi was right. He knew, and they are drawn from your race, they are Hindus, 50 or 60 million Hindus. He was right, and I agree with him. I begged of him in England. First he said: 'No, I will not divide the Hindus. I will never agree to this.' I begged of him. Believe me, I pleaded more for the Depressed Classes before Mahatma Gandhi than I did for the Mussalmans. But he was adamant, but ultimately he did realize, and I congratulate my Hindu brethren that they have, by recognizing and giving this protection and safeguard to the Depressed Classes, won them over, and to-day he is still working for their amelioration. Show us the same spirit, join hands with us and we are ready (Hear, hear).[13]

Just as the provisions that had been given to Muslims as a minority could inspire Dalit politics, then, so could the latter's negotiations with Congress be held up as an example by the League. But this sort of cross-referencing was not random, and Ambedkar himself would make it clear in his book on Pakistan that the Muslim League was committed to generalizing its brand of politics on the model of the Minorities Pact between the 1937 elections, which we have already considered in chapter two, and the Lahore Resolution of 1940, when the demand for Pakistan was first made.[14] During this period, when the League did not have the unstinting support of the Muslim majority provinces and was in search of allies, it turned to the other minorities, including the Dalits. Choudhry Khaliquzzaman writes in his memoirs that he was responsible for this decision, which was taken in June 1938 in response to the Congress keeping the League out of government by claiming "national" status in representing these very minorities, saying that "I thought it was very unfair for the Congress to secure favour with the 'other minorities' at the cost of the Muslim League. As such my view that we should also court them was accepted and the resolution went through."[15] The courting of these other minorities, then, seems to have been considered only so as to achieve some degree of parity with Congress, though principles were also involved. So as late as 1943, Jinnah's lieutenant in Calcutta, M. A. H. Ispahani, wrote his leader describing a successful attempt to woo some Hindus into supporting the League in Bengal, commenting that "I wonder if it is the right thing to do—to divide the Hindus. We are playing their game, which we resent and condemn."[16]

The year before, Ispahani had written to the Qaid informing him that the League government in Bengal had elected J. N. Mandal as Mayor of Calcutta, saying "In the Calcutta Corporation, we achieved a great victory. We established the principle of mayoralty by rotation by electing a Scheduled Caste man as the First Citizen of Calcutta. Never before in the history of this city was an 'Achutya' elevated to the mayoral chair."[17] Mandal would be made law minister by the League in the interim government of 1946, move to Pakistan, preside over its constituent assembly and become its first law minister as well, the very role that Ambedkar played in India. He would however eventually leave Pakistan, disillusioned by the anti-minority turn taken by politics there after Jinnah's death.[18] It was also with Mandal's and thus, indirectly, the Muslim League's support that Ambedkar himself was first elected to India's constituent assembly from Bengal, a province he didn't know and whose language he didn't speak. Even after 1940, then, the League continued to engage in caste and minority politics, though its stance had changed significantly in the meantime. For the high point of the kind of Minorities Pact politics that had emerged during the Round Table Conferences came in 1939, when Congress resigned office in protest at India's being taken into the Second World War without her consent or even the promise of freedom. Seeing this move as an attempt on the part of Congress to blackmail Britain into making it more concessions on the eve of war, Jinnah organized a "Deliverance Day" to be celebrated across the country, in which parties as diverse as the Hindu Mahasabha and the Dalits joined the League. This is what Ambedkar, for instance, had to say about Jinnah's announcement of Deliverance Day and call for an inquiry into alleged Congress atrocities in an interview with *The Times of India* on 19 December 1939:

When I read Mr Jinnah's statement, I felt ashamed to have allowed him to steal a march over me and rob me of the language and the sentiments which I more than Mr Jinnah was entitled to use. Whatever anyone may say with regard to the tyranny alleged to have been practiced by the Hindus over the Muslims during the Congress regime no one can entertain any doubt as to the position of millions of Untouchables who had the misfortune to be ruled by the Congress government in this province in common with some others. If Mr Jinnah and the Muslims can prove five out of 100 cases of oppression, I am prepared to place 100 out of 100 cases before any impartial tribunal. I, therefore, am anxious more than Mr Jinnah can ever be, for the appointment of a Royal Commission to investigate the cases of tyranny and oppression by the Congress government.[19]

What is interesting about the passage quoted above is its rhetoric of theft, with Muslims seen as stealing both the claims of oppression and the demands for justice from their Dalit compatriots. Whatever it might say about Ambedkar's own anxieties regarding the enforced subordination of his constituency to the political terms set by the larger and more powerful one represented by Jinnah, this statement points to the possibility that the League relied upon the vicarious fear of Muslims suffering the fate of pariahs. And indeed Jinnah's claims of Congress tyranny after the 1937 elections, and his forecast of "Hindu Raj" in an independent India, have always puzzled observers, with Nehru and others in the Congress likening them to the Nazis' atrocity propaganda during the same period. Even before the violence that would give such fears their reality among Indians of all religious persuasions, however, the paranoia fanned by the League possessed, as Ambedkar seems to suggest, a certain reality in the plight of "Untouchables." Muslims, in other words, had before them a concrete example of the kind of oppression they were told to fear, and it was to avoid being reduced to the status of pariahs that they were asked to support the League.

If this is indeed the case, then the curiously intermittent relations that Muslim politicians enjoyed with Dalit organizations must be attributed to something more than opportunism on their part, since at a popular level such relations would have been based as much upon a desire to escape the fate of "Untouchables" as to join them in a common cause. In other words the demand for solidarity was consistently undercut by the desire to distinguish oneself from those inferior in status, a kind of "fear of falling" which is in fact essential to caste thinking and prevents ties between groups that might otherwise support one another. But might not Jinnah's references to such oppression also have been an indirect call to the low caste Muslims who would have suffered similar treatment at the hands of high-ranking Indians of any denomination? The answer to this question will have to await more research on the politics of caste among Muslims in the run-up to partition and independence.[20] In any case, Aamir Mufti has made an elegant case for a number of Muslim intellectuals who rejected both Pakistan as well as the status of a national minority in India, adopting instead the role of "conscious pariahs" in their turn to religion, communism or literature, and thus universalizing the figure of the Dalit like a number of their Jewish peers had done in Europe.[21] But the figures of the Jew and the "Untouchable" had been brought together by Muslim writers even before the First World War, as illustrated in a letter by an anonymous Muslim, "a man both of European education and very wide knowledge of his Indian co-religionists, with whom he enjoys exceptional credit."[22] Valentine Chirol, an important British journalist who quoted this letter in *Indian Unrest*, his famously alarmist book on India, included it in a section titled "The Fate of the Spanish Moors." However, he might with equal if not more justice have substituted Iberian Jews for Muslims, given the reference the letter he quotes makes to the fate of minorities in modern European nationalism:

English observers must not forget that there is throughout India amongst Hindus a strong tendency towards imitating the national movements that have proved successful in European history. Now, while *vis-à-vis* the British the Hindu irreconcilables assume the attitude of the Italian patriots towards the hated Austrian, *vis-à-vis* the Moslems there is a very different European model for them to follow. Not only Tilak and his school in Poona, but throughout the Punjab and Bengal the constant talk of the Nationalists is that the Moslems must be driven out of India as they were driven out of Spain.[23]

Chirol's book had adopted an increasingly familiar justification for British rule, one founded on the protection of Muslims and "Untouchables" in particular from the supposedly violent designs of upper-caste Hindu nationalists. And it is the putative link between these two groups that is brought forward in the passage that immediately follows the one quoted above. For here the Muslim letter-writer moves from the figure of the mobile European minority, exemplified in the text by the Moors and, by implication, Jews, to that of the immobile and immiserated caste. For he mentions the fate of his poor and low-caste co-religionists in terms that more appropriately belong to Chirol's chapter on the "Untouchables":

This is no invention of ours. Nor is it quite so wild as it appears at first sight. I have gone into the matter carefully and I can certainly conceive circumstances—fifty or 100 years hence—that would make India intolerable for our upper middle classes; and once you get rid of the intelligent and wealthy Moslems the masses could be reduced to absolute subjection in the hands of Hindu rulers.[24]

Precisely because it was so hedged with taboos and fears of all kinds, then, the comparison between Dalits and Muslims, which was further internationalised in the figure of the Jews, was an immensely powerful one. Indeed, if I am correct it alone lent some degree of reality to the paranoid style that Muslim politics was increasingly taking in India.[25]

## A politics of sacrifice

While Ambedkar was concerned with securing the place of his people within a common front that would, of necessity, be dominated by the Muslim League, his rival Gandhi had a somewhat different reason for supporting it. For the Mahatma quickly realised that Jinnah's apparent effort to resuscitate the Minorities Pact he had himself killed at the Round Table Conferences could now save India's unity. So on 16 January 1940 he wrote to the Qaid, enclosing an article he had written in the *Harijan* supporting the Deliverance Day celebrations:

179

I know that you are quite capable of rising to the height required for the noble motive attributed to you. I do not mind your opposition to the Congress. But your plan to amalgamate all the parties opposed to the Congress at once gives your movement a national character. If you succeed you will free the country from communal incubus [*sic*], and in my humble opinion give a lead to the Muslims and others for which you will deserve the gratitude not only of the Muslims but of all the other communities.[26]

Gandhi's enclosed article elaborated upon the point made in his letter by arguing, much as Jinnah himself had done so many times, that communal majorities and minorities stood in the way of democracy and needed to be replaced by political and therefore changeable ones:

But the Quaid-i-Azam has given me special reason for congratulating him. I had the pleasure of wiring him congratulations on his excellent Id-day broadcast. And now he commands further congratulations on forming pacts with parties who are opposed to the Congress policies and politics. He is thus lifting the Muslim League out of the communal rut and giving it a national character. I regard his step as perfectly legitimate. I observe that the Justice Party and Dr Ambedkar's party have already joined Jinnah Sahib. The papers report too, that Shree Savarkar, the president of the Hindu Mahasabha, is to see him presently. Jinnah Sahib himself has informed the public that many non-Congress Hindus have expressed their sympathy with him. I regard this development as thoroughly healthy. Nothing can be better than that we should have in the country mainly two parties—the Congress and non-Congress or anti-Congress, if the latter expression is preferred. Jinnah Sahib is giving the word 'minority' a new and good content. The Congress majority is made up of a combination of caste Hindus, Muslims, Christians, Parsis and Jews. Therefore, it is a majority drawn from all classes, representing a particular body of opinion, and the proposed combination becomes a minority representing another body of opinion. This may one day convert itself into a majority by commending itself to the electorate.[27]

Gandhi's words would have been unlikely to elicit the approbation of those who led the Congress, men whose sometimes obsessive fear of India's fragmentation determined them upon achieving a kind of hegemony over her political life, and obtaining the country's freedom under a single party, which in Jinnah's eyes made it fascist. Nevertheless, the Mahatma's article was by no means unusual in its stance, as the communist leader M. N. Roy too wrote a couple of times to Jinnah proposing just such an alignment of forces against the Congress, as in the following passage from a letter of 1941, in which he recommended the formation of a National Democratic Union, saying:

As regards the personal composition of the projected movement, nobody can deny that yourself, a representative of the non-Brahmins, Dr Ambedkar, a Christian like Sir Maharaj Singh, an outstanding intellectual like Dr Paranjpye, a representative of the Sikhs and a representative of our party, can compose a government more representative than the national government of the Congress coterie. It is almost certain that the Hindu Mahasabha will fall in line with such a combination.[28]

And if communists were willing to entertain such an alliance with a combination of liberals, conservatives and reactionaries, so, apparently, were many of the Hindu capitalists who would otherwise support the Congress or Mahasabha. For taking their situation as itself a kind of political norm, rather than simply a temporary and exceptional condition under colonial rule, many Indians at this time were willing to consider the struggle of India's two great parties as being nothing less than the stuff of a democracy in the making. Capitalists, for example, did not seem to possess a particularly apocalyptic view of this struggle, as was made clear to the viceroy, Lord Wavell, who wrote the following entry in his journal on 30 November 1944:

Srivastava in a discussion with me today told me that, after the Congress success at the polls and assumption of office in U.P. in 1937, the leading industrialists—all I think Hindu—got together and decided to finance Jinnah and the Muslim League and also the Mahasabha, as the extreme Communal parties to oppose Congress who they feared might threaten their financial profits. I said I considered it a most immoral proceeding, and Srivastava merely said: 'But politics are immoral.'[29]

Further investigation will tell us how far Wavell's information was correct, though it was certainly true that Jinnah maintained excellent relations with one of India's wealthiest industrialists, Ramkrishna Dalmia, who unlike most of the Qaid's Muslim acquaintances was a personal friend of his, and who bought Jinnah's house in Delhi when the latter departed for Pakistan. The fact that Dalmia's great rival was a fellow Marwari industrialist, Ghanshyam Das Birla, one of the major financiers of the Congress, seems to lend substance to the viceroy's remark. Indeed, Dalmia appears to have been willing to serve as financier to an anti-Congress alliance led by the League, something of which Ambedkar, for one, was well aware, writing Jinnah as late as 1946 to plead with him to put in a good word with Dalmia, saying that:

I saw him today and placed before him my appeal for funds for the college. He has expressed his desire to do something but he said that he will consult you before he makes his decision. I was glad to hear from him that you had already spoken to him about the matter. I have to collect about twelve lakh [1,200,000 rupees] for the college. Out of this, I am expecting at least three lakh [300,000 rupees] from Mr Dalmia. I was glad to find that he has a great regard for you and also has great faith in your judgement. I have no doubt that if you put in a word, he will not hesitate to give the amount I have mentioned.[30]

I have cited this letter at length because it provides a good illustration of the complex interconnections between Indian politics and finance during this period, with the Qaid acting as the member of the trading caste he was by becoming a middleman and in effect guarantor for Ambedkar's scheme to found a college for Dalits.

But perhaps Gandhi should not have rushed into print in an effort to push Jinnah's politics in a "national" direction, for the reply he received from the Qaid on 21 January 1940 was uncompromising:

It is true that many non-Congress Hindus expressed their sympathy with the Deliverance Day in justice to our cause, so also the leaders of the Justice Party and the Scheduled Castes, and the Parsis who had suffered. But I am afraid that the meaning which you have tried to give to this alignment shows that you have not appreciated the true significance of it. It was partly a case of 'adversity bringing strange bedfellows together', and partly because common interests may lead Muslims and minorities to combine. I have no illusions in the matter, and let me say again that India is not a nation, nor a country. It is a subcontinent composed of nationalities, Hindus and Muslims being the two major nations.[31]

Very much like Ambedkar, then, Jinnah was suspicious of his own allies among the "other minorities," and refused to be drawn into a ramshackle coalition with them that might easily come apart and leave Muslims at the mercy of a Hindu majority. For as the Congress Muslim D. G. Dalvi wrote him in 1941:

You seem to rely on the verbal support of the leaders of the non-Brahmins like Ramaswami Naicker and C. R. Reddy and of the Depressed Classes like Dr Ambedkar. But please assess, in your own mind, what real support they can bring to the realization of Pakistan. They may be individually inspired by their personal opposition to the Congress. Their support might have served the purpose at the Round Table Conference for giving effect to the preconceived plans of the British government. But let me assure you they will prove a broken reed when you come to brass tacks. Was it not the support of the vast mass of the non-Brahmins and Depressed Class electorate which gave the Congress its majority in Bombay and Madras Provinces at the last general elections?[32]

Yet his unwillingness to become a "national" leader by no means indicated Jinnah's desire to lend reality to Congress fears and fragment India as completely as his response to the Mahatma appears to indicate. Once the League adopted the "two-nation theory" in 1940, it could no longer engage in minority politics apart from in an opportunistic way, but this shift also opened the possibility of another kind of alliance, between groups that would divide India into more than two nations. From Ambedkar's concerns, then, which could only be linked to minority politics given the dispersal of Dalits across the country, the Qaid moved to considering those of E. V. Ramaswami Naicker, leader of the Non-Brahmin Movement in southern India. Unlike Dalits, the Non-Brahmins were a regional majority, and so Naicker was able to deploy the League's rhetoric of nationality to claim a "Dravidasthan" for his people there—in full consonance with the League's "Pakistan." Because of the curious demographic configuration that Muslims possessed in colonial India, they were able to deploy two kinds of political strategies, one defined by the category of minority and the other by that of the nation. And this meant that the Muslim League really could play the role of universal mediator in the country, linking up with the politics of Ambedkar as well as Naicker while remaining faithful to neither one.

Speaking to an audience of a hundred thousand in his presidential address to the Madras session of the All-India Muslim League in April 1941, Jinnah had vowed to support Naicker's Non-Brahmin Movement:

I give my fullest sympathy and support to the non-Brahmins. I say to them: The only way for you to come into your own, live your own life according to your own culture and according to your own language— thank God that Hindi did not go very far here—and your own history is to go ahead with your ideal. I have every sympathy for you and I shall do all I can to support you to establish Dravidastan. The seven per cent of Muslims will stretch their hand of friendship to you and live with you on lines of equality, justice and fairplay.[33]

After having supported Jinnah's politics for a number of years, and having enjoyed the Qaid's full support in return, Naicker wrote to him on 9 August 1944, saying:

Kindly excuse me for reminding you about our discussions relating to Pakistan and Dravidastan while we were at Madras and Delhi and your assurance that you would plead for both questions as one. Here in South India, I considered both the questions as one and done [*sic*] my best to solve the problem as far as possible. Yourself [*sic*] know very well that there could be no Pakistan and the independence of

Muslim India until and unless independence was achieved for the rest of the nations.[34]

Now unlike a coalition whose betrayal by one party would have left Muslims in the very position of minority that they sought to reject, there was nothing to lose in supporting another national movement, whether or not it had any chance of success, and indeed such support might do much to harass Congress and at best even accomplish India's fragmentation. But Jinnah would have none of it, writing back to Naicker on 17 August:

I am in receipt of your letter of August 9, thank you for it. I have always had much sympathy for the people of Madras 90 per cent of whom are non-Brahmins, and if they desire to establish their Dravidas-tan it is entirely for your people to decide on the matter. I can say no more, and certainly I cannot speak on your behalf.[35]

Is it possible that the Qaid's curious reluctance to support any other movement that might help destroy both Congress and its vision of India, including his well-known lack of seriousness when conducting desultory negotiations with the Sikhs to opt for a better deal in Pakistan, demonstrated the remnants of his loyalty to India in some perverse way? Or did he want to be the only one to destroy the country he had fought to keep united for so many years? Whatever the compulsions of Muslim politics, in other words, Jinnah had it within his power to involve Dalits, Non-Brahmins and others in his plans, but, as we have seen, was resolute in turning down the opportunities that were offered him to do so. But then the Qaid's attachments to his earlier days as an Indian nationalist were well known even among his associates in the League, with his secretary K. H. Khurshid writing in his memoirs that "Nationalism was Mr Jinnah's first love and continued to give him occasional pangs until late in life, as first love does."[36] And Jinnah himself, in a speech to the Old Boys Association of Osmania University on 28 September 1939, commented that "The words 'nationalism' and 'nationalist' have undergone many changes in their definition and significance. Some people have a dictionary of their own, but within the honest meaning of the term I still remain a nationalist."[37]

Perhaps, then, the Qaid continued to believe the words with which he ended a speech opposing Congress in the Legislative Assembly on 23 August 1938, saying "I hope that one day perhaps my friends will realise that I have acted with the same motives they claim for themselves and that I have done a service to the interests of India."[38] For we have already seen that Jinnah's insistence upon India's partition was also phrased as if he were doing the country a service, stating in his message to the Bombay Presidency Provincial Muslim League Conference in May 1940 that "Our ideals presuppose Indian freedom and independence; and we shall achieve India's independence far more quickly by agreeing to the underlined principles of the Lahore Resolution than by any other method."[39] We have already seen that his very persistence, even after partition, in naming both of British India's successor states when celebrating Pakistan's independence, can be judged as evidence of Jinnah's continued if distinctly peculiar attachment to India's freedom. And this he thought he had guaranteed by sacrificing the majority of her intractable Muslim population, because they were unable by their size and concentration to be a minority there. Given his own dislike of Muslims in general, or perhaps his shame and pity at their "backwardness," the Qaid's politics resembled that of Zionism's founder. Along with Herzl, then, his actions might well have been informed by the desire to remove the problem that Muslims in India, like Jews in Europe, posed national movements in either place, as much as it was dedicated to winning new states for these minority populations.[40] For in the end both projects were meant to do nothing more than create friendly relations between groups torn apart by violence.

*Changing places*

By choosing to push the demand for Pakistan, Jinnah in effect abandoned the League's old politics, which had consisted of evading the status of minority for Muslims, and therefore of majority for Hindus as well. He sought instead to lend some reality to these categories by "smashing" the power of India's Muslims and finally reducing them to what he called a "sub-national" minority. And in doing so he also guaranteed Hindus the status of a majority. But the Pakistan of his original conception, in which Hindus would have constituted a much more significant population than Muslims ever had in India, could do no more than reverse the roles that these groups played in the Raj. Did the Qaid think that he would continue the League's old politics in his new country? Given the reduced territory that he received in the end, and the large-scale expulsion of Hindus and Sikhs that followed its transformation into a nation state, this was not a question Jinnah ever had to answer. It is clear, nevertheless, that what he accomplished was not simply the partition of India, but that of its Muslims also, whose demographic weight in the subcontinent was destroyed by Pakistan's founding. And it is entirely in keeping with the Qaid's ambiguous character that we are unable to tell if this is what he wanted, to save India from Muslims while at the same time saving the latter from being dominated by Hindus.

Once he had opted to instantiate majorities and minorities as religious rather than political categories in a divided subcontinent, as his famous speech made to Pakistan's constituent assembly on 11 August 1947 suggested, Jinnah's politics of demographic evasion suddenly became available for another kind of occupation. And in the rest of this chapter I will argue that Ambedkar took over the problem of Muslim politics and brought it to a quite different resolution. Indeed, I want to make the point that Pakistan made an autonomous Dalit politics possible by removing the dominating example and even hegemony of Muslim concerns over all other oppositional movements in colonial India. Unfortunately this complex and competitive link between Dalit and Muslim politics has rarely been explored or even recognized by scholars, who in this respect have done little more than follow the line of Indian prejudice by dividing the two in purely religious terms. Even more than his Muslim predecessors, Ambedkar's politics was defined by an effort to avoid being assimilated by a more powerful rival, whether this was identified with class, as with the communists and socialists, or religion, as with Hindus, Muslims and Christians. Without a secure base of his own, Ambedkar during the early period of his career was constantly flirting with all manner of established movements, including even Gandhian non-violence, though never fully identifying with any of them. And it was the Mahatma who recognized this evasive strategy for what it was, criticising Ambedkar in articles published in his journals, some of which the latter then included as an appendix to his book *The Annihilation of Caste*.[41]

When remonstrating with Ambedkar about his desire to leave Hinduism, Gandhi suggested that however cruel the Dalit leader might think this religion to be, he would be unable to forsake it without destroying his own history and identity as well. Hinduism, in other words, gave Dalits their sense of self even when they opposed it, so that any attempt to reject the religion would only leave them rootless and rudderless, capable of being seized by momentary or ill-advised passions and seduced by a superior force like the colonial state or Christianity into losing themselves utterly in the flotsam of modern history. In a sense, this was a deliberate challenge cast down before Ambedkar, but it was also the kind of appeal to a common tradition and origins that Gandhi made to Muslims in particular, most of whom had, after all, converted from Hinduism. And like Jinnah, his Dalit peer thought that he had no choice but to reject the call of history, which for him too was nothing but a record of oppression, something purely negative and therefore worthless. Of course Ambedkar converted to Buddhism late in life, and made of it a new order of belonging for his people, just as the famously "secular" and "nationalist" Jinnah ended up embracing the Muslim politics and identity he had spent so many decades fighting. But like the turn to the Prophet's life and rule in Medina among Muslims at that time, it is not evident that Ambedkar's turn to Buddhism had anything to do with the notion of history and tradition. For in both cases the resort to this mythical past was made possible by a deliberate repudiation of all received history, so that the social order apparently enunciated by the Buddha or Muhammad served more as a juridical or constitutional vision of a just polity, than the romantic exposition of one's ancestral glory in the manner of nationalism. In this sense, the Muslim and Dalit past was more akin to an Enlightenment theory or philosophical presupposition, like that of Rousseau's "noble savage," than to history properly speaking.

Unlike the Qaid, however, Ambedkar's repudiation of history did not result in a "fanatical" politics of the idea, not only because he didn't have the luxury of removing Dalits from their Indian context, but also because he was always concerned chiefly with the particular and corporeal discriminations of caste, and seemed to have no desire to transcend the material world in which the body existed. And this meant that the turn to Buddhism, itself as radically new as the League's claim for Pakistan, given the fact that neither could be justified by the logic of historical recovery, became an act of self-making and self-transcendence that was not merely abstract. For the new religion chosen by Ambedkar could be owned and reinvented by Dalits precisely because it had no living presence in peninsular India, thus allowing Buddhism's new adherents to make a distinct and polemical claim on the Indian past without assimilating to any existing order of identification there. But how was Ambedkar able to resist the logic of minority politics that had dogged India's Muslims until their fragmentation as a political category in 1947? To begin with, he always looked back with regret to the effort at creating a grand coalition against a Hindu-dominated Congress that would render India's religious demography a political irrelevance. So in the 1945 edition of his book on Pakistan Ambedkar, unlike any leader of the League, even goes so far as to acknowledge the low-caste status of the majority of Indian Muslims:

There are many lower orders in the Hindu society whose economic, political and social needs are the same as those of the majority of the Muslims and they would be far more ready to make a common cause with the Muslims for achieving common ends than they would with the high caste Hindus who have denied and deprived them of ordinary human rights for centuries. To pursue such a course cannot be called an adventure. The path along that line is a well-trodden path. Is it not a fact that under the Montagu-Chelmsford Reforms in most provinces, if not in all, the Muslims, the non-Brahmins and the Depressed Classes united together and worked the reforms as members of one team from 1920 to 1937? Herein lay the most fruitful method of achieving communal harmony among Hindus and Muslims and of destroying the danger of a Hindu Raj.[42]

But while the Dalit leader was happy to participate in the Minorities Pact style of politics that had emerged from the Round Table Conferences, he also suspected from the start that the Muslim League would simply use the "other minorities" for its own ends against the Congress. Indeed, Ambedkar realized that the League was more interested in reaching an arrangement with Congress and its upper-caste leadership than with advancing the cause of any other party, telling the *Bombay Chronicle* on 20 October 1938 that:

Mr Jinnah is totally carrying the Muslims on the wrong path. I do not understand what differences he has with Congress. If the League really stands for the interests of the minorities, I welcome Mr Jinnah to join hands with other sections who differ from the Congress, and make a united front of all these sections against the Congress. The Muslim League, to my mind, is fighting for elections and ministry. Mr Jinnah is on one side fighting with Congress; while on the other side he intends to come to a pact with the Congress, which is entirely meaningless. Appeal to him to learn a lesson from the Poona Pact.[43]

And indeed Jinnah can be seen as following in Syed Ahmed Khan's footsteps in this respect, though his arena of action was much wider than the latter's, for that celebrated Muslim "reformer" too had sought to bind together high-ranking Hindus and Muslims in a pact.

It was not simply because the League insisted on coming to an arrangement with Congress by sacrificing Dalit and other interests that Ambedkar distrusted it but, crucially, because this agreement entailed Muslims receiving concessions from out of what he saw as the share of the "Untouchables," since Muslims received more reserved seats in the legislatures or in the Viceroy's Executive Council than did Dalits as a proportion of their respective populations. Indeed, Dalits were in fact entirely excluded from the latter in 1941, much to Ambedkar's fury. Writing to the Secretary of State for India in complaint, he stated that "Your flouting of 60 million Depressed Classes altogether and giving 43 per cent representation to Muslims, which is nearly equal to that of Hindus, is astounding. Government appears to have been mortgaged to some communities only."[44] In a letter to Wavell on 7 June 1945, Ambedkar was still complaining about Dalit representation on the viceroy's council in comparison with that given to Muslims, writing:

Five seats to 90 million Muslims, one seat to 50 million Untouchables and one seat to 6 million Sikhs is a strange and sinister kind of political arithmetic which is revolting to any ideas of justice or common sense. I cannot be a party to it. Measured by their needs, the Untouchables should get as much representation as the Muslims, if not more.[45]

Of course the allotment of seats was decided by the political power of the parties involved, not by the actual need or demographic strength of their constituencies, and so Ambedkar had no option but to link his demands to Muslim ones in a competitive fashion, eventually claiming a share for his people that was, as a matter of principle, not less than half of what the Muslims received.[46] In other words, Ambedkar was compelled to follow in the wake of the League, receiving benefits measured according to its demands in a curiously negative way that could not but give rise to resentment. So on 26 August 1946 he could tell *The Times of India* that "If the Muslims are justified to claim equality with the caste Hindus, then there is more justification for the Scheduled Castes to claim at least 50 per cent of the representation given to the Muslims."[47]

Ambedkar was clearly unable to find any autonomous political space for himself, the very position that Jinnah feared so much, and by doing so no doubt recognizing in the fate of Dalits the future of his own Muslims. Searching to find a foothold for his politics, Ambedkar seems to have turned outward the fear he so lucidly analyzed as determining the relations of caste, trying to instil some version of it in the relations of his enemies and rivals. So in 1936, when discussing the possibility of Dalits converting to Sikhism with Dr Moonje, a leader of the Hindu Mahasabha, he said:

Conversion to Islam or Christianity will denationalize the Depressed Classes. If they go to Islam the number of Muslims will be doubled and the danger of Muslim domination also becomes real. If they go to Christianity, the numerical strength of Christians becomes five to six *crores* [fifty to sixty million]. It will help to strengthen the hold of the British on the country. On the other hand, if they embrace Sikhism they will not harm the destiny of the country. They will not be denationalized. On the contrary they will be a help in the political advancement of the country.[48]

Playing upon Hindu fears of Islam and Christianity, Ambedkar was trying to negotiate a space for Dalit politics while avoiding the threat of assimilation into some larger group, since like the Buddhism he would eventually accept, Sikhism could be taken over by Dalits if they joined it in sufficiently large numbers as to outnumber existing Sikh communities. Of course, Ambedkar's promises to deliver his people over to a new religion were doubtful in the extreme, but then his object was simply to reach the kind of agreement with Hindus that he was forever accusing Jinnah of doing:

The third question is, if it is the interest of the Hindus, that the Depressed Classes should go over to Sikhism, are the Hindus prepared to make Sikhism as good an alternative to the Depressed Classes as Islam or Christianity is? If they are, then obviously they must try to remove the difficulties which lie in the way of Sikhism, as compared with Islam and Christianity. The deficiencies are financial, social and political.[49]

Ambedkar deployed this rhetoric of fear in all directions and throughout his career, on the one hand threatening to convert to Islam while pointing out the harm this would inflict upon Hinduism, and on the other warning Muslims about the evil designs of caste Hindus and urging them to ally with the Dalits in order to counter it. Were it not for his desperate efforts to find a political place for his people in India, this rhetoric could easily be described as one of "divide and rule," the very procedure that Indians routinely accused the British of practising. So even in 1946 he was capable of saying in a typically assertive yet unctuous manner:

Could not I and my community decide to become Muslim converts? If I adopt Mr Jinnah's religion I will not stand to lose in any measure and, indeed, he might nominate me as a Muslim member to the Executive Council. I have not taken that drastic step because I want to save the Congress from total degeneration.[50]

As Ambedkar's threats do not appear to have been taken very seriously either by the League or Congress, he ratcheted up the rhetoric of fear to such a degree as to come close to propounding "communal" hatred, though for the completely instrumental reasons we have already noted. This was probably why the famously sensitive Jinnah seems not to have objected to Ambedkar's negative comments on the League, even going so far as to recommend the first edition of his book on Pakistan, published in 1941, to Gandhi during their talks of 1944.[51] Similarly, Ambedkar consulted the Qaid in 1946 before making demands of the British prime minister to create two seats for Dalits in the interim government that would be filled by non-Congress representatives.[52] As we have seen, however, it was the Muslim League that nominated a Dalit out of its own seats in the government, thus setting the precedent for Ambedkar's elevation to a position in Nehru's cabinet after independence. And as late as 1 January 1947 the League's newspaper *Dawn* was printing coy statements about Ambedkar, stating that:

The Scheduled Castes leader has denied any secret pact between the Scheduled Caste Federation and the Muslim League. What pact, secret or otherwise, can there be except that they are both alive to the common peril that faces them and the country by the imposition of caste Hindu Congress rule over this subcontinent?[53]

The culmination of Ambedkar's paradoxically anti-Muslim rhetoric came in his book on Pakistan which, as we shall see, also allowed him, finally, to find his political feet in India. While he did spend some pages describing how the Pakistan Movement was both produced by the monopolistic politics of caste Hindus, and destined to destroy it in Bengal and the Punjab,[54] Ambedkar was more concerned with frightening Hindus into agreeing to Jinnah's demand. In other words, his support for Pakistan was ambiguous if not contradictory, since the book played on every stereotype of Muslim barbarity to agree with Jinnah's two-nation theory—while at the same time accusing the Qaid of modelling his politics on Hitler's.[55] Its fourth chapter is dedicated to the history of Muslim invasions and their animosity against Hindus, chapter five to Muslim dominance in the Indian army and the threat it posed a free India, chapter seven to the increasing spate of riots between Hindus and Muslims and their inability to live together, and chapter eight to the frightful fate of Hindus were Pakistan not to be created. Or as Ambedkar puts it:

How far will Muslims obey the authority of a government manned and controlled by the Hindus? The answer to this question need not call for much inquiry. To the Muslims a Hindu is a Kaffir. A Kaffir is not worthy of respect. He is low-born and without status. That is why a country which is ruled by a Kaffir is Dar-ul-Harb to a Musalman. Given this, no further evidence seems to be necessary to prove that the Muslims will not obey a Hindu government.[56]

This was the kind of argument that had been common among colonial officials like W. W. Hunter at the end of the nineteenth century, one that had been debated extensively and refuted by Muslim intellectuals, so Ambedkar was being disingenuous in stating it as an uncontested fact.[57] But he went further in playing to the fear of pan-Islamism that had also emerged out of colonial rule but was much invoked by the Hindu Mahasabha among other groups:

The Hindus see that the Muslim move for independence is not innocent. It is to be used only to bring the Hindus out of the protecting shield of the British Empire in the open and then by alliance with the neighbouring Muslim countries and by their aid subjugate them.[58]

One reason why Ambedkar was so keen on supporting the Pakistan Movement had to do with the fact that he seems to have recognized that the destruction of Muslim politics in India would finally give him the opportunity to insert Dalits into the space it would vacate, even suggesting that the communal problem of India could only be solved by a wholesale exchange of Hindu and Muslim populations between the two successor states of the Raj, on the model of the large migrations that had occurred in Europe after both world wars.[59] Yet he didn't hasten to occupy this space without looking back regretfully at the squandered opportunity of building the kind of Minorities Pact that he had been the first to scupper, by noting that "The Muslim League started to help minority Muslims and has ended by espousing the cause of majority Muslims. What a perversion in the original aim of the Muslim League! What a fall from the sublime to the ridiculous! Partition as a remedy against Hindu Raj is worse than useless."[60] Ambedkar was the only politician who recognized that there existed a hidden agreement behind the Congress-League wrangles of the 1940s, one that allowed Jinnah to see Pakistan as a bizarre fulfilment of his Indian nationalist past.

From 1946, once Pakistan, in one form or another, had become a certainty, Ambedkar again started demanding separate electorates for Dalits, the constitutional safeguard that had been created for Muslims and that they would in effect be vacating with partition. So on 4 July 1946 he proposed a resolution to the Working Committee of the All-India Scheduled Castes Federation, saying that:

The fear which the Scheduled Castes have of the Hindu majority is far greater and far more real than the Muslim community has or can have. The Scheduled Castes have been arguing that the only effective protection they can have is representation through separate electorates and the provision of a separate settlement.[61]

More than this, he started arguing for the creation of separate Dalit settlements, indeed even for a single settlement where they might comprise the majority, thus doing nothing more than establishing some version of the Muslim majority provinces of colonial India.[62] Not by coincidence, this Dalit-only area was to be called "Dalitsthan," a term that, like "Dravidasthan," was nothing if not a gesture of homage to the idea of Pakistan, which after all served to "magnetize" these categories politically by the very immensity of its consequences.[63] For whether or not Dalit and Dravidian politics was named by or modelled on that conducted by the Muslim League, it was the latter's importance that made its more grandiose or separatist claims possible, which is why the followers of Periyar and Ambedkar were in the habit of writing letters to Jinnah asking for his support but not the reverse. Here, for instance, is a passage from a letter to the Qaid of 1946 by V. Veeraswamy, Secretary of the Dr Ambedkar's Students Home, thanking him for nominating J. N. Mandal to the law portfolio in the interim government:

It is with a high sense of gratitude and homage to you, the accredited leader of the ten million [*sic*] Muslims of this country, that I write this letter to pay my humble meed of tribute and heartfelt thanks to you for your broad-mindedness by having so generously sacrificed a high office on the interim government from the quota of five seats allotted to the League. The Scheduled Caste people did not expect such a great boon as the nomination to the interim government by you of a Scheduled Caste member working under the banner of the All-India Scheduled Castes Federation and a humble and faithful follower of our leader, Dr B. R. Ambedkar. [...] We look forward to a bright future and a respectable place in the national life of the subcontinent. This will be quite possible provided we, seven crores [70 million] of the Untouchables, embrace Islam as Dr B. R. Ambedkar indicated in London and Mr [J. N.] Mandal at the New Delhi meeting.[64]

It is instructive to note that with Pakistan's creation both Dravidasthan and Dalitsthan died quick deaths. I would also like to contend, however, that the Dravidian and Dalit adaptation of Muslim politics represented the latter's alternative fulfilment, as well as being its missed opportunity. Choudhry Khaliquzzaman, who led the Muslim delegation to India's constituent assembly in 1947, describes the final act in this politics of trading places. Ambedkar, he tells us, approached him suggesting that Muslims and Dalits should support each other's requests for separate electorates:

He took out a note from his pocket dealing with the rights of Scheduled Castes and the Muslims in the Indian Dominion. Briefly stated he wanted Muslim support to the claim of the Scheduled Castes for reservation of seats in the provincial and central legislatures as well as reservation in the services, in return for similar support to the League by his group in the constituent assembly. [...] My party supported Dr Ambedkar's demands but when the case of Muslims came up for discussion and voting, Dr Ambedkar abstained and his party remained neutral.[65]

But if Khaliquzzaman was unable to retain separate electorates for Muslims in independent India, neither was Ambedkar able to gain them for Dalits, thus illustrating how perversely interrelated the politics of both groups continued to be:

Both my demands for separate electorates and reservation in the services were rejected. Sardar Patel closing the debate on this question said: 'Those who want separate electorates should go to Pakistan. They are not wanted in India.' The Scheduled Caste representatives again abstained from voting with us. When lastly the Scheduled Caste matter came up, Dr Ambedkar claimed reservation of seats in the legislature and the services. I was in a temper and opposed both of them on the ground that Scheduled Castes were part and parcel of Hindu society and did not require any separate rights to safeguard their interests. If the Muslims could not claim them, then surely the Scheduled Castes were not entitled to any special safeguards. This happened on 29 July 1947.[66]

Indeed, Ambedkar was unable to take the League's place even after Pakistan had come into existence, and in a letter to Nehru from 18 December 1947 he complained that even now, during the violence of partition, Muslims were, as they always had, being given preference to Dalits, saying:

So far all care and attention has been bestowed by the government of India on the problem of the Muslims. The problem of the Scheduled Castes has either been supposed not to exist, or deemed to be so small as not to require special attention. Although some people do not like to mention the problem of the Scheduled Castes nonetheless those of us who are concerned with the Scheduled Castes know that the problem exists and it is much more acute than the problem of the Muslims.[67]

Despite his claim to separate electorates and even weightage, the one thing Ambedkar did not want to inherit from the League was minority politics, which was the very thing that Muslim leaders had always tried to escape.[68] This identity was left for Muslims in independent India, with Dalits breaking with their colonial history by avoiding the category altogether, and their former rivals degenerating into a merely religious and thus politically disempowered group—the fate that we have seen Jinnah had feared for them since the days of the Khilafat Movement.

While the subcontinent's partition, then, resulted in the mutual betrayal of Dalits and Muslims, recent years have seen a new relationship develop between these groups in certain parts of India, prompted by the victorious emergence of low caste politics in the country's north. But this time it is the system of reservations lying behind Dalit politics that has become a model for Muslims, thus reversing the trajectory of influence that had linked the two in colonial times. Since Dalits are not constituted as a minority, however, Muslim politics too can only follow their example by abandoning the category. And this seems to be happening among some activists, who insist on disaggregating the community by identifying low caste Muslims who require reservations, and whose natural allies are therefore seen as being Dalits rather than the North Indian Muslim elites who have by and large continued to represent their co-religionists since independence. Given the inability of this negatively defined "Muslim community" to defend the interests of its members, which have increasingly been defined in purely religious-symbolic terms since 1947, its breakup is probably a desirable thing. Already issues such as social and economic discrimination, that are today linked with caste politics, seem to have replaced the old debates over mosques and personal law at the top of the Muslim political agenda, and it remains to be seen if the role of religious minority can finally be shuffled off after more than a century of representative government in India. But whatever happens, caste politics is the true heir of at least one of the promises held out by the Muslim League before it adopted Pakistan as an ideal, with Dalits having supplanted Muslims as potentially the universal mediators of Indian society. No more significant an inheritance from Muslim political thought exists in either India or Pakistan.

6

# THE SPIRIT OF ISLAM

An eminent jurist, historian and founding member of the Muslim League, Syed Ameer Ali was also one of the most popular authors in the Muslim world. His much translated apologetic work *The Spirit of Islam*, for example, first published in 1891 and running into innumerable editions, remained as late as 1946 "the most widely quoted modern book on the religion" in Egypt.[1] Ameer Ali's great merit was to go beyond defending Islam from its European critics and take the battle into their own camp, by deploying the tools of modern scholarship to prove its superiority to all other religions. In a passage considering Islam as a proper name from this, his most famous book, Ameer Ali writes that "The religion of Jesus bears the name of Christianity, derived from his designation of Christ; that of Moses and of Buddha are known by the respective names of their teachers. The religion of Mohammed alone has a distinctive appellation. It is Islam."[2]

Having no doubt excluded Hinduism from his review because it was a foreign name for that religion, and dismissed other cults as beneath his notice, Ameer Ali was intent on demonstrating that Islam was the only one that possessed a proper name. This in the sense that it stood for a set of principles or ideas in its own right and not simply as part of an inheritance or legacy from its founder. We shall see later in this chapter how such an attempt to separate Islam from its prophet in this way ended up making him even more important for Muslims, but for the moment let us look at how Ameer Ali defines his religion:

In order to form a just appreciation of the religion of Mohammed it is necessary to understand aright the true significance of the word Islam. *Salam (salama)*, in its primary sense, means, to be tranquil, at rest, to have done one's duty, to have paid up, *to be at perfect peace*; in its secondary sense, to surrender oneself to Him with whom peace is made. The noun derived from it means peace, greeting, safety, salvation. The word does not imply, as is commonly supposed, absolute submission to God's will, but means, on the contrary, *striving after righteousness*.[3]

Rejecting the definition of Islam as a passive subjugation to some inflexible command, which he attributes entirely to European scholarship, Ameer Ali emphasizes its meaning as peace. And we shall soon see, when studying Jinnah's views on the matter, that this definition became the standard one for Muslim nationalists. But as with the Qaid, for Ameer Ali peace was not to be seen as a kind of stasis or end result. Instead Islam had to be conceived of as a form of action or striving. Whatever its historical precedents, this view made the religion into an ethical as much as political phenomenon of a distinctly modern sort. And this was particularly the case because as a form of action Islam was no longer derived from old-fashioned sources like the traditions of the Prophet, various schools of law, mystical orders or, indeed, the Quran as traditionally interpreted. Rather it was Islam newly conceptualized as a system that now prompted action in its name alone. Ameer Ali summarizes the ethical foundations of this system in the following way:

The principal bases on which the Islamic system is founded are (1) a belief in the unity, immateriality, power, mercy, and supreme love of the Creator; (2) charity and brotherhood among mankind; (3) subjugation of the passions; (4) the outpouring of a grateful heart to the

Giver of all good; and (5) accountability for human actions in another existence.[4]

We might see these five bases, entirely conceptual in character, as replacing the traditional five pillars of Islam, with their heavily ritualistic emphasis on actions like fasting and pilgrimage. Indeed, Ameer Ali and his successors in the Muslim League routinely stripped such ritual acts of all intrinsic merit to make them mere carapaces for everyday virtues, if not bland social functions; they were quite unlike the mystics of the past in this regard, for whom the externalities of religion served as signs of an esoteric reality. As the name of a system, Islam was so encompassing as to deprive all traditional authorities, such as clerics and mystics, of any real hold over it, thus permitting laymen like Ameer Ali to take the views of these worthies into account when writing about Muslim history, but quite ignore their modes of analysis and actual opinions to claim a kind of secular authority over the religion. And it is the consequences of turning Islam into a proper name of this kind, one referring to a system lacking traditional authority, that I want to show in this chapter allowed for its politicization in colonial India.

## The proper name

In a famous essay of 1948 on the word Islam, the historian of religion Wilfred Cantwell Smith suggests that it was reduced to a proper name as late as the nineteenth century.[5] Pointing out that the word's grammatical status is that of a verbal noun, which refers therefore to an individual act rather than an entity or institution, Cantwell Smith mentions its rare appearance in the Quran, where Islam was linked to a personal profession of loyalty or submission. Indeed he notes that the terms *iman* (belief) and *mumin* (believer), which are often paired with Islam and Muslim in the holy book, occur forty-five and five times as often as the latter there, whereas today, especially in Pakistan, the situation has been completely reversed and *iman* simply included in the category of Islam.[6] Rather than Islam, then, it may well have been the word for religion, *din*, which was more popular in pre-colonial texts, at least in India, though on anecdotal evidence this too seems to have been absorbed and even eliminated by the former. Looking at the German Semiticist Carl Brocklemann's famous list of 25,000 Arabic books from the earliest times to 1938, the *Geschichte der arabischen Literatur*, Cantwell Smith notes that the word Islam occurs in only eighty-four titles, of which fifteen alone can be said to treat it as a proper name. In another list, compiled less systematically, of Arabic works dating from the nineteenth century, Smith finds that the term Islam is not only used far more frequently in book titles, but that half of these concern works either translated from European languages, written by non-Muslims or responding to European authors and arguments.[7]

Cantwell Smith sums up his preliminary investigation by claiming that:

there has been a tendency over the centuries, and especially in modern times for the connotations of the word 'Islam' gradually to lose its relationship with God, first by shifting from a personal piety to an ideal religious system, a transcendent pattern, then to an external, mundane religious system, and finally by shifting still further from that religious system to the civilization that was its historical expression.[8]

By the end of the nineteenth century, therefore, Islam's earlier meanings had not simply lost pride of place to its significance as a proper name, thus including all of its other aspects under this identity, but had also come to be seen primarily as a kind of historical and sociological category which could describe even heretical practices and other forms of sin. It now became commonplace, in other words, to talk about the history of deviation or falsity in Islam, which therefore no longer referred to the truth alone. In modern times, argues Cantwell Smith, Islam can be seen in this particular way as if from outside itself. Leaving aside the question of how and why Islam came to be a category of this sort, I want to argue in this chapter that it named a new kind of totality which was crucial to the conceptualization of Muslim politics in colonial India.

As a proper name, Islam referred to a closed or impermeable entity, one we shall see was conceived of as a system. However vast the realm it might claim, then, Islam in the form of religion could only distinguish itself as one kind of particularity from another, its allegedly impermeable character serving as the mark of defeat for any universal project of an intellectual kind. This was arguably not the case in earlier times, when even the most acrimonious controversies between believers of different types still presumed a common truth they were all in search of. But today, in countries ranging from Pakistan to Indonesia, it has become common for a number of believers to claim that Islam, its prophet and indeed God himself when addressed by his Arabic name, belong solely to Muslims and thus cannot be invoked by anyone else. Indeed, we have already seen in chapter four how the laws banning Ahmadis from calling themselves Muslim were drawn from existing legislation on patents and copyright, making both the controversy and its apparent resolution about the problem of naming. Expressed though it is as a form of intolerance, this demand for the exclusive ownership of Islam also entails the recognition of that religion's particularity within an oddly pluralistic universe. The closing up of Islam, I would like to speculate, had much to do with the defeat and decline of royal power in its domains, for this had always striven to prevent the consolidation of Islam as a totality by staking the claims of profane authority over both Muslims and their faith.

This is probably why the great institutions of modern Islam in India, from the seminary of Deoband to Aligarh Muslim University, were all founded in British territory rather than within Muslim princely states and they were, in this sense, the products of colonial secularism, much like the religion named Islam was.

The only religious movement to emerge from a Muslim principality was the small, puritanical and controversial sect of the Ahl-e Hadis, or partisans of the prophetic tradition, who were supported by the female rulers of Bhopal, probably as part of the begums' effort to legitimise and indeed augment their position in the Muslim world.[9] It is interesting to note that the Ahl-e Hadis reject the traditional schools of Muslim jurisprudence altogether, and thus seem to hold on to a remarkably anti-pluralist form of their faith, which is conceived of as an absolute singularity suitable, we might say, to a proper name. Islam in its modern usage may therefore be described as the historical residue of Muslim history, though as a remnant of its own past it was incapable of opening itself up in any serious way to those outside its boundaries. C. A. Bayly notes in his recent study of Indian liberalism, for example, how with very few exceptions, even the most "progressive" Muslim thinkers in the nineteenth and twentieth centuries found it difficult to make room for others as equals in their visions of an Islamic order.[10]

Only in British India could religion become a closed and self-authorizing system removed from the interference of royal power, to be led by religious experts or laymen alone. It is not that these systems were absent in previous times, but they seemed to be confined to specialized forms of learning or activity rather than pertaining to something as grand as "Islam" taken as a whole. And such systems, in addition, tended to be structured in linear, causal, hierarchical or genealogical ways, for instance in the form of a circle or tree, where one thing led to the other by way of a unidirectional movement. Thus in an arboreal system one had to move from root to branch and twig, in that order, as in a family tree. Getting to another branch, then, required retracing one's steps, as it were, and going back to the root first. Modern systems, however, dispense with totalities constructed on the model of a step-by-step movement in a single direction that ends with a return to the beginning. Instead they enclose a set of relations between entities each of which mutually implies the existence of the others. In Islam as a modern system, then, one no longer has to do what the Neoplatonists did, and move in turn from God's command to various kinds of creation, to man, the prophets, Muhammad and the Quran, etc. Whatever their genealogies, in other words, the various aspects of Islam now stand together in a systematic and so strictly contemporary relationship with one another, and in this way they make up a totality, which is what allows Muslims to do novel things like speak about their religion as a "complete way of life."

One example of this shift can be seen in the way that the terms "Islam" and "Muslim" come to displace "Mohammedanism" and "Mohammedan" in twentieth-century India. Though they were British by origin, we have seen that these words were also popular among anglicized Muslims in the nineteenth century, as evidenced by institutions like the Mohammedan Anglo-Oriental College and the Mohammedan Educational Conference. By naming the religion after its founding prophet, of course, the use of "Mohammedanism" not only made it comparable to Christianity, but also prevented Islam from becoming the proper name of a closed and unique system. Yet the disappearance of this term, which was seen by its critics as implying the Prophet's deification, occurred at the same time as Muhammad was made into practically the sole object of devotion by Sunni reformers at least, for whom Shia imams and Sufi saints were no longer to be considered figures of veneration. I would like to suggest here that one reason why the Prophet becomes such a focus for identification, and therefore a flashpoint for controversy during this period, is because he is no longer connected to traditional schemas of religious order. Instead of seeing him as a link in some Neoplatonist chain of emanations, then, or as the founder of a sacred lineage, and so being able to relate to him by way of mystical visions, saintly charisma or dreams, Muhammad becomes a solitary and therefore vulnerable figure within Islam as a system made up of relations of implication.

If the set of qualities that constitute Islam as a totality, including texts, doctrines, practices or whatever they happen to be, can no longer be related by genealogy, linearity or causality, but rather by mutual implication in a purely contemporary or non-temporal way, then their relationship is neither mechanical nor instrumental but instead loving. For the different parts of such systems are so much in need of each other in ways that are neither causal, temporal nor linear, that they can only be linked by love, which makes of the system a space of freedom rather than of compulsion as it would otherwise be. And so the Prophet, for instance, was now related to the other elements that made up Islam, as much as to his followers, by the links of love alone and not as part of any juridical order or mystical genealogy. The ideological and indeed existential power of such a desire-filled conception of Islam as a totality should be clear, though this very virtue puts into question all traditional authorities in the Muslim world. For if Islam now exists as a proper name that refers to something more than the sum of traditional fields of expertise, each in the hands of a particular group of professionals, then who can speak for it? Both the men of religion gathered in a place like Deoband, who were traditionally entitled to speak in the name of Islam, but also the lay "reformers" associated with Aligarh, now struggled to represent Islam, and were soon joined in this enterprise by other groups as well.

But in the end Islam as a totality had to speak for itself, or rather its various elements were to be taken together, and interpreted as producing a unified message or speaking in a single voice. The Quran provides one example of what this meant, since like Islam itself it was made to express a unity of intention in the nineteenth century. In his book *Islam and Modernity*, for example, the Pakistani theologian and historian of Islam Fazlur Rahman, who was also my teacher, complains that traditional

Muslim scholarship always treated the Quran atomistically, dealing with its verses in isolation rather than considering the book a purposive unity.[11] No doubt used to avoid and discredit any alternative or heretical interpretation, this episodic mode of reading was not confined to scripture, but was applicable to all texts as a strategy that permitted one to thwart the author. So Rahman notes that traditional scholarship managed to absorb even the most radical narratives by declaring offending statements to be idiosyncratic.[12] Such an episodic reading presumes a text more or less independent of its creator, one that does not have to be arranged as a unity in terms of authorial intention or explained in terms of the author's life.

The lack of textual authority meant that truth was in some sense immanent in narrative and so could be dissociated from authorial arrangement and intention. But from the nineteenth century authors and their intentions suddenly became important and the Quran, like other texts, had now to be understood in light of its author's purpose, while at the same time being aligned with the Prophet's biography. And what was true for the Quran went for Islam as whole, both being required to speak as unities defined by intention. A common way to describe this intention was to call it a spirit, for how else could the sheer materiality of a system made up of all sorts of elements, from biographies and scriptures to events and beliefs, be made to speak as a unity except in a spiritual way? It became fashionable, then, to adopt European usage and talk about the "spirit" of Islam or indeed of the Quran. How did this happen and what did it entail as far as Muslim nationalism was concerned?

## Infernal machines

In an essay of 1889 published in the *Sirmoor Gazette*, Syed Ahmed Khan set out to criticize the twelfth-century thinker Abu Hamid al-Ghazali's concept of spirit.[13] Perhaps the most important theologian in Muslim history, Ghazali represented the orthodoxy that Sir Syed was trying to reform, in however respectful and admiring a manner. According to his critic, Ghazali defined spirit as being neither body (*jism*) nor accident (*arad*), but an essence (*jawhar*) that knows itself and its creator because it is capable of learning and change.[14] And yet spirit does not occupy any space, since this would make it into something divisible and thus another kind of body.[15] The relationship of spirit and body, thought Ghazali, was like that of an image in a mirror.[16] This was a familiar comparison, especially among mystics, of whom Ghazali was also one, and had become a standard literary trope, with virtue described as the polishing of the heart so that it might reflect the light of divinity more resplendently. In fact nature itself could be described as this kind of mirror, something one of Sir Syed's old but "unreformed" friends, the nineteenth-century poet Ghalib of Delhi, does in the following couplet:

> *Jalwa az baske taqaza-ye nigah karta hay*
> *Jawhar-e ainah bhi chahe hay mizhgan hona*

> The light makes such efforts to see
> The grains of the mirror also want to become eyelashes[17]

The light here, which represents God, is set opposite a mirror representing creation, in which the deity tries to see himself. But the mirror of nature is also overcome by God's desire to view his reflection and thus strives to become an eye looking back at him. And this effort Ghalib describes by a conceit. The tiny grains or scratches on the mirror's polished metal, which constitute its essence and align themselves along its edges, around the light's reflection, he compares to lashes. When a light is placed facing a mirror, then, the subsequent arrangement of the striations on its surface resemble the opening of an eye. The divine gaze, in other words, infuses the mirror of creation with its effulgence to such a degree that nature itself becomes self-conscious and looks back at the God whom it reflects. The image, in other words, while it literally enlivens the mirror, can be identified neither with it nor the light of God. It is in this sense a truly spiritual being, one that exists in its own right and yet does not, because unlike the bodies of created things it is eternal. So Ghalib conducts an ironic dialogue with the deity, one that aestheticizes the struggle to grasp autonomy from God as the only true self:

*Che tamashast za khud rafteh khishtan budan*
*Surat-e ma shudeh aks-e tu dar aineh-e ma*

What a spectacle it is to be a self without oneself
My appearance has become your image in my mirror[18]

Familiar though he no doubt was with this way of thinking, Syed Ahmed Khan asks only one question of Ghazali, wondering how the spirit, which was not a body but only a reflection, might undergo any change.[19] He then goes on to compare spirit to steam and the body to a steam engine, which allows the former to assume a different aspect despite its sameness.[20] Another example he gives is that of electricity, which, like spirit, exists independently of a body that has to be prepared to receive it according to its potential.[21] Of course, one could argue that traditional conceptions like polishing the mirror of the soul by virtuous actions performed the same task as Sir Syed's mechanical bodies. Apart from deploying very modern metaphors to describe spirit in the context of colonial India, however, Sir Syed also conceives of it in social rather than individual or even cosmological terms. But more importantly, he replaces the old erotic and aesthetic relationship that defined a certain kind of selfhood in the trope of reflection, with a functional and productive one appropriate for the industrial age. Modern as it undeniably was, however, Syed Ahmed Khan's reflections on spirit did not make any explicit reference to Islam as a totality whose agency was manifested spiritually. Yet he managed to set up the image of a discrete totality, the body, as a machine whose purpose was to be revealed only in the interaction of its many working parts, by spirit understood as steam or electricity.

It was left to Sir Syed's younger contemporary, Syed Ameer Ali, to make the connection between Islam as a system and spirit as its voice. In his celebrated book *The Spirit of Islam*, Ameer Ali not only turned Islam into a system but also imagined it as producing spirit in the form of what we may describe as structural agency. This is how he writes about it in the book's preface:

In the following pages I have attempted to give the history of the evolution of Islam as a world-religion; of its rapid spread and the remarkable hold it obtained over the conscience and minds of millions of people within a short space of time. The impulse it gave to the intellectual development of the human race is generally recognized. But its great work in the uplifting of humanity is either ignored or not appreciated; nor are its rationale, its ideals and its aspirations properly understood. It had been my endeavour in the survey of Islam to elucidate its true place in the history of religions[22]

Having discarded Syed Ahmed Khan's mechanistic metaphors and turned Islam into an organism, Ameer Ali was able to describe it as an actor whose purpose was manifested as spirit. It was the very totality of Islam as a religion, comprising as it did so many interacting elements related by mutual implication, which allowed it to function spiritually as the sum or distillation of these numerous parts that were no longer related in a linear or causal fashion. While religious specialists or mystics might be hold sway over certain kinds of practices and knowledge, in other words, Islam spoke directly to its believers, and its larger purpose could therefore be interpreted by anyone willing to argue their case, including politicians who no longer needed to claim religious authority in order to do so. It is this view of things that still allows statements like "Islam says such and such" to be made by all manner of Muslims. Men like Ameer Ali, who came from a Shia background, were also responsible for making Islam into an ecumenical phenomenon, since he wrote well even of figures from early Muslim history who the Shia otherwise execrated. This did not mean that Ameer Ali, like the Aga Khan, Ispahani, Raja of Mahmudabad and perhaps even Jinnah, did not hold fast to a Shia view of history, only that they were happy to construct a non-sectarian version of it for the sake of Muslim unity. This attitude, however, did not often go the other way, as the ecumenical Islam propagated by Shia thinkers was more inclusive of Sunni beliefs than the reverse, and we have already seen how it was a letter from Ameer Ali and the Aga Khan, in support of the Caliphate, that persuaded the Turkish Assembly to abolish this most Sunni of institutions.[23]

## Ecumenism and heresy

A more prosaic example of Muslim ecumenism as a Shia attitude may be seen in the Aga Khan's controversial speech of 1951 in Karachi, when he urged that Arabic rather than Urdu be made the country's national language.[24] In one sense this astounding advice belonged entirely in the anti-territorial and anti-historical world of ideas that I have described in the previous chapters as being characteristic of Muslim nationalism, and it may indeed be considered the failed equivalent to the adoption of Hebrew as a national language by Israel. For like its biblical cousin, Arabic was a ritual language for Pakistan's Muslims, one understood only by their religious specialists and a few scholars. Dismissing Urdu as the language of Muslim downfall in post-Mughal India, the Aga went on to point out that it had no real presence in Pakistan, and would indeed be resented by those who spoke Bengali, Punjabi, Sindhi, Baluchi or Pashtu there. Arabic, on the other hand, could not only unite these various peoples by its everyday strangeness as much as ritual familiarity, but also connect them to Muslims in other parts of the world. A perfect illustration of pan-Islamism in its liberal manifestation, one might think, except that the Aga Khan's own language, which he continued to treasure, was Persian rather than Arabic. Perhaps given its association with Shia Iran, the Aga chose not to recommend Persian as a national language for Pakistan, despite recognizing its historical role as the official language of government in India over many centuries. Moreover the commercial and other links that continued to subsist between his Ismaili followers in India and Pakistan, to say nothing of East and Central Africa, were premised upon their communication in languages like Gujarati and even English, which the Aga made no attempt to suppress in favour of Arabic. So his call for Muslim solidarity in a primarily Sunni context by no means suggested that the Aga wanted to turn Pakistanis away from India or even destroy regional languages, only that "while Arabic as a universal language of the Muslim world will unite, Urdu will divide and isolate."[25] Indeed we may even see in the Aga's rejection of Urdu a recrudescence of the criticism we have already seen him express of its North Indian speakers in chapter two.

The dissimulation of one's inner truth, even when this is not required for the purposes of protection, is in theory a cardinal tenet of the Shia, for whom this truth can only become public with the coming of the messiah. Dissimulation, of course, does not mean denying one's sectarian identification, but rather adopting an ecumenical if disbelieving attitude towards the Islam of the majority. It represents an esoteric interpretation of religion that is characteristic of a sect whose formative history was one of defeat and exclusion from power. So Ameer Ali writes approvingly that:

takeyyè, 'the natural offspring of persecution and fear', has become so habitual with the Persians that they conform to it even in circumstances when there is no necessity. They practice it to avoid giving offense or wounding susceptibilities, just as the modern Protestant shows a certain deference to Romish rites in Catholic countries.[26]

And while this doctrine has arguably played a more important role among its Sunni critics than Shia adherents, it was probably the latter who were largely responsible for turning Islam into an ecumenical category, one that could become politically effective by uniting a number of disparate groups of believers under it. For even if such a vision does not require doctrinal justification, and cannot be attributed solely to members of the Shia sect, it must presume their existence as a distinct element in Muslim society in order to exist. Perhaps the most interesting illustration of the fate of ecumenism in the making of Pakistan were the judicial investigations conducted between 1968 and 1984 to determine Jinnah's sectarian identity for the purpose of distributing his estate among relatives who belonged to both Ismaili and Ithnashari forms of the Shia denomination.[27] When the Qaid had died in 1948, his property was divided according to a will made in 1939 that had followed no Islamic precedent by leaving the bulk of his property to his daughter and only one of his sisters, rather than any male relatives, including his brother. And this was strange enough, given that it had been Jinnah who had piloted the Shariat Application Act of 1937 through the Legislative Assembly, one of whose aims was to place all of India's Muslims under religious rather than customary law as far as marriage, divorce and the inheritance of non-agricultural property was concerned—and thus giving women more inheritance rights than customary law allowed. But then Jinnah was keen not to have such a law forced upon all Muslims, and so in addition to agricultural land, which according to the Shariat would have to be split up in every generation, only the property of those who had made a declaration to be governed by it, and who had died intestate, could be brought under its purview. And this meant that in disposing of his own property against the dictates of Muslim personal law, the Qaid was in fact continuing the received practice of the Khojas, who had been legally exempted from the Shariat's rules of inheritance in the past. When one of Jinnah's two major legatees, his sister Fatima Jinnah, died intestate, however, there was a controversy among some of her descendants over who inherited how much of it, as Shia law differed from Sunni in granting more of an estate to female heirs in the absence of close male relations. The High Court of Sindh, therefore, had to determine what sect Fatima Jinnah had belonged to, and by extension the Qaid's religious affiliation as well, giving rise, in the process, to considerable controversy.

While the many witnesses called, Shia and Sunni, gave conflicting testimony, generally according with their own sectarian identity, it soon became evident that neither Jinnah nor his sister had ever publicly declared their religious denomination, having apparently been indifferent to it while practising Sunni forms of prayer on the rare public occasions they indulged in such practices, though in an affidavit relating to the disposal of the Qaid's property after his death, Fatima Jinnah had declared him to be governed by Muslim personal law as it applied to the Shia Khojas, no doubt to ensure her claim to his estate in the context of sectarian competition. But given the importance that the Shia doctrine of dissimulation possessed for its Sunni critics, this non-sectarian identification with their religion could simply mean that they had concealed their true beliefs out of consideration for the feelings of the Sunni majority and in order to proclaim Islam's unity. And so the hearing was dominated by a peculiar anxiety about the Qaid's intent, since even his most ostentatious gestures of Sunni piety, such as they were, could be interpreted as indicating exactly the opposite belief. And yet sectarian sensitivities were such that not even the word dissimulation (*taqiyya*) was uttered in court. Nevertheless, in line with the deep suspicion of this practice among many Sunnis, who saw it as being nothing less than hypocrisy, many witnesses from that sect proclaimed that the Qaid never was a hypocrite, this being a code word for a Shia. On the other hand, a number of Shia witnesses were eager to prove that their denomination did not place so much importance on ritual forms and thus allowed them to adopt Sunni ones as a courtesy to the Muslim majority—thus doing nothing more than demonstrating the hypocritical nature of their sectarian belief to their adversaries.

Jinnah had himself been faced with this kind of suspicion during his own lifetime, and one of the exhibits presented to the court consisted of letters exchanged between him and one Zafarulmulk. The latter had written to the Qaid in September 1944, remonstrating with him for having put off a meeting with Gandhi because it fell on 21 Ramadan, the death anniversary of Ali, the first Shia imam whose status among Sunni sectarians is only that of the fourth caliph:

Muslims have nothing to do with the twenty-first Ramzan. This is a purely Shia function. Islam does not permit any mourning day. In fact the very spirit of Islam revolts against such Jewish conceptions. I know you belong to the Khoja community, a sect of the Shias, but, pardon me, you have no right to impute a Shia belief to Muslims.[28]

Though he had probably postponed meeting Gandhi for reasons other than the religious one given, and perhaps even in order to match the Mahatma's various religious observances and days of silence with his own, Jinnah's response was couched in the manner typical of Muslim ecumenism, arguing that:

It is not a question at all of Shia belief. Hazrat Ali was the fourth Caliph, and I know as a matter of fact that the twenty-first day of Ramzan is observed by a large body of Mussalmans, irrespective of the question of Shia or Sunni belief, and I am really surprised that you should have taken up the attitude you have shown in your letter.[29]

Rather than being considered efforts at surmounting the sectarian divide, such evidence, including another letter in which Jinnah declined to attend a Shia function, was used in court to demonstrate that the Qaid was a "pure" Muslim if not a crypto-Sunni, thus claiming his allegiance to the majority sect in exactly the same way as this correspondence might equally have been used to paint him as a dissimulating Shia. But the latter possibility was something the Shia witnesses, wedded as they were to an ecumenical vision of Islam, were not prepared to entertain, at least in public, and so the suspicion about Jinnah's sectarian identity had to remain unexpressed in court.

Even among the Shia there was a game of concealment being played, as the Ismaili sub-sect into which Jinnah had been born, and of which the Aga Khan was the spiritual head, made no claims on him at all, and seems deliberately to have kept out of a controversy that might have affected Jinnah's reputation negatively while pushing them into some unwanted limelight. And this was despite the fact that some of Jinnah's Ismaili relatives were among the claimants to his estate. So nothing was done when a credible Ismaili witness, praised by the judge in his summation, stated that Shirin Bai, one of Fatima Jinnah's sisters who claimed the entirety of her estate, had been an Ismaili before she arrived in Pakistan to stake her claim as an Ithnashari entitled to the property in a way that Ismaili women, who still fell under the Hindu law which had defined Khoja and Memon inheritances, couldn't do.[30] And Shirin Bai herself, who refused to take the stand, remained silent on these matters. It was the more populous Ithnashari sub-sect, to which Shirin Bai now said she belonged, that was represented in court, which suggests that there might have been multiple forms of dissimulation being practiced here, with Shirin Bai becoming Ithnashari to inherit an estate that might otherwise have gone to her male relatives who were Ismailis. It soon became evident that Jinnah's wife, a Parsi heiress, had converted to the Ithnashari branch of the Shia sect in order to marry him. Was this because the Ismaili branch of the Khoja caste to which Jinnah belonged looked askance at marriages outside the group and required lengthy periods of trial and training for conversion? Or was it because Jinnah, as his friend Kanji Dwarkadas recounted, suddenly realized that that those wedded under the Civil Marriage Act of the time would have to declare themselves as belonging to no religion, which would thus imperil his standing as a Muslim representative in the system of separate electorates?[31] As it turns out this caution was well advised, since in later years the Qaid's enemies among pro-Congress Muslims, including the rector of Deoband, would attack him in the press precisely for marrying a non-Muslim under the Civil Marriage Act.[32] Ruttie Jinnah was buried in the Khoja Ithnashari cemetery of Bombay. And when Jinnah died his last rites were performed in private according to the practice of this sub-sect, while the public funeral was conducted following Sunni rites. The same was true of Fatima Jinnah's burial in 1967, though by this time sectarian tensions over the Qaid and his family violently came out into the open. Pakistan's president at the time, Ayub Khan, who had defeated Fatima Jinnah in elections that had probably been rigged some years before, described the scene in his diary:

There was an initial *Namaz-e-Janaza* [funeral prayer] at her residence in Mohatta Palace in accordance, presumably, with Shia rites. Then there was to be *Namaz-e-Janaza* for the public in the polo ground. There an argument developed whether this should be led by a Shia or Sunni; eventually Badayuni was put forward to lead the prayer. As soon as he uttered the first sentence the crowd broke in the rear. Thereupon, he and and the rest leaving the coffin high and dry. It was with some difficulty that the coffin was put on a vehicle and taken to the compound of the Quaid's *Mazar* [mausoleum], where she was to be buried. There a large crowd had gathered and demanded to converge on the place of burial. This obviously could not be allowed for lack of space. Thereupon, the students and the *goonda* [hooligan] element started pelting stones on the police. They had to resort to *lathi* [stave] charge and tear gas attack.[33]

Although the complexity of Jinnah's religious identification had a great deal to do with the nineteenth-century history of the Khojas and their internal divisions, it was also illustrative of his relative indifference to sectarian forms and indeed religion in general.[34] But what came through most clearly in the court case over his estate was the increasing polarization of Pakistanis over religious matters, which indicated the breakdown of this form of "tolerance," seen as a kind of esoteric or internal reservation. Given the violence at Fatima Jinnah's funeral, sectarian animosity could not openly be voiced in court, with the dying conception of an ecumenical and public Islam itself becoming a sign of heresy by being especially prominent amongst Shia witnesses. Thus M. A. H. Ispahani, who we have already seen had been a close associate of Jinnah's, tried in his testimony to dismiss all particularly Shia forms of religious practice as being inessential to his faith, and so of no real relevance in defining who might belong to it:

I am a Shia by birth, and continue to be so, but I do not wear black clothes or green clothes during the Moharrum days. According to me, it is not necessary that a Shia should do so. [...] I do attend majlis, but do not consider it to be mandatory on Shia to attend majlis. [...] I also think that it is not obligatory on a Shia to offer prayers in separate mosques reserved for themselves.[35]

I do not know whether the Quaid-e-Azam declined to attend a Shia conference or not, but I can say that I am a Shia and I also declined to attend that conference, because I did not believe in creating differences among the Muslims.[36]

I am not aware if the Quaid-e-Azam ever declared himself publicity [sic] to be a Shia, nor do I think that it was necessary.[37]

The more they affirmed their ecumenism, however, the more dissimulating did such Shia witnesses appear, as if they were intent on claiming the Qaid for themselves by turning even his more "Sunni" pronouncements to their own account. The court's verdict was an interesting one, pronouncing both Jinnah and his sister to have been generic Muslims, practising the same faith as Muhammad had before the emergence of sectarian distinctions in Islam. In the initial judgment of 1976, Fatima Jinnah's property was nevertheless divided according to Shia law, allowing her sister Shirin Bai to inherit the whole of it. But in a subsequent judgment of 1984, the same reasoning about Jinnah and his sister's generic or non-sectarian Islam was used to determine that the latter's estate be apportioned according to the Quran's prescriptions alone, which in the court's interpretation essentially meant in conformity with Sunni law and thus favouring her male agnates, whose Ismaili affiliation had to be concealed under the rubric of this denomination. And so the generic Islam created by Muslim nationalism as an ecumenical religion was finally conflated with the form of Sunnism that happened to be practised, in theory at least, by the majority of Pakistanis. This is in fact indicative of a larger shift in Pakistan, where the ecumenical Islam so important to Muslim nationalism and tied to the presence of the Shia has been increasingly narrowed in sectarian terms, in yet another example of that religion's particularization and the defeat of its universal aspirations.

Instead of seeing Islam from the outside therefore, as Cantwell Smith argues, it may well have been the reverse that was true, with Muslim thinkers in colonial India establishing a new kind of public religion from the inside, while reserving their own devotions to a private faith. And I would like to repeat that this move might have had as much to do with Shia doctrine as with some liberal principle of dividing public from private in a secular way. Ameer Ali, for example, clearly draws this conclusion from his analysis of Muslim sectarianism, following up his study of the "solidarity of the Sunni church," which he attributes to that sect's worldly triumph, resulting in the unity of religious and political authority, with a very different vision of the defeated Shia minority:

Shiahism, on the other hand, shows how the church and the state have become dissociated from each other, and how the 'Expounders of the Law' have assumed, at least among a section, the authority and position of the clergy in Christendom. The freedom of judgment, which in Protestantism has given birth to 180 sects, has produced an almost parallel result in Shiahism, and the immense diversity of opinion within the church itself is due to the absence of a controlling temporal power, compelling uniformity at the point of the sword.[38]

Ameer Ali was suggesting that the historical defeat of the Shia actually made them into progenitors of Islam's future, representing as the sect did a more "modern" yet entirely indigenous or authentic division of religion and politics. But by mapping such a division onto a Christian model, he somewhat vitiated its properly "Islamic" or at least non-secular character, and so it was left to a Sunni thinker to make the case in a more sophisticated way. Indeed, Mohammad Iqbal, who we have seen was a stern critic of European secularism as a spatial and metaphysical division, was not averse to propounding the Shia separation of public religion and private faith in its stead, one he thought was temporal and functional in character. For it was the absence of the vanished Imam that made a profane world possible within a horizon of expectation, one in which religion could not fully instantiate itself without denying the authority and necessity of this messianic figure. Thus in his letter to Nehru that we have already studied when discussing the Ahmadis, Iqbal notes:

Nor is the idea of separation of church and state alien to Islam. The doctrine of the major occultation of the Imam in a sense affected this separation long ago in Shia Iran. The Islamic idea of the state must not be confounded with the European idea of the separation of church and state. The former is only a division of functions as is clear from the gradual creation in the Muslim State of the office of Shaikh-ul-Islam and Ministers; the latter is based on the metaphysical dualism of spirit and matter.[39]

## The idol destroyed

Iqbal was indeed one of the rare Sunni thinkers and public men who was willing to include explicitly Shia themes in the generic Islam that came eventually to hold the political loyalty of India's Muslims, though without in the least implying their religious unity. Perhaps because he realized the fundamentally Shia character of modern Islam as a category, Iqbal wrote verses of praise to a number of the Shia Imams, only to be accused of having converted to that sect as a consequence. But his repudiation of "the metaphysical dualism of spirit and matter" also tells us that Iqbal's vision was rather different from Ameer Ali's. In one of the lectures he delivered in Madras in 1934, and which were collectively published under the title *The Reconstruction of Religious Thought in Islam*, Iqbal seems to begin where Ameer Ali left off. Significantly called "The Spirit of Muslim Culture," this lecture commences with the following statement:

The idea is not to give you a description of the achievements of Islam in the domain of knowledge. I want rather to fix your gaze on some of the ruling concepts of the culture of Islam in order to gain an insight into the process of ideation that underlies them, and thus to catch a glimpse of the soul that found expression through them.[40]

Let us note in passing that Islam here has been turned from a religion into a culture, which is a much more generic and capacious category than the former. But rather than singing the praises of Muslim culture, as Ameer Ali had done, Iqbal is more interested in distilling its history into a set of ideas or principles that can then be identified as Islam's spirit, which is to say its voice, agency or purpose. And this can be done only by destroying or at least rendering into spirit the materiality of Muslim culture, with Iqbal continuing his lecture by saying that "The first important point to note about the spirit of Muslim culture then is that, for the purposes of knowledge, it fixes its gaze on the concrete, the finite."[41] Instead of simply entering or animating a body, then, as it had done with Syed Ahmed Khan, or being produced by it, as with Ameer Ali, spirit in Iqbal's view was meant to penetrate this and all other bodies and convert them into itself: "Knowledge must begin with the concrete. It is the intellectual capture of and *power* over the concrete that makes it possible for the intellect of man to pass beyond the concrete."[42] In doing so Iqbal was making a larger historical argument, in which he opposed Islam's quest for infinity, which must spiritualize all matter, to the Greek and more generally classical concern with finitude and proportion, that led to theoretical knowledge alone and as a consequence the "idolatry" of matter. So in the next lecture he says in a very Hegelian way that "There is no such thing as a profane world. All this immensity of matter constitutes a scope for the self-realization of spirit."[43]

Having eliminated the dualism of spirit and matter, and destroyed the last remaining causal or chronological relations between the elements that made up the content of Muslim culture, Iqbal was able to enunciate the spirit of Islam in a way that was deeply religious while at the same time being utterly profane. Reduced as it was to an illustration of spirit, the content of Muslim culture could now be deployed in all kinds of ways, because it lacked any intrinsic virtue or sacredness as part of a pre-modern system of linear or cosmological relations. But rather than becoming dispensable as a result, this generic content, the customs, practices and texts inherited from the past, were all the more important, because they could now be related to one another by love as a form of mutual implication. Their links, in other words, had become intuitive and existential in nature, thus making Islam into a phenomenon far more combustible emotionally than it had ever been before. This attachment, then, to repeat a point made in chapter four, was not historical in any conventional sense, for the new kind of identification that Muslims now had with their religion went well beyond some kind of resuscitation of the past. On the contrary, it was the spiritualization of everything Islam had been given by history that made possible such novel forms of attachment to the detritus of its past. But by recommending the spiritualization of matter in the manner of European idealism, Iqbal was also rejecting the traditional notion of an esoteric dimension of knowledge, one that existed underneath the exoteric reality of everyday life and constituted a space of freedom and interiority. Linked to Shia and Sufi forms of religion in particular, this bifurcation of knowledge continued to play a role in Iqbal's poetry and aesthetics, but in future would no longer inform "reformed" or "modern" Sunni ideas of Islam.

Recondite as it may seem, this way of thinking about Islam, as a system secreting spirit, had become commonplace by the twentieth century. Indeed, it was the only form that religion took in political life, allowing Muslim leaders to make statements in its name while relegating traditional authorities, like divines and mystics, to subordinate if sometimes locally important roles. Unlike the rulers of the past, then, these politicians did not try to keep Islam open-ended or attempt to interrupt its rulings with their own profane law, but instead to voice its spirit as a closed totality. The very dominance that the relatively new word Islam came to occupy in Muslim political life suggested that its modernity had conquered all the resources of tradition, to constitute a novel reality that was shared by the most diverse actors. Even Jinnah, who was not otherwise known to pay much attention to religious language, had become accustomed to this way of deploying it, as we shall note below. We have seen in the previous chapter Gandhi commending Jinnah for his Id day broadcast of 1939, a speech that indeed struck many of the Qaid's own associates as the most religious one he ever gave. Delivered as an oration to the young, who were to bear the burden of Muslim aspirations, Jinnah's broadcast was a classic statement of the new kind of system Islam represented, and the spirit it was meant to produce. The Qaid began his commentary on Islam with the following words:

The discipline of the Ramzan fast and prayer will culminate to-day in an immortal meekness of heart before God, but it shall not be the meekness of a weak heart, and they who would think so are doing wrong both to God and to the Prophet, for it is the outstanding paradox of all religions that the humble shall be the strong and it is of particular significance in the case of Islam, for Islam, as you all know, really means action.[44]

Let us remember that for a layman with no religious background to be speaking about Islam in this way, sociologically as much as devotionally, was something extraordinary in itself and only possible from the end of the nineteenth century. Having invoked discipline, one of his favourite political terms (as in the League's credo, "Unity, Faith, Discipline") with reference to the fast, Jinnah goes on to mention how the paradox of religion is to make the humble strong, thus immediately linking Islam to politics, not least by defining it as action. Yet this way of describing religion cannot be seen as politicizing it in any way, as Islam's transformation into a system made such a connection almost inevitable. He then continues:

The discipline of Ramzan was designed by our Prophet to give us the necessary strength for action. And action implies society of man. When our Prophet preached action he did not have in mind only the solitary life of a single human being, the deeds he accomplishes only within himself, the prayer and all it involves spiritually.[45]

Religious practices, then, are important because they have social functions, again a very sociological way of looking at them, and taken together it is these functions that constitute Islam's spirit. The difference between this instrumental way of considering the relations of spirit and matter is striking, compared with the visual relationship depicted by Ghazali, one in which transformations occur by the medium of sight alone. But the Qaid went further in laying out the social meaning of prayer:

Five times during the day we have to collect in the mosque of our mohalla [neighbourhood], then every week on a Friday we have to gather in the Juma mosque; then again once a year we have to congregate in the biggest mosque or *maidan* [arena] outside the town on the Id day, and lastly there is the Hajj to which Muslims from all parts of the world journey, once at least in their lifetime, to commune with God in the House of God. You will have noticed that this plan of our prayers must necessarily bring us into contact not only with other Muslims but also with members of all communities whom we must encounter on our way. I don't think that these injunctions about our prayers could have been merely a happy accident. I am convinced that they were designed thus to afford men opportunities of fulfilling their social instincts.[46]

While this way of bringing the non-Muslims "whom we must encounter on our way" into the circle of Islam's totality was ingenious, the Qaid's observations on the purpose of prayer are not so different in kind from popular theories, like that about the movements of ritual prayer being designed to give Muslims the most effective and health-giving form of exercise. But Jinnah had something more interesting to say about the duties to mankind that he thought Islam preached:

Man has indeed been called God's caliph in the Quran and if that description of man is to be of any significance it imposes upon us a duty to follow the Quran, to behave towards others as God behaves towards His mankind. In the widest sense of the word, this duty is the duty to love and to forbear. And this, believe me, is not a negative duty but a positive one.[47]

It is no wonder that Gandhi admired the Qaid's broadcast, for he of all men would have understood that if the sentiments it expressed seemed to be so unusual coming from Jinnah, this was because such words as love and forbearance could not be uttered in a political speech without sounding cynical. Only a religious register, one in which Jinnah rarely indulged, allowed him to express such feelings. And he did so, interestingly enough, by comparing man to God, not a very pious thing to do as far as Sunni orthodoxy was concerned, but a comparison that Iqbal might have appreciated. Like Iqbal, the Qaid also moved from the Muslim community to humanity itself, in that longing for the wider world that we have seen belongs so close to the heart of a minority:

Not seldom will your minds be assailed by doubts. There will be conflicts not only material which you perhaps will be able to resolve with courage, but spiritual also. We shall have to face them, and if to-day, when our hearts are humble, we do not imbibe that higher courage to do so, we never shall. All our leaders both Muslims and Hindus continue to be pained at communal strife. I shall not enter into the history of its causes but there will arise moments when the minds of men will be worked up and when differences will assume the character of a conflict. It is at such moments that I shall ask you to remember your Id prayer and to reflect for a while if we could not avoid them in the light of the guidance given to us by our Quran and that mighty spirit which is Islam. I would ask you to remember in these moments that no injunction is considered by our holy Prophet more imperative or more divinely binding than the devout but supreme realization of our duty of love and toleration towards all other beings.[48]

However uncertain the Qaid's theology, the effectiveness of his speech, comparable in its own way to anything the Mahatma might have said, resided in its invocation of Islam's "mighty spirit." For the rituals of prayer, fasting and pilgrimage he refers to serve both as exercises producing this spirit and as illustrations of it. And it is because Islam manifests itself as spirit that it can inform everyday life and politics in such general yet varied ways, though Jinnah's treatment of Muslim practices as if they were nothing but aids to memory was certainly curious.

*Politics withers away*

An infernal machine producing voice and purpose in the form of spirit, Islam as a system is no longer in need of God, but has in some sense become a version of the clockwork universe conceived of by Enlightenment thinkers. And this is one possible consequence of naturalizing religion, as so many Muslim thinkers were doing from the nineteenth century in order to make it modern. We have already seen, for example, how Iqbal kills off the deity, at least in his received incarnation, by glorifying human freedom in themes like Adam's fall, the Devil's disobedience and Muhammad's finality. While Iqbal, however, was interested in man's divinization or partnership with God, the "fundamentalist" thinkers who emerged during this period were more concerned with ensuring the working of this system by subordinating Muslims to it. And in this section I wish to examine the way in which Abul Ala Maududi, founder of the subcontinent's first "fundamentalist" organization, the Jamat-e Islami, imagined turning Pakistan into an Islamic state meant to do nothing more than guarantee the functioning of Islam as a system, one that could be thought of in both organic and mechanical metaphors.

Since the idea of an Islamic state is often seen as being theocratic, by its supporters as much as its detractors, let us attend more closely to this word. Coined by the first-century Jewish-Roman historian Josephus as an addition to the conventional political forms, such as monarchy, oligarchy, aristocracy and democracy, to say nothing of tyranny, theocracy was meant to name a state ruled by God's law. Josephus saw in the biblical kingdom of Judaea the instantiation of this novel political form, and theocracy has been associated with prophetic Judaism since then. By the time Josephus was writing about it theocracy was already dead, assuming it had ever existed, and it only became a living political concept with the Reformation, and in particular during the sixteenth and seventeenth centuries in Europe, when, as the political philosopher Eric Nelson has recently written, it came to provide the model for new ideas of republicanism.[49] One of the markers of theocracy was its exclusiveness, or rather its inability to recognize the plurality of political forms. For in the face of God's rule, no other form of government could be legitimate. Equally illegitimate was an ecclesiastical order like that of the Catholic Church, which sought to monopolize divine authority while sharing temporal power with kings. Protestant radicals in the sixteenth and seventeenth centuries, then, saw in the "Hebrew republic" a model of exclusive and unmediated rule that allowed the people to be governed by God's law directly, so being able, legitimately, to unseat and execute kings as well as alter the social order by doing things like redistribute wealth, and finally to tolerate religious difference by leaving the chastisement of sinners to God and the afterlife.

Nelson's account of the role that theocracy played in Western Europe is of course freighted with liberal sentiments, since he sees popular rule, social justice and toleration emerging from it well before the Enlightenment to which these conceptions are usually and uncritically attributed. But the revolutionary potential of a theocratic imagination also possessed another trajectory in the Reformation, one leading, at least in the eyes of its enemies, to disorder, injustice and intolerance. Indeed by replacing a plurality of political forms, each mediated by a particular authority, with a single, abstract one whose unmediated character allowed for endless claims to represent it, theocracy could well be seen as opening the door to anarchy as well as tyranny. Even its justification of religious toleration, for example, can be seen as relying upon the unquestioning or "fundamentalist" and therefore undemocratic primacy of divine law. And it is this ambiguous heritage of the concept that is particularly noteworthy, for Muslim theorists of the Islamic state in the twentieth century faced a very similar set of questions.

These men, too, had an exclusive and republican vision of theocracy, one that also entailed, on occasion, the radical transformation of society in the name of social justice, something previously unknown in Sunni political thought. Toleration might not have been their strong suit, but we have seen that the conception of Islam as a totality and proper name did ensure at least some degree of diversity among Muslims themselves in the political arena. Like the attitude their Christian predecessors of the Reformation adopted towards the biblical past, the Muslim partisans of theocracy, too, looked back to the origins of their faith to find a political model for the present in Muhammad's rule over Medina. And given the familiarity of men like Maududi with an eclectic range of European political texts dating from the seventeenth to the nineteenth centuries in particular, there is every reason to think that their version of theocracy was based at least in part on that of Christian Europe. Moreover the Western scholarship on their religion, which Muslims accepted and contested in equal measure, explicitly made the connection between Jewish theocracy and early Islam, suggesting therefore that by returning to Mecca and Medina, both "modernist" and "fundamentalist" Muslims were at the same time returning to Jerusalem. Indeed with the idea of such a political form having become naturalized, Maududi needed only to refer to the Quran to derive the origins of Muslim theocracy from Judaea.[50]

Positing a theocratic link between Judaism and Islam was also to deliberately exclude Christianity as a religion falling outside the bounds of law, whatever else these Muslim thinkers had taken from it. And this inheritance was so great as to radically transform even the Islamic past under colonial rule, so that interesting about the theorists of an Islamic state was the modernity of their vision. Crucial about Maududi's conception of theocracy, for instance, was his distrust of politics in general and democracy in particular. We have already seen how Muslim nationalism, like its Dalit rival, was suspicious of a politics based on numbers, and in this sense Maududi was simply following established tradition, though in his own peculiar way. His dislike of politics also had a nineteenth-century genealogy, for this term possessed a very particular meaning in colonial India. With the subordination or displacement of "native" and especially Muslim rulers by the British, politics conceived of as *siyasat* or a branch of ethics dealing with the pastoral care of a people broke down. Not only was the traditional realm of ethics now fragmented and confined to the private life of Indians, but *siyasat*, which survived as a name for the virtue of principled or rule-bound government, came to be overshadowed by the English word politics, with which it did not entirely coincide, and which referred to an utterly unprincipled practice of gaining and using power. Indeed, the term politics is still used in this sense throughout the subcontinent, and in popular usage it is difficult to associate it with anything like thought, principles or ethics. As a cynical practice, of course, politics is morally ambiguous, constituting a field of its own like modern politics in general, and is therefore threatening to religion, which had itself also become a closed field with the decline of Indian monarchies.

From the middle of the nineteenth century, especially following the Indian Mutiny of 1857, and even into the first decade of the twentieth, Indian public figures, and Muslim ones in particular, had studiously avoided dabbling in "politics," not least because this was seen as a dangerous enterprise that might put in question their loyalty to the Raj. They were instead assiduous in calling everything they did religious, cultural or traditional, thus increasing to a remarkable degree the role these supposedly unexceptionable categories played in social life. And this was simply another way in which colonial rule exaggerated the importance of religion and tradition in general within Indian society. Indeed the personal or family regulations having to do with marriage, divorce, inheritance and the like, which had been drawn from Muslim legal texts and codified under the name Anglo-Mohammedan Law, were throughout British rule and much later seen as posing limits to the state and its politics. What came to be known as Islamic law, in other words, represented a protected area of Muslim life in which no state could interfere. However expanded its reach, then, such a legal order was not meant to take the state's place, only to prescribe its limits, and Maududi's otherwise novel idea of an Islamic state does nothing but follow this inherited logic.

Leaving aside his elaborate vision of what an Islamic state should look like, one which drew upon Christian as well as Muslim sources, and followed the institutional logic of the modern state (with executive and judicial branches of government, ministries of domestic and foreign affairs, etc.), what can we learn from Maududi's theoretical justification of this political form? In a text from 1963 entitled *A Method for Islamic Movements in the Muslim World*, which had initially been delivered as a speech in Mecca, Maududi describes the "secular" Muslim elites who were then in charge of countries like Pakistan as victims of colonialism insofar as they had derived all their categories and methods of rule from their former masters. Indeed, he goes further and says that the independence movements led by these elites represented the fulfilment rather than defeat of imperialism, since the British, French or Dutch had not been able to mobilize their Muslim populations and thus did not possess any hegemony over them, having to tread carefully as far as interfering in the religious lives of their subjects was concerned:

In this manner generations passed their lives under Western laws, but to this day they have neither accepted the truth of these laws nor the supersession of Islamic law. Whatever faith the westernized elite might have in European laws, the generality of common Muslims today, as always, believe only in Islamic law and desire its protection.[51]

Given their inability to mobilize Muslims on the basis of European law, these elites, like those of other colonized countries, had to appeal to religion in order to enlist common people into their national movements:

Wherever an independence movement arose, its leaders, westernized though they may have been, could not mobilize common Muslims or demand sacrifices of them without religious appeals. On the contrary, they had everywhere to mobilize people in the name of Islam. They had everywhere to appeal to the names of God, the Prophet, and the Quran. Everywhere they had to pattern the independence struggle on that of Islam and infidelity.[52]

But of course this nationalism based on an anti-national mobilization meant that the ruling class of newly independent countries like Pakistan continued to depend upon the West both in military and ideological terms. For it was their inability to exercise hegemony that led these rulers to an unquestioning acceptance of European models of governance:

The truth is that no matter how opposed these people may be to Western rule, the Western ruler is for them dearer than anything else in the world. They die upon his every style. They consider his every word the absolute truth. They copy his every act. The only difference between him and them is that while he thinks, they only blindly follow. They cannot shift even an inch away from the paths he has laid out to find some new road.[53]

All of which entails the inevitable ideological failure that prevents even the will for development:

The result is that nowhere are the hearts of Muslim nations with their leaders. Governments become stable when the exercise of rule and national feeling are joined in the effort to build a common livelihood. For where heart and hand are occupied in fighting each other their whole strength is exhausted in battle, and progress along the road of construction and development becomes impossible.[54]

Not only did their failure to achieve hegemony confine indigenous elites to a narrow class identity that could not open itself even superficially in parliamentary democracy, it also resulted in a politics of coups d'état as one small group snatched power from another:

In the beginning for some time leadership remained in the hands of this group's politicians, who ran these Muslim countries through civilian governments. But it was a natural result of this state of affairs that the armies of these Muslim countries should very quickly come to feel that the rule of this class depended upon itself. This feeling soon brought army officers into the political arena, and they began the practice of overthrowing governments in army actions to put their own juntas in power.[55]

Naturally, the very conditions that made military coups possible also made the army itself susceptible to takeovers, thus throwing such regimes into an even more dependent relationship with the West.[56] And it was the debilitating character of this situation that permitted Maududi to propose an ideology that might address the problem of hegemony and popular will:

The hearts of the Muslim peoples are perfectly protected, for they never fully accept these so-called revolutionary leaders. And from this fact all the possibilities suggest that if a peaceable group were to ideologically assume leadership among ordinary Muslims and intellectuals, then it would eventually triumph and deliver the Muslim peoples from a baleful and vicious leadership.[57]

Whatever his views about its inherent virtue, then, Maududi argues for an Islamic State by pointing to the failure of the nationalist one to mobilize people behind modern forms of government that were, he thought, essentially colonial in nature. Rather than appealing to the particular if superficial forms of territorial belonging that nationalists did, he also sought to oppose the universality of modern politics with an equally capacious Islamic alternative. And in doing so, of course, Maududi fell heir to the anti-territorial dimension of the very nationalism he criticized, at least in Pakistan. This is how he describes the universal and ideological task of the Islamic State in a speech from 1952:

This means that the main objects of an Islamic State are to enforce and implement with all the resources of its organized power that reformatory programme which Islam has given for the betterment of mankind. Mere establishment of peace, mere protection of national frontiers, mere endeavour to raise the standard of living of the common man do not form its ultimate goal, nor do they constitute the characteristics which distinguish the Islamic State from the non-Islamic states. Its distinction lies in the fact that it has to encourage and popularize those good practices which Islam desires humanity to adopt and to discourage, eradicate and crush with full force all those evils of which Islam aims to purge mankind.[58]

If the nationalist elite were unable to exercise hegemony and transform society by mobilizing people behind it, how would the Islamic State do so? Maududi suggests that Muslims can be mobilized by identifying with the sacred law itself as a universal form, and not by way of blood and soil, custom or history. So far, so familiar, but identifying with the law in this unmediated way is important because it eliminates all particularity of class, ethnicity, etc. from politics, thus giving it an unshakeable legitimacy and making for an apparently harmonious society. By identifying directly with the neutrality of God's law, in other words, whose archaic nature becomes a virtue by putting it above all sectional interests, the people are able to constitute themselves as a whole in the most disinterested manner imaginable.[59] But this constitution of the people through divine law by the same token denies them sovereignty, which Maududi feared because it might urge them to approve of un-Islamic moves like legalizing alcohol. It is this paradox of the people mobilized against itself that makes the Islamic State into a theocracy, assuming, of course, that everyone could be brought to agree upon the definition of what counted as sacred law. Maududi's justification for his theory of state, however, is a sophisticated one, and depends on his criticism of the idea of sovereignty.

Having examined the legal doctrine of European sovereignty, with all its extraordinary powers, Maududi asks "Does such sovereignty really exist within the bounds of humanity? If so, where? And who can be construed and treated as being invested with it?"[60] Sovereignty, he recognizes, can never be fully manifested in political life because it presumes a power too great to be realized, which is to say the mastery of an entire society. In fact if such a power were to be instantiated it could only lead to tyranny. The sovereign, whether king or president, was therefore unable in actuality to exercise the power vested in him, and this difference between what political theory called for and what really was the case could only result in corruption and violence, as "he who is really not sovereign, and has no right to be sovereign, whenever made so artificially cannot but use his powers unjustly."[61] Sovereignty, then, properly belongs to God alone, who has sole decision over life and death, since to give such powers to mortals would be to create the possibility of a dictatorship. But "There is no place for any dictator in Islam. It is only before God's command that mankind must bow without whys and wherefores."[62]

In an effort to prevent dictatorship of an individual as well as popular kind, Maududi embodies the people's will in God while at the same times annulling it. For God here is not sovereign in any traditional way, for instance as the "unmoved mover," but solely as a displacement for the will of the people, which can only manifest itself by identifying with the divine will, and in doing so to un-will itself. In the Islamic State, in other words, Muslims must destroy their particularity by identifying with God's universality. And even though Maududi never achieved his Islamic State, it was largely because of his doing that Pakistan's constitution reserves sovereignty for God.[63]

Running counter to the idea of Islam's "politicization," therefore, Maududi's conception of theocracy is anti-political in nature, as the views of religious experts had always been in colonial India. But rather than simply placing limits on the invasive power of the sovereign, which is what these men had done in earlier times, Maududi's project was paradoxical in its attempt to achieve a non-political state by way of political action. It is as if he recognized that limits were no longer sufficient, and that the sovereign power had to be rolled back together with its governing institutions before the divisiveness of politics could be neutralized in a theocracy. Indeed, Maududi's idea can even be seen to represent a bizarre version of Lenin's thesis about the "withering away" of the state under communism, just as the Bolshevik leader's notion of the party as a vanguard was explicitly adopted by the former for his own Jamat-e Islami.[64] Like his more famous revolutionary predecessor, Maududi is also filled with anxiety about the domination of the strong over the weak, which he describes in theological terms as the sin of men claiming to be gods, something he thinks happens whenever one individual or group assumes absolute authority over another:

All persons who exercise unqualified dominion over a group of men, who impose their will upon others, who make them their instruments and seek to control their destinies in the same manner as Pharaoh and

Nimrod did in the heyday of their power, are essentially claimants to godhood, though the claim may be tacit, veiled and unexpressed. And those who serve and obey them admit their godhood even if they do not say so by word of mouth.[65]

Rather than being an extravagant and anachronistic claim, in other words, Maududi sees the sin of man becoming god (*ilah*) as occurring so easily that it can manifest itself within individuals as well as between them, writing that "Even if he secures deliverance from the service of other *ilahs*, he becomes a slave to his own petty passions and exalts the devil in him to the position of a supreme Lord."[66] In order to prevent the domination of man over man, then, as well as of an individual over himself, all mortals need to be subjected to God as a purely external, and in this way mythical figure, one embodied in an archaic and therefore non-partisan law that preserves society from internal division:

If people observe these just limits and regulate their affairs within these boundary walls, on the one hand their personal liberty is adequately safeguarded and, on the other [*sic*] possibility of class war and domination of one class over another, which begins with capitalist oppression and ends in working-class dictatorship, is safely and conveniently eliminated.[67]

This obsession with harmony led Maududi to recommend the kind of separation between social and religious groups, and even between genders, that might prevent conflict and domination among them. Remarkably similar to contemporary Hindu visions of a harmonious society of castes, some of which were shared by figures like Gandhi, Islamic models of coexistence in this period made every effort to prevent both desire and conflict between groups by a segregated form of pluralism that took caste and class, as well as community and gender into consideration. Maududi's advocacy of separate legislative assemblies for men and women, therefore, extended to a defence of separate electorates. But the reasons for supporting such a constitutional system have now changed, as is inevitable in a situation where Muslims are a majority, so Maududi links separate electorates to Pakistan's curiously anti-territorial or rather ideological character:

[Joint electorates] will strengthen, in both the geographically distant wings of the state, the consciousness of territorial nationhood at the cost of Islamic fraternity. And, as this feeling will grow in strength and intensity, Muslims of the two different areas who have nothing in common except religion, will be driven farther and farther away from their own brothers-in-faith and nearer to the people belonging to their own *territory* who have almost every factor common with each other except religion.[68]

Having zeroed in on the anti-territorial dimension of Muslim nationalism, Maududi is able, in an extraordinary achievement, to recover the paranoia that marked minority politics in India and instil it in the heart of Pakistan's majority. Unlike the fears of an exploding Muslim population that haunt the nightmares of Hindu nationalism, however, it is not the number of non-Muslims that concerns Maududi, but instead that of his own co-religionists. For as a majority Muslims are capable of destroying what he sees as their religious distinctiveness by democratic means, something they would have been unable to do as a minority in India. They might, for instance, start identifying as Bengalis in East Pakistan, or neglect properly Islamic principles of "harmonious" governance. And so the Muslim majority requires protection from itself, just as the Pakistani people needs to divest itself of sovereignty by reserving this attribute for God. All of which suggests that despite having tried to surmount it for decades, the language of minority politics and protections continues to inform Pakistani debates, with "fundamentalists" in particular setting themselves against a heedless Muslim majority that has taken the place of its erstwhile Hindu foe. The only way to avoid this threat, we have seen, is by eliminating all notions of popular sovereignty and the social conflict that inevitably follows it, and instead to identify directly with the divine law. Yet this surely does nothing more than allow Muslims to take God's place and thus commit the very sin that Maududi most fears. To reject "man-made" legislation, after all, and enforce divine law in defiance of it, as those did who attacked Ahmadis in the 1950s, or who do today when punishing "blasphemy," is to act as nothing less than the hand of God smiting down sinners. In a perverse fulfilment of Iqbal's vision, in other words, those who would enforce God's law in Pakistan by repudiating popular sovereignty in fact end up acting the part of God in that country. Their very rejection of human agency and mediation has made such Muslims divine. Is this surreptitious pleasure, then, part of the secret of theocracy?

# CONCLUSION

I wish to compound my impertinence in beginning this book with a quotation from Hegel by ending it with another, not least because the German philosopher had by the end of the nineteenth century acquired a large following among Indian thinkers. Writing about the Crusades, surely an early example of the "return" to an unknown homeland that we have been exploring in the preceding chapters, Hegel notes that it signalled a desire to grasp the deity in sensuous form, and thus to unite the secular and the eternal. But to seek God in the Holy Sepulchre was a vain enterprise, for a grave cannot be the site of new life:

Christendom was not to find its ultimatum of truth in the grave. At this Sepulchre the Christian world received a second time the response given to the disciples when they sought the body of the Lord there: '*Why seek ye the living among the dead? He is not here but is risen.*' You must not look for the principle of your religion in the sensuous, in the grave among the dead, but in the living Spirit in yourselves. [...] Christendom found the empty Sepulchre, but not the union of the secular and the eternal; and so it lost the Holy Land. [...] The West bade an eternal farewell to the East at the Holy Sepulchre, and gained a comprehension of its own principle of subjective infinite Freedom. Christendom never appeared again on the scene of history as *one* body.[1]

For Hegel, then, Christendom's abandonment of a sensuous homeland, and its consequent disappearance from the "scene of history" as a single body, represented the final victory of the

West as a spiritual entity. And this meant that the Occident's eventual command over the things of the world was due precisely to its refusal to be embodied in them. Very likely drawing upon this and other passages from thinkers like Hegel, Iqbal too had warned Muslims about the seduction of objects, among which he counted the nation state as the most dangerous. Indeed, Iqbal turned repeatedly in his work to the story of the Prophet's abandonment of Mecca as providing a model for the leave-taking of such a homeland. Having initially left the town of his birth in a migration from which the Islamic calendar begins, Muhammad returned as Mecca's conqueror only to forsake it again, having literally destroyed the holy city's obduracy as a material entity. Iqbal's poem *Wataniyyat* (Nationalism), from the collection *Bang-e Dara* (Call of the Caravan-Bell), for example, contains the following hemistich:

*Hay tark-e watan sunnat-e mahbub-e ilahi*

To abandon the homeland is to follow the example of God's beloved[2]

He suggests that Muhammad abandoned Mecca not because it was the home of idolatry so much as because the very idea of a homeland was idolatrous. Being Muslim, then, meant following the Prophet's example by abandoning the familiarity of a Mecca for some alien Medina. That this abandonment had nothing to do with a rejection simply of worldly attachment is evident from the poem's title, invoking as it does the national movements with whose ideal of patriotism, as the belonging to a state, Iqbal so actively opposed. For we have already seen him rejecting any homeland defined by the state as a manifestation and guarantor of property in all the relations of modern life. By abandoning the familiar for the alien, Iqbal forsakes belonging to the homeland of which he had in fact already been dispossessed by the Raj. And the freedom of this dispossession allowed him to abandon that entire politics of identification within which the familiar and the alien are opposed, since these terms have undergone a strange reversal here, with the familiar becoming alien and the alien familiar, in a travesty of identification as an act of recognition. Indeed, Iqbal's emphasis on the act of departure over that of arrival, in the line quoted above, puts being itself into question by abandoning all belonging.

What is it to be without belonging in a national state? How is it possible to belong independently of this state? Such are the questions that for Iqbal characterize the sentiment of homelessness as a denial of national belonging. A complicated sentiment that is too often simplified into the pan-Islamic passion, minority disaffection, or class interest that supposedly became Muslim separatism in colonial India. Yet this sentiment did not subsist in some facile rejection of the homeland, but rather in a struggle with it, almost as a kind of imponderable fate. So in Iqbal's hemistich abandonment itself comes to belong in the homeland of tradition, the founding event that is the Prophet's emigration from Mecca to Medina, which means that the familiar and the alien here posit and destroy one another in a vicious circle, making of Muslim identification itself a nation in suspense. Indeed, politicians like Liaquat Ali Khan, who would become Pakistan's first prime minister, invoked this anti-territorial vision to propound a supposedly "ideological" nationality, saying in his presidential address to the All-India Muslim Educational Conference in Agra on 27 December 1945 that "the principle of territorial nationalism is opposed to the Muslim view of nationalism which is based on a philosophy of society and outlook on life rather than allegiance to a piece of territory."[3]

It is possible to see Iqbal's struggle with nationality working itself out in Pakistan, where the rejection of history and territory as the foundations of nationality makes for a paradoxical relationship with the present. Unlike Gandhi's rejection of history, which was meant to recover the present as a site of moral action, Muslim efforts to shuffle off the past were intended to grasp the future. Is it because of this repudiation of the past as much as the present that Pakistan appears to possess no history, properly speaking? Similar in this respect to the Israeli narrative of living under a continuous existential threat, the country's popular as well as academic histories are circular and so unchanging in character, made up as they often are of repetitive accounts about the dismissal of civilian governments and the imposition of military rule. And this narrative is in its turn premised upon other, equally recurring themes, such as an Indian threat or an American intervention leading to yet another instance of martial law. This might be why Pakistani history, despite its many theatrical features, tends to be so tedious to read however skilled the author writing it. And perhaps this also explains why so much historical narrative in that country is dominated by a salacious interest in the corrupt practices and sexual escapades of its various leaders.

Indeed the only element of such narratives that can be said to possess a historical trajectory has to do with the rise of Islamic politics, which thus assumes the role of Pakistan's only national project. Ferociously interested in matters of external observance like dress codes, sexual segregation, dietary rules and pious speech, those who manage the country's religious movements are interested in creating the national majority and uniform citizenship that the Muslim League had lacked in colonial times. Instead of constituting a threat to such a state, in other words, Islam in Pakistan might well be its only true supporter, trying as its upholders do to nationalize people by inculcating among them a set of comportments making for a collective sense of citizenship. Islam in Pakistan has become, like Judaism in Israel, a national religion in such a strong sense as to take the place of citizenship. And yet this obsession with external observance also suggests that Islam is not in fact a political entity. The chief concern of Islamic parties, after all, is with social regulation, for which the state is meant to act merely as a guarantor, without any sovereign power of its own. But they are not particularly original in this claim, with Liaquat Ali Khan himself acknowledging in his convocation address to Aligarh Muslim University on 16 February 1947 that "According to Islam no one can wield authority in his own right, as all authority is derived from God and can be exercised only on His behalf."[4]

But an anti-political Islam turns out to be the very image of Hegel's grave. For the investment of religious movements in outward observances, especially if only in a nominal way, entirely ignores the spiritual dimension of inner life, and thus the individual freedom that Iqbal had hoped Islam would instantiate in a post-national future. Yet we have already seen in the last chapter that by seeking to spiritualize the world of matter, Iqbal had himself abandoned the traditional bifurcation of knowledge that divided a *zahir* (exoteric) realm from a *batin* (esoteric) one, thus implying the former's lack of autonomy if not its illegitimacy. But the reverse was also true, since by spiritualizing the outer world Iqbal eliminated the inner one as well. And it is indeed this latter which is now viewed with suspicion by Sunni radicals. So the "deviant" beliefs of those who belong to the Ahmadi or Shia sects offer reason enough for Sunni radicals to condemn them to obloquy, and increasingly even to death for their inner beliefs rather than outward observances. For in a remarkable departure from Sunni tradition, it is no longer the offending practices of these groups, but rather what is seen as their invisible faith in the prophetic stature of Mirza Ghulam Ahmad or the primacy of Ali that is considered sinful. More than the particularity of such beliefs, it is the very existence of an inner life, whether of an esoteric or spiritual kind, that causes offense, since it gives rise to the possibility of hypocrisy, a term specifically associated today with the Shia doctrine of dissimulation, and one which has come to name the gravest of sins in the lexicon of Sunni militancy. Dissimulation, of course, presupposes and indeed fosters the existence of an inner life, while hypocrisy destroys the distinction between what is true and false, inner and outer, by robbing its own agent of this recognition and thus wholly preventing the exercise of virtue.

Now hypocrisy, as Hannah Arendt pointed out in her book *On Revolution*, emerged as a political theme in Europe during the French Revolution, whose leaders were dedicated to stripping off its mask and revealing the truth lying underneath. But as she notes:

However deeply heartfelt a motive may be, once it is brought out and exposed for public inspection it becomes an object of suspicion rather than insight; when the light of the public falls upon it, it appears and even shines, but, unlike deeds and words which are meant to appear, whose very existence hinges on appearance, the motives behind such deeds and words are destroyed in their essence through appearance; when they appear they become 'mere appearances' behind which again other, ulterior motives may lurk, such as hypocrisy and deceit.[5]

Any attempt to erase the distinction between personal and public life, then, is bound to be endlessly circular because these realms are incommensurable. And to lay bare all inner life is in fact to destroy the very character of a public space made possible by the "mask" of a legal personality. Arendt goes on to describe how in totalitarian societies this effort to strip off hypocrisy's mask is transformed into the rather different enterprise of searching out traitors whose existence is demanded by the laws of historical necessity.[6] While her view of public life and anxiety to defend its autonomy are open to criticism, two elements of Arendt's analysis interest me. One has to do with the fact that her analysis can also take for its subject the kind of historiography I have been keen to reject, one whose hunt for interests, motives and intentions is no less about the impossible desire of making the inner life amenable to scholarly judgement modelled on law. The other matter of interest in her study of hypocrisy has to do with the very different role the word plays in Pakistani politics, where it is never simply about revealing what should remain hidden.

CONCLUSION

If there is no gap between the outward observance of Islam and the believer's inner life, then the ecumenical religion we saw being put in place by the League's early leaders must collapse, and with it Muslim politics itself in the way it was practised in colonial India. Yet the Islam promoted by militant Sunni groups is not about replacing one kind of belief with another. What they object to is the inner life itself, whose freedom is now identified with heresy. But why should this be the case? Perhaps an inner life is the last remaining vestige of all that is simply given or *a priori* within Muslim nationalism. We have already seen, after all, that the Muslim League had been dedicated to eliminating every manifestation of such "dark matter" from its ideology, whether this was a geographical, historical or even demographic inheritance. In this sense the execration of inner life by Sunni militants can be seen as part of the logic of Muslim nationalism, which would replace every blind or taken for granted inheritance by a fully visible and self-conscious artifice, but one that by this very token can never be fully naturalized. And it is the absence of such an inner life, mixing tradition and freedom in equal measure, which makes the outward observance of Islam such a raw, passionate affair, with its great dramas of blasphemy and desecration demonstrating the urge to externalize religion completely as a kind of citizenship without politics. The passion for outward observance proceeds from an effort to replace inwardness, though it has ceased to be concerned with targeting sectarian minorities alone, since nowadays accusations of desecration and blasphemy can and are being launched by individuals against rivals from their own communities, thus illustrating the disintegration of Sunni forms of religiosity from within. Manifested only by such external forms, Islam becomes a never-ending effort to extirpate inner life, though in doing so occult elements like a belief in jinns and magic sometimes lodge themselves more firmly in the places vacated by the mystical commentaries of Sufi saints or Shia imams.[7]

We might say that Pakistan represents the sepulchre of Muslim nationalism, which to my knowledge has inspired only one Muslim politician outside the subcontinent. Bosnia's first president, Alija Izetbegovic, gave his misguided approval in the 1960s to a Pakistani model for his country's future, one that was used to justify Serbian atrocities after the collapse and fragmentation of Yugoslavia, in an eerie echo of the partitions of Ireland, India and Palestine.[8] But though Pakistani forms of Islam, and Sunni sectarianism in particular, have had a much greater and sometimes violent success abroad, the country is also the grave of Islam as an ecumenical religion with its own form of politics. And so the history of Muslim nationalism ends with Pakistan's founding, its anti-historical and anti-geographical themes leading a life there that is disconnected from any coherent political project. For in many ways Pakistan, both as a secular and religious ideal, serves as an illustration of the failure to escape or transcend the problem of minority politics in India, within whose ambit, after all, did these themes possess any meaning. Indeed the hatred of inner life in militant Sunnism might be seen as a final effort to rid Islam not only of sectarian minorities like Ahmadis and the Shia, but of the minority itself as a category that retains the role of an alter-ego and reminder of Islam's colonial past. But this attempt to exit history can never be fulfilled. Even at a theoretical level, for example, as we have seen from his hemistich quoted above, Iqbal's attempt to avoid the idea of a homeland proved to be a circular one, with territorial citizenship simply replaced by a religious form of nationality.

If the role of religion in a Muslim-majority state like Pakistan is a national one, though perhaps by default rather than by design, then perhaps it is simply as a non-nation and thus a non-majority that Islam might exist as a global phenomenon. For seen as a global fact, in the way that Muslim activists of all kinds now routinely do, this religion does indeed exist only as a demographic minority. Dispossessed of its geographical weight in the global arena, and therefore of a merely cartographic vision of universality, Islam, despite the fantasies of conversion that some of its upholders share with Christianity, can no longer claim to represent the future of humanity in any conventional sense. Liaquat Ali Khan, for example, had spoken to the students of Aligarh Muslim University on 22 September 1945 about Pakistan representing the future of humanity in this merely cartographic and international fashion, saying:

In the world there are all kinds of experiments being made—Fascism, Nazism, Bolshevism, Capitalism, Shintoism and a number of other isms. All these isms are out to destroy each other. Islam gave a message of peace nearly 1,400 years ago. We owe a debt to Islam. We have to show by our precept and example by working in the laboratory of Pakistan that the future of humanity lies in the teachings of Islam.[9]

Such geographical visions of universality belong to a time long gone by, with Islam no longer confined to expanses of territory or identified with any political order. And if today Islam as a global fact takes the shape of a demographic minority, then its homologue in the world of national politics is surely provided by the world's largest Muslim minority, which is still to be found in the Indian Union.[10] As Iqbal had himself realized when in a speech to the Muslim League in 1930 he spoke about India as "the greatest Muslim country in the world," it was the status of his co-religionists as a minority that made them into the most Islamic of populations, precisely because it was only an idea that united this diverse and dispersed community.[11] Indeed, even Liaquat Ali Khan, in his speech of 1945 to the All-India Muslim Educational Conference, was clear about the "ideal" character of the minority, saying about India's Muslims that "Religion is their sheet anchor and the only enduring force which has welded together Muslims living in far-flung localities into a virile brotherhood and has given them a strong sense of national and cultural unity overriding all those factors of race, blood, territory and even language which tend to divide."[12] But instead of protecting Islam as an abstract idea, Pakistan has only nationalized it. Its true home remains with the Muslim minority of India, which thus portends the future of Islam itself as a global entity, one that can no longer be brought together in some traditional way, whether as a caliphate, empire or indeed a set of nation states.

# NOTES

## INTRODUCTION

1. G. W. F. Hegel, "Is Judaea, then, the Teutons' Fatherland?" in *Early Theological Writings*, trans. T. M. Knox (Philadelphia: University of Pennsylvania Press, 1975), p. 147.
2. Ibid., p. 146.
3. See for this Amnon Raz-Krakotzkin, "The Zionist Return to the West and the Mizrahi Jews," in Ivan Kalmar and Derek Penslar (eds), *Orientalism and the Jews* (Lebanon, NH: Brandeis University Press, 2005), pp. 162–81.
4. Aamir R. Mufti has written an important book on this theme, *Enlightenment in the Colony: The Jewish Question and the Crisis of Postcolonial Culture* (Princeton: Princeton University Press, 2007).
5. Jacqueline Rose, *The Question of Zion* (Princeton: Princeton University Press, 2005), p. 83.
6. For a fine discussion of the ambiguity of national belonging in Israel, see Zali Gurevitch, "The Double Site of Israel," in Eyal Ben-Ary and Yoram Bilu (eds), *Grasping Land: Space and Place in Contemporary Israeli Discourse and Experience* (Albany: State University of New York Press, 1997), pp. 203–16.
7. Theodor Herzl, *Old-New Land*, trans. Lotta Levensohn (New York: Markus Wiener, 1987).
8. Gabriel Piterberg, *The Returns of Zionism: Myths, Politics and Scholarship in Israel* (London: Verso, 2008), p. 246.
9. *The Economist*, Dec. 12, 1981, p. 48.
10. M. R. T., *Pakistan and Muslim India* (Bombay: Home Study Circle, 1943), pp. 17–18.
11. Ibid., p. 91.
12. Rose, *The Question of Zion*, p. 67.
13. See Farzana Shaikh, *Making Sense of Pakistan* (London: Hurst, 2011).

14. The chief exponent of this view is Ayesha Jalal, especially in her book *The Sole Spokesman: Jinnah, the Muslim League and the Demand for Pakistan* (Cambridge: Cambridge University Press, 1994).

15. This view is best represented by David Gilmartin's *Empire and Islam: Punjab and the Making of Pakistan* (Delhi: Oxford University Press, 1989).

16. Perhaps the most succinct statement of this position, together with a general critique of historical or "dialectical" reason, remains the last chapter of Claude Lévi-Strauss, *The Savage Mind* (London: Weidenfeld and Nicolson, 1966).

17. Mohammad Ali Jinnah, "Speech at a public meeting in Dacca: 21 March 1948," in S.M. Burke (ed.), *Jinnah: Speeches and Statements, 1947–1948* (Karachi: Oxford University Press, 2000), p. 149.

18. Rose, *The Question of Zion*, p. 67.

## 1. ANOTHER COUNTRY

1. E. S. Reddy, "The Jew and the Arab: Discussion with Mr Silverman and Mr Honick, March 1946, report by Pyarelal from Louis Fischer papers," in *Gandhi, Jews and Palestine: A Collection of Articles, Speeches, Letters and Interviews* (http://gandhiserve.org/information/writings_online/articles/Gandhi_jews_palestine.html)

2. Ibid.

3. Ibid.

4. Ibid.

5. Choudhry Khaliquzzaman, *Pathway to Pakistan* (Lahore: Longmans, 1961), pp. 198–9.

6. B. R. Ambedkar, *Pakistan or the Partition of India*, in Vasant Moon (ed.), *Dr Babasaheb Ambedkar: Writings and Speeches*, vol. 8 (1990) p. 120.

7. M. R. T., *Pakistan and Muslim India*, p. 57.

8. Ibid., p. 66.

9. Ibid., p. 5.

10. See Muhammad Zafrulla Khan, *Palestine at the U.N.O.* (Karachi: The Pakistan Institute of International Affairs, 1948).

11. Ibid., p. 8.

12. Muhammad Zafrulla Khan, ed. A. H. Batalvi, *The Forgotten Years: Memoirs of Sir Muhammad Zafrulla Khan* (Lahore: Vanguard Books, 1991), p. 182.

13. See Shamim Akhtar, *Quaid-i-Azam's Personal Collection of Books in Dr Mahmud Husain Library: A Catalogue* (Karachi: Research and Publications Section, Dr Mahmud Husain Library, University of Karachi, 1982).

14. Ibid.

15. See, for instance, the statement by Liaquat Ali Khan in Jamil-ud-din Ahmad, (ed.), *Quaid-e-Azam as Seen by his Contemporaries* (Lahore: Publishers United, 1976), p. 225.

16. Hannah Arendt, "The Balfour Declaration and the Palestine Mandate," in Jerome Kohn and Ron H. Feldman (eds), *The Jewish Writings* (New York: Schocken Books, 2007), p. 205.

17. Penderel Moon (ed.), *Wavell: The Viceroy's Journal* (London: Oxford University Press, 1973), pp. 251–2.

18. Arendt, "Peace or Armistice in the Near East," in *The Jewish Writings*, p. 425.

19. See, for instance, Nadav G. Shelef, *Evolving Nationalism: Homeland, Identity, and Religion in Israel, 1925–2005* (Ithaca: Cornell University Press, 2010).

20. Chaudhary Rahmat Ali, *The Millat and the Mission: Seven Commandments of Destiny for the Seventh Continent of Dinia* (Cambridge: Pakistan National Movement, 1944).

21. Chaudhary Rahmat Ali, *India: The Continent of Dinia or the Country of Doom* (Cambridge: Dinia Continental Movement, 1946).

22. Theodor Herzl, trans. Sylvie d'Avigdor, *The Jewish State: An Attempt at a Modern Solution of the Jewish Question* (London: Henry Pordes, 1993), pp. 63–4.

23. Jamil-ud-din Ahmad (ed.), *Some Recent Speeches and Writings of Mr Jinnah* (Lahore: Sh. Muhammad Ashraf, 1942), p. 213.

24. Rajendra Prasad, *India Divided* (New Delhi: Penguin Books, 2010), p. 273.

25. J. Ahmad, *Some Recent Speeches and Writings of Mr Jinnah*, pp. 163–4.

26. Cited in R. Prasad, *India Divided*, p. 11.

27. All-India Muslim League, *Jinnah-Gandhi Talks* (Delhi: Muslim League Printing Press, 1944), pp. 30–1.

28. Cited in R. Prasad, *India Divided*, p. 504.

29. See Alan Campbell-Johnson, *Mission With Mountbatten* (London: Robert Hale, 1951), pp. 27 and 56.

30. R. Prasad, *India Divided*, pp. 38–9.

31. Beni Prasad, *The Hindu-Muslim Questions* (Allahabad: Kitabistan, 1941), p. 86.

32. Jawaharlal Nehru, *The Discovery of India* (New Delhi: Oxford University Press, 1999), p. 536.

33. M. R. T., *Pakistan and Muslim India*, p. ii.

34. Ibid., p. 3.

35. Ibid., p. 70.

36. Ibid., p. 71.

37. Arendt, "The Crisis of Zionism," in *The Jewish Writings*, p. 335.

38. Ibid.
39. Ibid.
40. Cited in R. Prasad, *India Divided*, p. 413.
41. J. Ahmad, *Some Recent Speeches and Writings of Mr Jinnah*, pp. 40–1.
42. Ibid., p. 247.
43. Ibid., pp. 153–4.
44. Ibid., p. 84.
45. Cited in Jyotirmaya Sharma, *Hindutva: Exploring the Idea of Hindu Nationalism* (New Delhi: Penguin Viking, 2003), p. 170.
46. B. Prasad, *The Hindu-Muslim Questions*, p. 69.
47. Ibid., p. 72.
48. Aga Khan, *The Memoirs of the Aga Khan: World Enough and Time*, with a foreword by W. Somerset Maugham (London: Cassell and Company Ltd., 1954), pp. 264–5.
49. J. Ahmad, *Some Recent Speeches and Writings of Mr Jinnah*, p. 229.
50. Marie Tyler-McGraw, *An African Republic: Black and White Virginians in the Making of Liberia* (Durham: North Carolina University Press, 2007), p. 2.
51. See Hannah Arendt, *On Revolution* (London: Penguin Books, 1990).
52. See, for example, Yvonne Chireau and Nathaniel Deutsch (eds), *Black Zion: African American Religious Encounters with Judaism* (New York: Oxford University Press, 2000).
53. See Dawn-Marie Gibson, *A History of the Nation of Islam: Race, Islam, and the Quest for Freedom* (New York: Praeger, 2012).
54. Tyler-McGraw, *An African Republic*, p. 6.
55. See, for example, Vazira Zamindar, *The Long Partition and the Making of Modern South Asia: Refugees, Boundaries, Histories* (New York: Columbia University Press, 2007).
56. Tyler-McGraw, *An African Republic*, p. 165.
57. Herzl, *The Jewish State* pp. 19–20.

## 2. THE PROBLEM WITH NUMBERS

1. For a discussion of the early links between Jewish politics and the British Empire, see, Abigail Green, "The British Empire and the Jews: An Imperialism of Human Rights?" in *Past and Present*, no. 199, May 2008, pp. 178–205.
2. See for this Bernard Cohn's classic essay, "The Census, Social Structure and Objectification in South Asia," in *An Anthropologist Among the Historians and Other Essays* (Delhi: Oxford University Press, 1998), pp. 224–54.
3. For the best discussion of the politics of representation in Muslim North India, see Farzana Shaikh, *Community and Consensus in Islam: Muslim*

*Representation in Colonial India, 1860–1947* (Cambridge: Cambridge University Press, 1989).

4. C. F. Andrews, *Zaka Ullah of Delhi* (Cambridge: W. Heffer and Sons, 1929), p. 114.

5. For a fine discussion of the place of numbers in the political imagination, see Arjun Appadurai, *Fear of Small Numbers: An Essay on the Geography of Anger* (Durham and London: Duke University Press, 2006).

6. Sayyid Ahmad Khan, "Political umur awr Musalman," in *Khutbat-e Sir Sayyid*, vol. 2 (Lahore: Majlis-e Taraqqi-ye Adab, 1973), pp. 34–5.

7. Sayyid Ahmad Khan, "Siyasat awr ham," in *Khutbat-e Sir Sayyid*, vol. 1 (Lahore Majlis-e Taraqqi-ye Adab, 1973), p. 34.

8. Khan, *Khutbat*, vol. 2, pp. 14–15.

9. Khan, *Khutbat*, vol. 1, pp. 35–36.

10. Ibid., pp. 48–50.

11. See, for instance, Mahdi Ali Khan, *Majmua-e Lectures-o Speeches*, vol. 1 (Lahore: Nawal Kishore Gas Printing Works Press, 1913), pp. 484–5.

12. Shan Muhammad, *The Indian Muslims: A Documentary Record*, vol. 1 (Meerut and New Delhi: Meenakshi Prakashan, 1983), p. 29.

13. Ibid., p. 40.

14. Ibid.

15. Ibid., pp. 42–43.

16. Ibid., p. 44.

17. Mahdi Ali Khan, *Majmua-e Lectures-o Speeches*, p. 418.

18. Ibid., p. 484.

19. Ibid., p. 489.

20. Ibid., p. 492.

21. Ibid., p. 405.

22. Ibid.

23. Ibid., p. 406.

24. Ibid., p. 404.

25. Shan Muhammad, *The Indian Muslims*, pp. 175–176.

26. For the Muslim deputation and its aftermath, see Matiur Rahman, *From Consultation to Confrontation: A Study of the Muslim League in British Indian Politics, 1906–1912* (London: Luzac and Co., 1970).

27. Ibid., p. 192.

28. Ibid., pp. 198–199.

29. See, for instance, "Speech at a Function in Honour of the Deputation of the Hindu University, Bombay, 23 February 1913," in K. K. Aziz (ed.), *Aga Khan III: Selected Speeches and Writings of Sir Sultan Muhammad Shah*, vol. I (London and New York: Kegan Paul International, 1998), pp. 410–15.

30. "Interview with *The Times of India*, Bombay, 8 March 1912", in ibid., pp. 396–7.

31. Ibid., p. 397.

32. Ibid., pp. 397–8.

33. Shan Muhammad, *The Indian Muslims*, pp. 275–6.

34. For the working class see, for instance, Dipesh Chakrabarty, *Rethinking Working-Class History: Bengal 1890–1940* (Delhi: Oxford University Press, 1989), and for capitalists, Ritu Birla, *Stages of Capital: Law, Culture and Market Governance in Late Colonial India* (Durham, NC: Duke University Press, 2009).

35. See, for instance, Soumen Mukherjee, "Being 'Ismaili' and 'Muslim': Some Observations on the Politico-Religious Career of Aga Khan III," in *South Asia: Journal of South Asian Studies*, vol. 34, no. 2, July 2011, pp. 188–207.

36. For an account of the ambiguity of Shia politics in northern India during this period, see Justin Jones, *Shi'a Islam in Colonial India: Religion, Community and Sectarianism* (New Delhi: Cambridge University Press, 2012).

37. See for this Nikki Keddie, *Sayyid Jamal-ad-Din "al-Afghani": A Political Biography* (Berkeley and Los Angeles: The University of California Press, 1972).

38. Aga Khan, *India in Transition: A Study in Political Evolution* (London: The Medici Society, 1918), pp. 6–7.

39. Ibid., p. 169.

40. Ibid., p. 18.

41. "Letter to *The Times*, London, 12 August 1917", in Aziz, *Aga Khan III*, pp. 525–9.

42. Aga Khan, *India in Transition*, p. 37.

43. Ibid., pp. 171–2.

44. Ibid., pp. 76–7.

45. Ibid., p. 24.

46. Ibid., pp. 10–11.

47. See for this the second and third chapters of Faisal Devji, *The Impossible Indian: Gandhi and the Temptation of Violence* (London: Hurst, 2012).

48. Aga Khan, *The Memoirs of the Aga Khan*, pp. 150–51.

49. Ibid., p. 151.

50. Ibid., p. 152.

51. Arendt, "Can the Jewish-Arab Question be Solved?" in *The Jewish Writings*, pp. 196–7.

52. Ibid., p. 196.

53. Ibid., p. 197.

54. Syed Abdul Vahid (ed.), *Thoughts and Reflections of Iqbal* (Lahore: Sh. Muhammad Ashraf, 1992), pp. 371–2.

55. Cited in C. A. Bayly, *Recovering Liberties: Indian Thought in the Age of Liberalism and Empire* (Cambridge: Cambridge University Press, 2012), p. 323.

56. Ibid., p. 174.

57. Ibid., p. 324.

58. Patrick Lacey, *Fascist India* (London: Nicholson and Watson, 1946).

59. See for this M. Naeem Qureshi, *Pan-Islamism in British India: The Politics of the Khilafat Movement, 1918–1924* (Karachi: Oxford University Press, 2009).

60. Aga Khan, *India in Transition*, pp. 23–4.

61. See "Ameer Ali's Letter with the Aga Khan to His Excellency Ghazi Ismat Pasha, the Prime Minister of Turkey," in Shan Muhammad (ed.), *The Right Hon'ble Syed Ameer Ali: Political Writings* (New Delhi: Ashish Publishing House, 1989), pp. 288–90.

62. Zia-ud-Din Ahmad Suleri, *My Leader, Being an Estimate of Mr Jinnah's Work for Indian Mussalmans* (Lahore: The Lion Press, 1945), pp. 41 and 53.

63. J. Ahmad, *Some Recent Speeches and Writings of Mr Jinnah*, p. 88.

64. Ibid., p. 107.

65. Ibid., p. 41.

66. *Thoughts and Reflections of Iqbal*, p. 211.

67. J. Ahmad, *Some Recent Speeches and Writings of Mr Jinnah*, p. 226.

68. Ibid., p. 206.

69. M. R. T., *Pakistan and Muslim India*, p. 103.

70. J. Ahmad, *Some Recent Speeches and Writings of Mr Jinnah*, p. 233.

## 3. A PEOPLE WITHOUT HISTORY

1. S. M. Burke, *Jinnah: Speeches and Statements 1947–1948* (Karachi: Oxford University Press, 2000), p. 25.

2. Jawaharlal Nehru, *The Discovery of India* (New Delhi: Oxford University Press, 1999).

3. Ishtiaq Husain Qureshi, *The Development of Islamic Culture in India*, Pakistan Literature Series No. 9 (Lahore: Muhammad Ashraf, 1946), p. 1.

4. Ibid., pp. 11–12.

5. Ibid., p. 16.

6. Khaliquzzaman, *Pathway to Pakistan*, p. 237.

7. Ibid., p. ix.

8. Ibid., pp. x-xi.

9. Ibid., p. 284.

10. Ibid., p. 400.

11. Craig Baxter (ed.), *Diaries of Field Marshal Mohammad Ayub Khan, 1966–1972* (Karachi: Oxford University Press, 2007), p. 319.

12. J. Ahmad, *Some Recent Speeches and Writings of Mr Jinnah*, p. 127.

13. Ibid., p. 161.

14. Cited in R. Prasad, *India Divided*, pp. 21–2.

15. J. Ahmad, *Some Recent Speeches and Writings of Mr Jinnah*, p. 153.

16. All-India Muslim League, *Jinnah-Gandhi Talks* (Delhi: Muslim League Printing Press, 1944), p. 31.

17. Burke, *Jinnah*, p. 22.

18. Ibid., p. 73.

19. John Morley, *On Compromise* (New Delhi: Rupa and Co., 2003), p. 21.

20. J. Ahmad, *Some Recent Speeches and Writings of Mr Jinnah*, p. 86.

21. Ibid., p. 117.

22. V. B. Kulkarni, *Is Pakistan Necessary?* (Bombay: Hind Kitabs, 1944), p. 36.

23. B. Prasad, *The Hindu-Muslim Questions*, p. 31.

24. J. Ahmad, *Some Recent Speeches and Writings of Mr Jinnah*, pp. 123–4.

25. Ibid., p. 29.

26. Khaliquzzaman, *Pathway to Pakistan*, p. 385.

27. Burke, *Jinnah*, pp. 25–9.

28. Ibid., p. 28.

29. J. Ahmad, *Some Recent Speeches and Writings of Mr Jinnah*, p. 72.

30. M. K. Gandhi, ed. Anthony J. Parel, *Hind Swaraj and Other Writings* (Cambridge: Cambridge University Press, 2003), especially chapter XIII.

31. B. Prasad, *The Hindu-Muslim Questions*, p. 69.

32. Vahid, *Thoughts and Reflections of Iqbal*, pp. 50–1.

33. Ibid., pp. 51–2.

34. Muhammad Iqbal, *Stray Reflections* (Lahore: Sh. Ghulam Ali and Sons, 1961), p. 15.

35. See, for instance, the second chapter of Iqbal's *The Reconstruction of Religious Thought in Islam* (New Delhi: Kitab Bhavan, 1990).

36. Cited in Souleymane Bachir Diagne, *Bergson Postcoloniale: L'élan Vital dans la Pensée de Léopold Sédar Senghor et de Mohamed Iqbal* (Paris: CNRS Éditions, 2011), p. 65.

37. See his *Reconstruction*, especially chapters two and five.

38. Vahid, *Thoughts and Reflections of Iqbal*, p. 75.

39. Ibid., p. 60.

40. Ibid., p. 163.

41. Ibid., p. 162.

42. Ibid., p. 193.

43. Iqbal, *Stray Reflections*, p. 29.

44. Muhammad Iqbal, *Kulliyat-e Iqbal Farsi* (Lahore: Iqbal Academy, 1990),

p. 134. The translation is by Arthur J. Arberry, in Muhammad Iqbal, *The Mysteries of Selflessness* (London: John Murray, 1953), pp. 40–1

45. Ibid., p. 51.
46. Vahid, *Thoughts and Reflections of Iqbal*, pp. 167–8.
47. Ibid., p. 173.
48. Iqbal, *Kulliyat*, pp. 554–5.
49. Iqbal, *Kulliyat*, pp. 551–2. My translation heavily modifies Arberry's in *Javid-Nama* (London: George Allen and Unwin Ltd., 1966), pp. 67–8. While the word "ayyam" literally means "days" in Arabic, in the locution "Days of the Arabs" it refers to a set of historical battles, and it is in this sense that I take Iqbal to be using it here.

4. THE FANATIC'S REWARD

1. See for this Denise A. Spellberg, "Islam on the Eighteenth-Century Stage: *Mahomet* as a Trans-Atlantic Case Study in the History of Ideas," *International Seminar on the History of the Atlantic World, 1500–1800*, Harvard University, Working Paper 00–05 (2000).
2. F. M. A. de Voltaire, *Zaïre, Le Fanatisme ou Mahomet le Prophète, Nanine ou L'homme sans Préjugé, Le Café ou L'écossaise* (Paris: Flammarion, 2004), pp. 152–3. All translations from this text are mine.
3. Ibid., p. 157.
4. See Jean-Jacques Rousseau, trans., with notes and an introduction, by Allan Bloom, *Politics and the Arts: Letter to M. D'Alembert on the Theatre* (Ithaca and New York: Cornell University Press, 1960), p. 30.
5. For a fascinating discussion of this event as a "myth" justifying the Prophet's finality, see David S. Powers, *Muhammad is Not the Father of Any of Your Men: The Making of the Last Prophet* (Philadelphia: University of Pennsylvania Press, 2009).
6. Voltaire, pp. 168–70.
7. Rousseau, p. 30.
8. Voltaire, p. 204.
9. Ibid., p. 210.
10. Rousseau, p. 25.
11. Edmund Burke, *Reflections on the Revolution in France* (Harmondsworth: Penguin Books, 1983).
12. G. W. F. Hegel, trans. J. Sibree, *The Philosophy of History*, (Buffalo, NY: Prometheus Books, 1991), p. 358.
13. Ibid.pp. 355–59.
14. G. W. F. Hegel, trans. A.V. Miller, *Hegel's Phenomenology of Spirit* (New York: Oxford University Press, 1977), pp. 355–63.

15. For the history of fanaticism as an idea, see Alberto Toscano, *Fanaticism: On the Uses of an Idea* (London: Verso, 2010).

16. Burke, *Jinnah*, p. 118.

17. Ispahani, M. A. H., *Qaid-e-Azam Jinnah as I Knew Him* (Karachi: Forward Publications Trust, 1967), p. 99.

18. J. Ahmad, *Some Recent Speeches and Writings of Mr Jinnah*, p. 442.

19. J. Ahmad, *Some Recent Speeches and Writings of Mr Jinnah*, pp. 28–30.

20. Z. H. Zaidi (ed.), *M.A. Jinnah-Ispahani Correspondence, 1936–1948* (Karachi: Forward Publications Trust, 1976), p. 449.

21. Syed Sharifuddin Pirzada (ed.), *Quaid-e-Azam Jinnah's Correspondence* (Karachi: Guild Publishing House, 1966), pp. 42–3.

22. K. H. Khurshid, *Memories of Jinnah* (Karachi: Oxford University Press, 1990), p. 35.

23. Ibid., p. v.

24. Suleri, Zia-ud-Din Ahmad, *My Leader*, pp. 54–5.

25. Ibid., p. 58.

26. All-India Muslim League, *Jinnah-Gandhi Talks*, p. 49.

27. J. Ahmad, *Some Recent Speeches and Writings of Mr Jinnah*, pp. 94–5.

28. John Morley, *On Compromise*, p. 3.

29. Ibid., p. 59.

30. Ibid., pp. 114–15.

31. Ibid., p. 78.

32. Ibid., p. 81.

33. See John Stuart Mill, *Considerations on Representative Government* (London: Longmans, Green, and Co., 1873).

34. Jawaharlal Nehru, *The Discovery of India*, p. 390.

35. Penderel Moon, *Wavell, the Viceroy's Journal*, pp. 348–9.

36. Suleri, *My Leader*, p. 1.

37. See, for example, Altaf Husain, "Memories of the Quaid-i-Azam", in Jamil-ud-din Ahmad (ed.), *Quaid-i-Azam as Seen by his Contemporaries* (Lahore: Publishers United Ltd., 1976), p. 76.

38. See, for instance, K. H. Khurshid, *Memories of Jinnah*, p. 53.

39. See All India Muslim League, *Jinnah-Gandhi Talks*, pp. 46–7.

40. J. Ahmad, *Some Recent Speeches and Writings of Mr Jinnah*, p. 76.

41. Vahid, *Thoughts and Reflections of Iqbal*, p. 42.

42. Ibid., p. 214.

43. Ibid., p. 78.

44. Iqbal, *Kulliyat e-Iqbal Farsi*, pp. 26–7.

45. The most sophisticated work on Iqbal now seems to be published in French. For a discussion of Iqbal's theology, see Abdennour Bidar, *L'islam Face à la Mort de Dieu* (Paris: François Bourin Editeur, 2010).

46. Muhammad Iqbal, "Jibril-o Iblis", in *Kulliyat-e Iqbal Urdu* (Aligarh: Educational Book House, 1997), p. 435. My translation.

47. Iqbal, *Kulliyat-e Iqbal Farsi*, p. 656. My translation is a heavily modified version of Arberry's in the *Javid-Nama*, p. 135.

48. S. Hasan Ahmad, *Iqbal: His Political Ideas at Crossroads* (Aligarh: Printwell Publications, 1979), p. 80. Iqbal's correspondence with Thompson forms part of the latter's papers in the Bodleian Library at Oxford, and facsimiles of it have been published together with a commentary in Ahmad's book.

49. Piterberg, *The Returns of Zionism*, chapter 5.

50. See Gershom Scholem, *Sabbatai Sevi: the Mystical Messiah* (Princeton: Princeton University Press, 1973).

51. See Naveeda Khan, "The Law and the Ahmadi Question," in *Muslim Becoming: Aspiration and Skepticism in Pakistan* (Durham: Duke University Press, 2012), pp. 91–119.

52. The most important scholarly discussion of this doctrine is David S. Power's book, *Muhammad is Not the Father of Any of Your Men: The Making of the Last Prophet*, cited above.

53. Iqbal, *The Reconstruction of Religious Thought in Islam*, p. 125.

54. Ibid., p. 126.

55. Mohammad Iqbal, *The Development of Metaphysics in Persia: A Contribution to the History of Muslim Philosophy* (Lahore: Bazm-i-Iqbal, 1959), p. 144.

56. For the changing tradition of being "crazy" with God but "careful" of Muhammad, see C. M. Naim, "Be Crazy with God..." in *Outlook India*, 27 Dec. 2012 (http://www.outlookindia.com/article.aspx?283453#1).

57. Vahid, *Thoughts and Reflections of Iqbal*, p. 249.

58. Ibid., p. 250.

59. Ibid., p. 252.

60. Ibid., p. 273.

61. Ibid., pp. 259–60.

62. Ibid., p. 260.

## 5. TO SET INDIA FREE

1. See Piterberg, *The Returns of Zionism*. chapter 1.

2. Arendt, "The Jew as Pariah: A Hidden Tradition," in Jerome Kohn and Ron H. Feldman, *The Jewish Writings*, p. 276.

3. See Mufti, *Enlightenment in the Colony*.

4. The only scholarship on this subject is to be found in Anupama Rao's *The Caste Question: Dalits and the Politics of Modern India* (Berkeley and Los Angeles: University of California Press, 2009), especially chapter 3.

5. See for this the first chapter of my *The Impossible Indian*.

6. "Mr Gandhi and the Suppressed Classes: A Chapter of Autobiography," in *Young India*, April 27, 1921, p. 4.

7. Vasant Moon (ed.), *Dr Babasaheb Ambedkar: Writings and Speeches* (hereafter *DBAWS*), vol. 2, part 2 (Bombay: Education Department, Government of Maharashtra, 1982), p. 451.

8. Sayyid Ahmad Khan, "Taqrir bajawab address-e anjuman-e Islamiyya Rae Bareilly," in *Khutbat-e Sir Sayyid*, vol. 1, pp. 365–9.

9. See, for instance, Moon, "Evidence Taken Before the Joint Committee on Indian Constitutional Reform," in *DBAWS*, vol. 2 (1982), pp. 714–29.

10. Moon, *DBAWS*, vol. 17, part 2 (2003), pp. 199–200.

11. For Gandhi's criticism of interest and contract, see the third chapter of my book, *The Impossible Indian*; and for Iqbal see Faisal Devji, "Illiberal Islam," in Saurabh Dube (ed.), *Enchantments of Modernity: Empire, Nation, Globalization*, (New Delhi: Routledge, 2009), pp. 234–63.

12. Vahid, *Thoughts and Reflections of Iqbal*, pp. 365–6.

13. J. Ahmad, *Some Recent Speeches and Writings of Mr Jinnah*, pp. 5–6.

14. Moon (ed.), *DBAWS*, vol. 8 (1990), p. 360.

15. Khaliquzzaman, *Pathway to Pakistan*, pp. 192–3.

16. Z. H. Zaidi (ed.), *M.A. Jinnah-Ispahani Correspondence, 1936–1948*, p. 205.

17. Ibid., p. 252.

18. See Dwaipayan Sen, "'No Matter How, Jogendranath had to be Defeated': The Scheduled Castes Federation and the Making of Partition in Bengal, 1945–1947," in *Indian Economic and Social History Review*, vol. 49 no. 3 (2012), pp. 321–64.

19. Moon, *DBAWS*, vol. 17, part 1 (2003), pp. 300–1.

20. For an example of the ambiguity of low-caste Muslim politics in this period, see Santosh Kumar Rai, "Muslim Weavers' Politics in Early 20th Century India," in *Economic and Political Weekly*, vol. XLVII, no. 15 (14 April 2012), pp. 61–70.

21. See Mufti's *Enlightenment in the Colony*.

22. Valentine Chirol, *Indian Unrest* (London: Macmillan and Co., 1910), p. 122.

23. Ibid., p. 123.

24. Ibid.

25. For a fine analysis of "Hindu" thinking on this issue, and in particular that of Tilak, see Shruti Kapila, "A History of Violence," in *Modern Intellectual History*, vol. 7 no. 3 (August 2010), pp. 437–57.

26. Pirzada, *Quaid-e-Azam's*, pp. 411–12.

27. Ibid., p. 413.

28. Z. H. Zaidi, *Jinnah Papers* (hereafter *JP*), third series, vol. XVI (Islamabad: Quaid-i-Azam Papers Wing, Culture Division, Government of Pakistan, 2008), p. 308.

29. Penderel Moon, *Wavell: The Viceroy's Journal*, p. 102.

30. Zaidi, *JP*, second series, vol. XIII (2006), p. 80.

31. Pirzada (ed.), *Quaid-e-Azam Jinnah's Correspondence*, p. 415.

32. Zaidi, *JP*, third series, vol. XVI (2008), p. 459.

33. J. Ahmad, *Some Recent Speeches and Writings of Mr Jinnah* p. 240.

34. Ibid., p. 225.

35. Ibid.

36. Khurshid, *Memories of Jinnah*, p. 53.

37. J. Ahmad, *Some Recent Speeches and Writings of Mr Jinnah*, p. 83.

38. Ibid., p. 57.

39. Ibid., p. 165.

40. See for this the first chapter of Piterberg's *The Returns of Zionism*.

41. See Moon, *DBAWS*, vol. 1 (1989), pp. 81–5.

42. Moon, *DBAWS*, vol. 8 (1990), p. 359.

43. Moon, *DBAWS*, vol. 17, part 1 (2003), p. 284.

44. Ibid., p. 340.

45. Moon, *DBAWS*, vol. 17, part 2 (2003), pp. 167.

46. See for instance his memorandum to the Cabinet Mission of 5 April 1946, in ibid., p. 180.

47. Ibid., pp. 256–7.

48. Moon, *DBAWS*, vol. 17, part 1 (2003), p. 241.

49. Ibid.

50. Moon, *DBAWS*, vol. 17, part 2 (2003), pp. 242–3.

51. See All India Muslim League, *Jinnah-Gandhi Talks*, p. 22.

52. Zaidi, *JP*, second series, vol. XIII (2006), pp. 254–5.

53. Moon, *DBAWS*, vol. 17, part 2 (2003), p. 286.

54. See, for example, Ambedkar's *Pakistan or the Partition of India*, pp. 123–5.

55. See, for instance, ibid., pp. 217 and 264.

56. Ibid., p. 301.

57. See Hunter's 1871 book, *The Indian Musalmans: Are They Bound in Conscience to Rebel Against the Queen?* (Delhi: Indological Book House, 1969). Also see Syed Ahmed Khan's response to it, *Review on Dr. Hunter's Indian Musalmans: Are They Bound in Conscience to Rebel Against the Queen?* (Lahore: Premier Book House, n.d.).

58. Ibid., p. 339.

59. Ibid., p. 115.

60. Ibid., p. 362.

61. Moon, *DBAWS*, vol. 17, part 2 (2003), pp. 219–20.

62. See for example his memorandum to the Cabinet Mission on 5 April 1946, in ibid., pp. 178–9.

63. See, for instance, ibid., p. 511.

64. Zaidi, *JP*, second series, vol. XIV (2006), pp. 318–19.

65. Khaliquzzaman, *Pathway to Pakistan*, p. 393.

66. Ibid., p. 394.

67. Moon, *DBAWS*, vol. 17, part 1, p. 374.

68. For an important discussion of the emergence and elaboration of minority rights in independent India, see Rochana Bajpai, *Debating Difference: Minority Rights and Liberal Democracy in India* (New Delhi: Oxford University Press, 2011).

## 6. THE SPIRIT OF ISLAM

1. Wilfred Cantwell Smith, *Modern Islam in India* (London: Victor Gollancz, 1946), p. 55.

2. Syed Ameer Ali, *The Spirit of Islam: A History of the Evolution and Ideals of Islam, With a Life of the Prophet* (London: Chatto and Windus, 1978), p. 137.

3. Ibid., pp. 137–8.

4. Ibid., p. 138.

5. See Wilfred Cantwell Smith, "The Historical Development in Islam of the Concept of Islam as an Historical Development," in *On Understanding Islam: Selected Studies* (The Hague: Mouton Publishers, 1981), pp. 41–77.

6. Ibid., p. 47.

7. Ibid., p. 62.

8. Ibid., pp. 63–4.

9. See Barbara Metcalf, "Islam and Power in Colonial India: The Making and Unmaking of a Muslim Princess," in *The American Historical Review*, Feb. 2011, pp. 1–30.

10. C. A. Bayly, *Recovering Liberties: Indian Thought in the Age of Liberalism and Empire*, pp. 236–7.

11. Fazlur Rahman, *Islam and Modernity: Transformation of an Intellectual Tradition* (Chicago and London: University of Chicago Press, 1982), pp. 2–3.

12. Ibid., p. 30.

13. Sayyid Ahmad Khan, "Ruh awr us ki haqiqat Imam Ghazali ke nazdik," Muhammad Ismail Panipati (ed.), *Maqalat-e Sir Sayyid*, vol. 3 (Lahore: Majlis-e Taraqqi-ye Adab, 1961), pp. 35–45.

14. Ibid., p. 35.

15. Ibid.

16. Ibid., p. 39.

17. Mirza Asadullah Khan Ghalib, *Divan-e Ghalib* (Aligarh: Maktabah-e Alfaz, 1990), p. 44.

18. Mirza Asadullah Khan Ghalib, *Ghazaliyat-e Farsi* (Lahore: Punjab University, 1969), p. 13.

19. Khan, *Maqalat*, vol. 3, p. 39.

20. Ibid., p. 42.

21. Ibid., pp. 44–5.

22. Syed Ameer Ali, *The Spirit of Islam: A History of the Evolution and Ideals of Islam with a Life of the Prophet* (London: Christophers, 1946), p. vii.

23. See "Ameer Ali's Letter with the Aga Khan to His Excellency Ghazi Ismat Pasha, the Prime Minister of Turkey," in Shan Muhammad (ed.), *The Right Hon'ble Syed Ameer Ali: Political Writings* (New Delhi: Ashish Publishing House, 1989), pp. 288–90.

24. "Speech before the Motamar-al-Alam-al-Islami, Karachi, 9 February 1951," in Aziz, *Aga Khan III*, vol. II, pp. 1272–75.

25. Ibid., p. 1275.

26. Ameer Ali, *Spirit of Islam*, p. 336.

27. For a transcript of the court proceedings see Liaquat H. Merchant, *Jinnah: A Judicial Verdict* (Karachi: East and West Publishing Co., 1990).

28. Ibid., p. 93.

29. Ibid., p. 94.

30. Ibid., p. 60.

31. Cited in Khwaja Razi Haider, *Ruttie Jinnah: The Story, Told and Untold* (Karachi: Pakistan Study Centre, University of Karachi, 2004), p. 47.

32. Ibid., chapter 7.

33. Baxter, *Diaries of Field Marshal Mohammad Ayub Khan, 1972*, pp. 115–16.

34. For the complex religious history of the Khojas, see Teena Purohit, *The Aga Khan Case: Religion and Identity in Colonial India* (Cambridge, Mass.: Harvard University Press, 2012).

35. Merchant, p. 28.

36. Ibid., p. 32.

37. Ibid., p. 33.

38. Ameer Ali, *Spirit of Islam*, p. 317.

39. Vahid, *Thoughts and Reflections of Iqbal*, p. 284.

40. Iqbal, *Reconstruction of Religious Thought in Islam*, p. 125.

41. Iqbal, *Reconstruction*, p. 104.

42. Ibid., p. 105.

43. Ibid., p. 123.
44. J. Ahmad, *Some Recent Speeches and Writings of Mr Jinnah*, p. 92.
45. Ibid.
46. Ibid., pp. 92–3.
47. Ibid., p. 93.
48. Ibid., pp. 93–4.
49. See Eric Nelson, *The Hebrew Republic: Jewish Sources and the Transformation of European Political Thought* (Cambridge, Mass.: Harvard University Press, 2010).
50. See, for instance, Sayyid Abul A'la Maududi, trans. Khurshid Ahmad, *First Principles of the Islamic State* (Lahore: Islamic Publications Limited), p. 34.
51. Sayyid Abul Ala Mawdudi, "Dunya-e Islam men Islami tahrikat ke liye tariq-e kar," in *Tafhimat*, vol. 3 (Lahore: 1965), p. 365.
52. Ibid., p. 366.
53. Ibid., p. 367.
54. Ibid.
55. Ibid., p. 368.
56. Ibid.
57. Ibid., pp. 369–70.
58. Maududi, trans. Khurshid Ahmad, *Islamic Law and Constitution* (Lahore: Islamic Publications Ltd., 1992), p. 231.
59. See for this Sayyid Abul Ala Mawdudi, "Islam awr adl-e ijtimai," in *Tafhimat*, p. 156.
60. Maududi, *Islamic Law*, p. 214.
61. Ibid., p. 216.
62. Mawdudi, *Tafhimat*, p. 164.
63. See Leonard Binder, *Religion and Politics in Pakistan* (Berkeley and Los Angeles: University of California Press, 1963).
64. See for this Seyyed Vali Reza Nasr, *The Vanguard of the Islamic Revolution: The Jama'at-i Islami of Pakistan* (Berkeley and Los Angeles: University of California Press, 1994).
65. Maududi, *Islamic Law*, p. 132.
66. Ibid., p. 142.
67. Ibid., p. 143.
68. Ibid., p. 309.

CONCLUSION

1. G.W. F. Hegel, trans. J. Sibree, *The Philosophy of History* (Buffalo: Prometheus Books, 1991), p. 393.

2. Iqbal, "Wataniyyat," in *Kuliyyat-e Iqbal Urdu*, p. 161.

3. Roger D. Long (ed.), *'Dear Mr Jinnah': Selected Correspondence and Speeches of Liaquat Ali Khan, 1937–1947* (Karachi: Oxford University Press, 2004), p. 237.

4. Ibid., p. 294.

5. Arendt, *On Revolution*, p. 96.

6. Ibid., p. 100.

7. For an example of this, see the fourth chapter of Naveeda Khan's *Muslim Becoming*.

8. Alija Izetbegovic, *The Islamic Declaration: A Programme for the Islamization of Muslims and the Muslim Peoples* (Sarajevo, 1990).

9. Long, p. 227.

10. To my knowledge the only scholar who recognized this homology was the historian of Islam, Marshall Hodgson, in his multi-volume work, *The Venture of Islam: Conscience and History in a World Civilization*, vol. 3 (Chicago: The University of Chicago Press, 1977), p. 440.

11. Vahid, *Thoughts and Reflections of Iqbal*, p. 162.

12. Long, p. 240.

# INDEX

INDEX

# INDEX

# INDEX

# INDEX